ELITE
BASTARDS

"He who is prudent and lies in wait for an
Enemy who is not, will be victorious."
                        – Sun Tzu, The Art of War

First published in Great Britain in 2023 by
PEN AND SWORD MILITARY
An imprint of
Pen & Sword Books Limited
Yorkshire – Philadelphia

ISBN 978 1 52678 965 5

A CIP catalogue record for this book is available from the British Library.

Typeset in Times New Roman 12/15.5 by
SJmagic DESIGN SERVICES, India.
Printed and bound in the UK by CPI Group (UK) Ltd.

Pen & Sword Books Limited incorporates the imprints of Atlas, Archaeology,
Aviation, Discovery, Family History, Fiction, History, Maritime, Military,
Military Classics, Politics, Select, Transport, True Crime, Air World, Frontline
Publishing, Leo Cooper, Remember When, Seaforth Publishing, The Praetorian
Press, Wharncliffe Local History, Wharncliffe Transport, Wharncliffe True Crime
and White Owl.

For a complete list of Pen & Sword titles please contact
PEN & SWORD BOOKS LIMITED
George House, Units 12 & 13, Beevor Street, Off Pontefract Road,
Barnsley, South Yorkshire, S71 1HN, England
E-mail: enquiries@pen-and-sword.co.uk
Website: www.pen-and-sword.co.uk

or

PEN AND SWORD BOOKS
1950 Lawrence Rd, Havertown, PA 19083, USA
E-mail: uspen-and-sword@casematepublishers.com
Website: www.penandswordbooks.com

MIX
Paper | Supporting
responsible forestry
FSC® C013604

ELITE BASTARDS

THE COMBAT MISSIONS OF
COMPANY F,
LRP TEAMS IN VIETNAM

EDWARD L. DVORAK

Pen & Sword

MILITARY

AN IMPRINT OF PEN & SWORD BOOKS LTD.
YORKSHIRE - PHILADELPHIA

Contents

CONTENTS

The First Three Principles of a Lurp's Field Manual

STEALTH is the foundation for all Lurp Teams. If the enemy doesn't know you are in the area or they can't find you, then you have a reasonable chance of completing your Recon/Intelligence Mission (Long Range Recon Patrol) without contact. If you elect to initiate a contact (Long Range Patrol) with the enemy, they'll never know what hit them until it's too late. It increases the effect of the second principle.

SHOCK caused by a sudden, violent attack is used as an effective weapon when the Team Leader elects to viciously strike the enemy!

DEATH of the enemy is the ultimate goal of a Lurp Team on an ambush mission. Of course, nothing in combat is guaranteed, so it's the team's operational skills along with some luck that ultimately provides the solution as to who lives and who dies.

A Combat Seasoned Lurp's Opinion

You've probably heard a lot of Vietnam war stories about alleged heroes who went through an entire year in the war zone, been involved in numerous firefights, possibly hand to hand combat, were wounded numerous times and who came home with a chest full of heroic medals. Well, I have to tell you that most of those stories are pure unadulterated Bull Shit! The true facts about combat are that you can be in the Top Tier, High-Speed-Low-Drag Special Ops Unit and **IF** and **WHEN** it's your time to get your "Ticket Punched", there's no denying fate.

Secondly, the longer you are in a combat unit in a combat zone, whether you're a grunt in the infantry, a Lurp conducting recon missions or a Green Beret Special Operator running cross border prisoner snatch missions, your mortality and/or wounded in action odds substantially increase. Somewhere along that "In Combat" time line, you will most likely get nicked by enemy or friendly fire; however, if your luck runs out completely, you could come home in the horizontal position with an American Flag draped over your coffin!

Every slang name has a story behind it. For the Lurp's in Company F 51st Infantry, LRP, Airborne being called Elite Bastards, it was coined by First Sergeant Walter P. Butts. If you asked him why he called his boys that name he would say; ELITE "For all the hell they raise in the field against the enemy" and BASTARDS "For all the hell they raise in the rear when on passes!"

Xin Loi GI!

Prologue

I grew up on a cattle ranch in south-central South Dakota. My only escape from hard work in the hay fields, fencing and working with cattle, was hunting. By the time I was 12 years old I was hunting with a real gun, a .22-caliber bolt-action rifle, which I still possess to this day. We owned 1,500 acres, so I had a lot of room to roam and hunt. The primary fall game was pheasant, grouse and of course white tail deer. If you had to draw a parallel between combat in Vietnam and hunting in South Dakota, the white tail deer with a touch of coyote thrown in for cunningness, it would definitely be the Viet Cong. They were smart and knew their area like the back of their hands. They would use their environment and their senses to try to outmaneuver and attack your force, or they would just disappear into the jungle. I guess the closest thing to the North Vietnamese Army (NVA) would have been the mountain lion. The NVA were definitely the apex predators of GIs in the jungle and vice versa. Of course, there were tigers, but they normally only hunted other animals, not humans!

I was always intrigued by war and had read some of the history of the Second World War and Korea. Vietnam was a different kind of war. I was essentially a weekend warrior at the beginning of long-term war, only later would a few National Guard (NG) and Reserve Units be moved into active war footings. I, along with a lot of other GIs of all ranks, had to learn how to fight a guerilla war in the dense jungles, rice paddies and swamps of South Vietnam. It was a very steep learning curve for everyone involved and, unfortunately, lethal for many.

Chapter 1

You're in the Army Now

Cherry/Cherry Boy/FNG (Fuckin' New Guy) DEFINITION:

> a soldier, sailor, marine, air force or coast guard person,
> who has yet to be directly involved in combat, which tests
> his metal and confirms that he can function while under
> hostile fire! This is a necessary experience, especially for
> the high speed, low drag units of Special Operation Forces
> such as Delta, SOG, Force Recon, LRP, Rangers and other
> un-named secret units of the Department of Defense.

To illustrate to you a "no shit" quick transition from my civilian life
to a combat trooper, I will list the relevant dates. On May 1, 1967, I
enlisted in the Regular Army and was released from my three-year
commitment to the National Guard. I was immediately sent to Fort
Leonard Wood, Missouri, for my clothing issue and shipped out the
next week to airborne training at Fort Benning, Georgia. Following
three weeks of airborne training and two weeks of leave I arrived
in Cam Ranh Bay, July 23, 1967. It was a short 11 weeks after my
enlistment day with only basic training, no AIT, and airborne training
under my belt. I had just turned a salty 19 years old. We only stayed
one full day at the Cam Ranh Bay Replacement Depot (AKA Repo
Depo), because they needed fresh meat for the grinder/combat and of
course we were "bad ass" paratroopers and were looking for a fight.

Half of the Cherries that arrived "in country" with me were
assigned to the 173rd Airborne Brigade at Bien Hoa, South Vietnam.
Because of my previous NG enlistment and on the job training, I had
a supply MOS and was immediately sent to the 4th Battalion Area,

1

when we arrived at Bien Hoa Army Base. When I got to the 4th Battalion Area, I told my supply sergeant that I did not want to be a supply clerk and that I wanted to go to the line. He looked at me with disbelief along with a statement of something like, "You got to be shitting me, troopers would kill for this assignment." When he saw I was serious, the transition was quickly made. I immediately had a change of my MOS to 11B, which is an infantryman, with the stroke of a typewriter. I was issued an "almost" complete set of used combat gear, which included load bearing equipment, canteens, ammo pouches, a mosquito net, a poncho, but no poncho liner. I was also issued a used M-16 rifle that looked like it had been left in a mud hole for six weeks and then baked in an oven for an hour or two. This was followed by an immediate assignment to guard duty within four hours of reaching Bien Hoa. I adjusted all of my web gear, which consisted of a pistol belt attached to a set of suspenders commonly called load bearing equipment (LBE), which had several ammo pouches and a canteen and pouch attached to the pistol belt. I had to adjust the belt to fit my torso size and started looking at the poor condition of my M-16. Several seasoned troopers, apparently back from Rest and Relaxation (R&R), came into the barracks where I was assembling my gear. They started preparing their gear to catch a ride back to their assigned units, all of which were at Dak To. One trooper in particular noticed that I was having some difficulty disassembling the M-16 to clean it and asked me what the problem was. I told him straight out that I had been trained on the M-14 in basic training and I had never held an M-16 let alone fired one. He basically said that he would give me a down and dirty quick session on how to clean and take care of the M-16, so that I could probably survive my first firefight. Within about 20 minutes I was given the complete M-16 training course, compared to several weeks in a Regular Army course, which included zeroing and numerous hours on the range for familiarization. I was issued some live ammo and after filling my four magazines, I was transported to a three-man bunker with another Cherry, on the north perimeter of Bien Hoa Army Base, South Vietnam.

Here were two Cherries, scared as shit, sitting in a blacked-out bunker so dark you couldn't see four inches in front of your hand, with two M-16s and a few mags between them, a crank telephone to the Guard HQ and a bunch of bad ass rats running around in the pallets under our feet. I don't think anyone in their right mind would have thought about falling asleep and I knew for damn sure that I wouldn't. We had been told at the guard briefing prior to being dropped off at our bunker, by an Officer of the Guard, a leg butter bar 2nd LT, about sappers crawling through the wire and cutting the throats of soldiers who had fallen asleep on guard duty. Total bullshit, but it did make you imagine crazy things in the middle of the night in a dark bunker!

There were a lot of the natural noises out front of the bunker and in the wire. There was everything from insects, to lizards to wild pigs that were feasting on stuff the GIs had thrown out into the wire, like half empty cans of C-Rats(C-Rations) and other types of pogie bait that they had lost interest in and were too damn lazy to take it back to the barracks with them at the end of their guard duty shift. Then there were the skeeters, some of which sounded like they were the size of hummingbirds and could suck out a pint of your blood in seconds. All of these distractions, along with the heat and man-made smells like piss in the bunker made for one damn miserable night. Of course, there weren't any toilets around so if you had to piss, you were supposed to go out of the bunker, but my nose told me that a lot of GIs just pissed on one of the interior walls. If you made your way up the several steps to the door that led into the bunker you could relieve yourself, like the other several hundred GIs before you had. You didn't have to see where to piss; all you had to do was follow the odor which, with the heat and humidity, was overpowering. Even though it was a hell of a lot cooler up behind the bunker, you didn't stay long, because there were lights from the base behind you and you were essentially "back lit", a perfect target for a sniper, which the LT also told us about at the guard briefing. Later, when I came back to Bien Hoa with Company F, Long Range Patrol, we made the Leg Officers of the guard pay for all the shit they had shoveled on us as Cherries.

3

Chapter 2

The 173rd Airborne Brigade (aka The Herd)

I survived several nights of guard duty in Bien Hoa in between other extra duty details like filling sandbags. Finally, I was told to pack my shit, that I was being sent to Dak To, to my new unit, without attending Jungle Orientation. I'm not sure why the Supply Sergeant was pissed off at me, but he never issued me a poncho liner and that must have had something to do with me being immediately shipped out.

Me, along with probably 20 other repo-depot Cherry replacements were driven to Bien Hoa Airbase in a deuce and a half-truck (2½ ton Army Truck), where we loaded onto a C-130 cargo plane. This would be my first ride in a C-130, because we had jumped from the C-119, the flying Box Cars, in jump school. Of course, the Army never let a free transportation effort pass, so loaded on the C-130 was a ¾ ton, basically a pickup with a trailer as well as a jeep with a trailer. Both of the vehicles and the trailers were loaded to the top with gear that was being sent forward to the 173rd Airborne Brigade at Dak To. If you've never flown in a C-130, it's a real trip. They're loud on the ground before they close the rear ramp and there is always the smell of JP-4 jet fuel exhaust that the four turboprops burn. They were built as an aerial work-horse, to haul just about anything that would fit on its cargo deck and to parachute equipment and men off its tail gate or just paratroopers out the two side doors. They weren't built for human comfort.

Prior to takeoff, an Air Force NCO/ Loadmaster showed us where to sit in the side seats that were attached to the exterior walls of the airplane. They were the standard issue aluminum frames with nylon type material seats and they aren't what you would call comfortable. Since the center area of the cargo deck on the aircraft was completely filled with the two vehicles and their trailers, all of our gear had to sit on the floor of the craft under our feet with no room to spare. The flight took several hours and of course none of the Cherries had slept a wink since yesterday, when we were told to prepare our gear for transportation to the 173rd Airborne Brigade Line Units.

As we prepared to land at Dak To, the Loadmaster told us to sit down, strap in and hang on for the landing. I thought that was rather curious, but since I had never flown in a C-130 before, I decided it was just standard Air Force procedure. As we came in to land you could feel the aircraft dramatically slowing down, like we were dropping out of the sky, which in fact we were. What we didn't know was that the airstrip at Dak To was short and the runway was made of PSP: interlocked, narrow metal sheets. The runway was not smooth and when the aircraft hit the runway, and I mean hit hard, everything inside the aircraft started to bounce up and down, including the two vehicles and their trailers that had been chained to the cargo deck. I had this flash moment, thinking that when the aircraft stopped tumbling from the crash, the rescuers would need a sponge to extract what was left of us after the vehicles and trailers broke loose from their chains and just rattled around inside the cargo compartment, with human bodies caught between the steel of the vehicles and the aluminum frame of the inside of the aircraft! We were very happy to exit the C-130 and we all thought that it couldn't get any worse than that landing! Dumbass Cherries, we were wrong again!

Ultimately, I ended up in 1st squad, 1st Platoon, Delta Company (aka Dog Company), 4th Battalion of the 173rd Airborne Brigade. My Buck Sergeant E-5, Squad leader (can't remember his name) was a gung-ho asshole of the first magnitude, who was hell bent on receiving the Congressional Medal of Honor at the cost of as many men as it took to get him there. Bear, the Specialist Four, assistant team leader was a little better, but he let me know right up front that a Cherry in a combat line squad was rated somewhere below fresh dog shit and that I was a liability to all of them. As soon as he was finished lecturing me on the finer points of the claymore mine and how to transport it on and off a helicopter, I was sent off to KP – Kitchen Police – which is essentially washing hundreds of pots, pans, trays, cups, silverware and whatever else the mess sergeants used to prepare and serve that particular meal.

I had only been in the company/battalion area for less than two hours when I went off for KP. I worked until late into the evening, probably around 2200 hours, before I was released by the Mess Sergeant to go back to my company. It was now dark as hell and I had to walk probably fifty or more meters just to get back to the general area of where the poncho hooches (two ponchos snapped together with a center, front and rear support to form a makeshift tent shared by two GIs) were for all four companies of 4th Battalion. I was clueless as to where I had come from in the daylight and it was very dark now. There weren't any guards around to ask where in the hell Dog Company was amongst probably 200 or more poncho hooches. It appeared that everyone was asleep and I sure as hell didn't want to wake anyone up and tell them I was lost!

Sleep is very precious in a combat zone, so disturbing a combat vet's sleep is a problem you don't want to cause.

I continued to walk through all of the hooches for probably a couple of hundred meters then I noticed that the hooches thinned out and eventually stopped. It should have been a clue to me that I was near the perimeter, but because of the lack of sleep and my inexperience, I did not pick up on that very important detail. I walked probably another twenty meters before I started hitting low brush and I was pretty noisy forcing my way through it. All of a sudden, I was through the brush and ran into a several rows of concertina wire. Even though I was just a fucking Cherry and hadn't slept in well over 48 hours, I realized that I was probably not supposed to be in this area. There was actually an angled opening in the wire where two separate rows of concertina came together. I thought about walking

6

through it because there had to be a guard shack or something there before I got to the tree line, which I could see in front of the wire. Something told me to turn back, even though the only thing I could see was by starlight and that was just outlines against the night sky. I decided to follow the inside of the wire to see if I could find someone that was awake and on guard duty, who could possibly direct me back to my company area. I hadn't walked more than ten feet when I heard this "Psst", and a whispered voice in broken English saying, "GI you no go there, VC there, you no go!"

I about shit my pants on the spot! As I looked to my left, I was able to make out a round mound about 10 meters away. I walked to the mound and realized that it was an open, sandbagged bunker sitting above ground. There were two Vietnamese soldiers sitting behind what appeared to be a World War II 30-caliber Browning machine gun pointed directly at me. I sidestepped the gun and the bunker and walked up to them. They again told me that the VC were out there and I needed to go back, pointing in the direction I had come from. I thanked them and, after my heart settled back to the interior of my chest, I started walking in the direction they had pointed. I was then struck with the realization that I had just missed being shot at point blank range with a 30-caliber machine gun and it would have been a justified/friendly fire shooting. Just some dumbass Cherry who wondered out of the perimeter for some stupid reason and got his ass fired up by the ARVNs (Army of the Republic of Vietnam soldiers). I'm guessing the only reason they didn't light me up was because I was making so much fucking noise going through the brush that they knew it couldn't be Vietcong or NVA. They correctly assessed the situation and decided that it had to be some stupid GI! This was one of many times I almost got wacked by "not so friendly" fire! I finally found my hooch by using the light from the mess tent to vector myself into the company area. Of course, I never told anyone about my near fatal mistake, because I already knew my life was worthless in the eyes of the rest of the squad.

Chapter 3

Dak To

Dak To is located in the Central Highlands of Vietnam. It is high in altitude (8,000 -10,0000 ft) with nothing but mountain ridges, valleys and very steep-ass elevations between the two. The jungle is triple canopy with the top of the tallest trees being well over 200 feet high. I believe some were mahogany or other types of hardwood trees, but I really didn't have the time or the disposition to be sight-seeing.

Everything was wet, the soil was red in color and the consistency of clay. It was greasy slick, stuck to everything, especially the bottom of your jungle boots, and was always willing and able to assist you in an uncontrollable fall, especially while on one of the very steep slopes. The floor of the jungle under the triple canopy was pretty much wide open because the sunlight hardly ever penetrated with any intensity down to the floor; therefore, very few small plants or bushes could grow there. There were some natural open areas and these were hell on earth, because that is where elephant grass liked to grow. It was a long-leafed plant that could grow to 6 feet or higher and its edges were razor sharp. I think it was designed by Mother Nature to cut dumb GIs who wandered into their patches. The elephant grass especially targeted your wrists and forearms, which within 24 hours became festered and infected wounds. With no way to keep the cuts clean they could easily become a serious medical problem in the near future.

In the open areas the brush and small plants were so thick that you literally could not fall down. In between the open areas and the triple canopy you had single and double canopy and that is where the vines were the thickest. The grunts called them "wait a minute vines" because they would catch on your rifle, your gear (striping any loose equipment off), your arms and legs. It is where I was taught the most important Jungle Fighting Lessons I ever received while in the Herd (the 173rd nickname). As we humped along through the endless jungle at 8,000 feet or higher, 100 plus degree heat and near 100 per cent humidity, carrying around 85 pounds of gear, water and C-Rats (C-Rations), you could quickly become over-heated if you didn't regulate your activity to a sustainable rate. A lot of the troopers became over-heated and irritated with the jungle, especially the Cherries. I was not exempt from that activity. It was when I was having one of my "kick your ass moments" with several vines that an old, grizzled lifer (Career Army) platoon sergeant walked up to me and said in the most clear and concise words, "Son, the jungle has been here long before you and it will be here long after you, so don't fight it!" He then calmly turned and agilely worked his way through the vines and brush with very little effort and making very little noise.

The heat, along with the heavy load on your back, the mud, the jungle vegetation and the constant threat of walking into an NVA ambush was enough to physically and mentally exhaust you, but the jungle left the best for last. There were numerous species of insects in the jungle, but the top of the "Screw a GI" list were mosquitoes and leeches, but Numero Uno were ants. The mosquitoes were pretty much a 24/7 harassment group, except for when it got cold, around 70 degrees at night in the higher elevations; however, you were then freezing your ass off and would have welcomed the heat and the mosquitoes. The leeches were a constant with the small – about an inch long – variety the most common. They managed to find a tear in your fatigues or crawl up a pant leg or sleeve and attach to your skin to suck out some blood. They were ruthless son of bitches and your crotch, testicles or armpits were the prime meal areas. We had small squirt bottles of bug spray, which would at least cause the leeches to release their bite on your skin, but it felt like you were spraying high-octane gasoline on your heat flushed skin and open pores. It burned like a bitch when you used it and some GIs preferred to burn the leeches off with cigarettes, but you weren't smoking while you were humping a ruck in the bush, so the leeches got a quick squirt of "bug juice" and you humped on.

There were two main varieties of ants in the Central Highlands; the red ants and the black ants. I'm not talking about the small North American variety, but ants about half of an inch long and probably about an eighth inch in diameter. The red ones liked to build their nests in the leaves of low hanging trees like a banana tree, which were about shoulder high on the standard GI frame. As you were passing through their neighborhood and unknowingly brushed against their nest, they would swarm you, and bite the shit out of your neck, shoulders and face. It was like getting instantaneously hit by a hundred miniature arrows! You needed assistance from a fellow GI to knock them off or kill them. Probably the king of the insect jungle world was the black ant. They not only bit you, but also stung you at the same time. They were the "bad ass Mo Fos" of the jungle floor and you avoided them at all cost. If you sprayed "bug juice" across their trail it just seemed to piss them off, and they charged across the line to get at you. Many times, I had to give up a near perfect fighting position as a Lurp because I had trespassed on their trail and they evicted me with extreme prejudice and with pain thrown in for good measure.

Added to all of the weight of your equipment, humping at high altitudes in high heat and humidity was the fact that you could never walk a straight line while on patrol in the Central Highlands. The topography would not allow this. Usually in the morning you were given your marching orders and you headed out on an approximate compass azimuth. Rarely was the route exactly where the Officers wanted you to go. It was usually straight up or straight down– and I mean probably a 10 percent plus grade – so you were using trees and bushes to help pull you up a mountain and whatever you could grab a hold to slow you down when headed down an incline. Most orders for route of march and distance came from the Battalion Commander, who had his ass in a Huey, several thousand feet above you. He would radio his orders down to the Company Commanders and they would say, "Airborne, Sir!"

I don't know if any Company Commander, who was normally a Captain, would ever question the Battalion Commander, who was probably a Lieutenant Colonel, but I doubt it. We would be given orders to hump to these particular coordinates on the topo map. It would show a straight-line distance of maybe 5 clicks (5 kilometers, which is equal to just a little over 3 miles), but in actuality it was more like 8 clicks (almost 5 miles) because you had to go up and down ridges and valleys to get to that point. I don't think we ever made it to a specific location in a single day of humping in the Highlands. Once you stopped for the night, you had to dig in with overhead cover for bunkers, fill sandbags you carried with you and, of course, dig your individual foxhole. We did this every night in the Herd while out on combat patrols. Once it became dark you hunkered down and pulled your assigned guard duty. It was so fricking dark in the jungle, you couldn't see your hand in front of your face and the jungle became alive at night with nocturnal animals, snakes and insects. We never got probed or hit at night in the two months I was with the Herd, but I knew it would have been a total cluster fuck. We couldn't see a damn thing and neither could the enemy. It would be several years before any kind of useable "night vision" equipment was developed, so the only thing that owned the night was the jungle and its nocturnal residents!

When you're stateside in an Airborne Unit, the NCOs, Officers and all of the enlisted personnel have to have "high and tight" haircuts, be close shaved and wear a squared away uniform at all times. In the bush it was different because there weren't any facilities to assist you with hygiene issues. In fact, I took one shower in the two months I was with the Herd in the Central Highlands. Everything else was what you would call "El Nat Ural"; basically, if you found a stream and had time you did a quick dunk, uniform and all, minus your equipment. I could roll tiny balls of dirt in my buzz cut hair most of the time and body odor was a standard issue with everyone, regardless of rank. It was the reason why you didn't wear any underwear and most of us, once our feet got sufficiently callused, didn't wear socks in our boots.

You've probably heard the term "Grunt" to describe an infantryman who was in a line unit in a combat zone. I'm not sure if the term came from the fact that you were down in the dirt, mud or swamp most of the time, like a pig on a farm, or if the term came from the fact that you were hauling a heavy load on your back up and down mountain slopes or through the jungle brush and you could be heard "grunting" as you tried to keep up with your fellow soldiers on a tough march through inhospitable land. Either way, being a Grunt in a combat zone is at the bottom of the lists of jobs/MOS in the military that anyone in their right mind would select as a career opportunity. Some GIs couldn't take it and actually gave themselves self-inflicted wounds, but the majority just buckled down, endured the pain and suffering and had the "Drive ON!" attitude.

Chapter 4

Walking point for the 4th Battalion of the 173rd Abn Brigade

After less than a week assigned to Dog Company of the 4th Battalion, we were deployed in the mountains to the west of Dak To. It was my first flight on a Huey and it was very exciting, but it didn't last that long. There were several Assault Helicopter Companies that were used to lift each line company from Dak To to the large LZ. I believe there were more then 50 Hueys sitting on the landing strip at Dak To with the idea being that they lifted an entire line company of soldiers (100 +) in one move so as not to piecemeal a company into a hostile location. It was amazing to see all of the Hueys sitting there and when they fired them all up at one time, there was a lot of noise, the smell of JP-4 in the air and as they all lifted off a lot of crap flying around. In the air the Hueys flew in a tight formation and you could see the troops sitting in the doors on the other helicopters that were flying in formation. Along the way we picked up Huey UH-1B Gunship helicopters who would be flying escort. If the LZ was hot they would be hitting it with machine gun fire and rockets.

I think we were the first company to get inserted on the large LZ and as soon as the troops left the helicopters, they immediately lifted off to retrieve the other companies still waiting at Dak To. Dog Company moved off the LZ and set up a secure perimeter on the west side of the LZ. Very shortly another company from 4th Battalion landed and they secured the perimeter just to our right. This continued and in little over an hour all four companies were on the ground and the battalion was ready to move out. All the fun stopped then and I got my first taste of humping in the mountains around Dak To. The mountains in this area have high peaks and steep valleys between them, with some connected by ridge lines, but not all of them. They definitely weren't one continuous mountain range. When I say mountains, I'm not talking about mountains like Denali in Alaska. No, they were more like the Tetons in Montana with higher peaks and connected by steep valleys. The topo maps showed some of them reaching 10,000 feet with the average being around 6,000 to 8,000 feet. They were high enough to have clouds cover their tops and for the ground temperatures to drop to around 70 degrees Fahrenheit at night.

We did a short march that day because it takes time to get the battalion lined up for a march. I was introduced to the facts of digging in at night with a fox hole and overhead cover. It took our company several hours to dig in while connecting to a company on each side of our positions. The battalion perimeter was a rough wagon wheel with the battalion CP in the middle. It wasn't that large of a perimeter nor was it a perfect circle because of the terrain, but it worked. As soon as it got dark, strict sound and light restrictions were put in place by the senior NCOs of each company. I was told that this was to prevent the enemy from finding us at night and attacking. Of course, we had been making a hell of a lot of noise while digging in.

One of many highlights I experienced during my "Walking Point" assignment was a wound to my left upper leg. We were again humping in the mountains around Dak To and I was walking point for the 4th Battalion. Behind me was a dog handler and his German Shepherd scout dog. The dog had a reputation of being a mean SOB and would bite anything and anyone who got near it, except the handler. We had been on the move for about 30 minutes when a halt was called. I was sweating profusely and just bent over with all my gear on and placing the butt of my M-16 on the ground to give my back some support. I didn't want to set down because I wasn't sure I could get back up without some help from another trooper. I had been in that position for about a minute when I detected movement to my left side and then felt a sudden pain in my upper left leg just below the knee. The dog had clamped onto my leg with a vicious bite. The sudden action and the movement of the dog caused me to lose my balance and fall backwards, the weight of my heavy pack too much to overcome. As soon as I hit the ground the scout dog let loose of my leg and launched an attack at my face and neck. I just had time to raise my right hand as I saw his open mouth coming right at my face. Out of instinct more then anything else, I grabbed at the dog's mouth and by pure luck I grabbed his tongue. He was trying to bite my hand, but I held on tight and twisted his tongue as hard as I could. That stand off lasted about 20 seconds, but seemed like a life time. I knew if I let loose of the scout dog's tongue that he would go for my throat and I would be in deep shit. All of a sudden, the dog handler was there and pulled the German Shepherd off of me by its heavy-duty choker chain. He held the dog suspended in the air until it was just about choked out and then lowered it to the ground where the dog just laid there trying to catch its breath. I had a very curt conversation with the dog handler which ended with me telling the dog handler that I would shoot and kill his dog if it every attacked me again!

I managed to dump my pack and get to my feet. I checked the wound and saw that I had a 2 inch tear in my fatigues just below the knee and an approximate 2″ long x ¼″ deep tear in my skin where the canine tooth had penetrated. It was slightly bleeding, so I just dumped some water on it from my canteen. By then I was given the order to move out so I slung my pack back on and moved out. I wasn't going to hold up an entire battalion because of the bite and I knew my Squad Sergeant would be on my ass for stopping and causing him and the squad to be embarrassed. We humped another 3 hours before we stopped for the over night, to dig in and secure the perimeter of the Battalion. By then the wound had dirt and other material on it and in it. I had the medic give me some antibiotic cream but never mentioned anything to anyone about the scout dog attack. Later, I learned that the scout dog had been turned loose by the dog handler on two separate occasions and the dog had run down and killed two VC. Because of that action, the scout dog had gone back to its wild state and was little more than a killer looking for a victim. That was the dog handler's fault and I would guess eventually that dog would have had to be euthanized because of how vicious it was. Maybe with luck it got killed on Hill 875 where 4th Battalion of the 173rd got seriously bloodied. They lost a lot of men when attacking a regiment of NVA dug in bunkers on the side of the mountain. Combat is vicious SOB and no man or animal is exempt from its deadly tentacles!

Chapter 5

My Fifth Act of Volunteering

I had volunteered to join the Regular Army (RA), to go to Jump School, to go to Vietnam and to become an infantryman (Grunt; 11 Bravo). Now I was going to volunteer for a new unit, a Long Range Patrol Unit (pronounced as Lurp) which was being formed from the 173rd Airborne Brigade. Someone from the outside world looking in at my decisions would think that I was slowly digging myself into a fatal hole and that I could not survive this last stroke of bad decisions. It turned out to be the best decision I ever made and I'm quite sure it saved my life. All of the 1st squad of Dog Company told me that I was a stupid Cherry for volunteering to go to a LURP Unit and that I was going to die! Sadly, within a month and a half after I left my squad, the 4th Battalion of the 173rd hit Hill 875 in the Central Highlands, and except for a trooper named Cal, all were killed as they made their assault. I was later told by Cal, who I accidentally met on a college campus in California, that the squad leader/Sgt 'I want to be a Hero', was hit in the head by an RPG as he charged up the hill.

In the month and half prior to the Hill 875 Operation, the entire 4th Battalion of the 173rd was on a stand down at Dak To, to rest and obtain new/used equipment for everything that had been damaged or destroyed by the jungle. As luck would have it or maybe fate, I was pulling extra duty again, cleaning a 50-caliber machine gun during the stand down. I was still considered a Cherry even after having humped with the 4th Bn for almost two months in a combat zone with no action except for distant sniper fire and some dead gooks lying in a ditch in a Montagnard village.

There was a battalion formation and several men got up to speak about a Long Range Recon Company that was being formed from volunteers in the 173rd Abn Brigade. After the formation, the officers and NCOs from the new company sat up a table next to the tent where I and some other Cherries were pulling extra duty. As I came out of the tent, Sergeant First Class (SFC) Butts saw me and asked me if I wanted to volunteer for the LRRP Company. He explained what the LURP Company's mission would be and how it would operate. I told SFC Butts that it couldn't be any worse than what I was now doing and signed my name on the line. It was one of those split-second decisions you make in your life that changes everything. First of all, I received some of the best combat jungle fighting techniques and Recondo Training ever developed at the 5th Special Forces MACV Recondo School in Nha Trang, South Vietnam. That training saved my life numerous times. Secondly, I became a Team Member. What I thought and did was important to everyone on the team. I wasn't just some piece of meat that was thrown into the grinder and used up.

On or about 1 October, 1967, I again arrived back at Bien Hoa Airbase via a C-130 aircraft. The airbase was located next to, but with shared perimeters of the Bien Hoa Army Base and the Long Binh Supply Depot. Housed on Long Binh was the Headquarters for II Field Force, the 199 Light Infantry Brigades, and numerous other smaller units. The three complexes were huge, probably 7 plus miles wide and 5 plus miles long. I along with other "Volunteers" from the 173rd were picked up in a deuce and a half and driven directly to the Company F Compound. This was rather unique in itself because up to that point we had been moved around en-masse aboard trucks or buses like cattle being sent to the market. I noted this as did other Troopers, because in civilian life it would be like the difference of being driven by a limo than by a taxi, albeit an open air one at that.

When we arrived at Company F, we unloaded and were taken to the supply room by one of the Company's new NCOs. We drew sheets – holy shit – actual white sheets and a pillow. Yes, a real fricken pillow. This was very significant, because for the last two months I along with the rest of the troopers had been sleeping on good old Mother Earth with my pack as a pillow, a poncho liner as my blanket and a poncho as my half of a roof for a hooch. I decided right then and there that I had made a damn good decision to join the Long Range Patrol Company, aka LURPs. We were then taken to an actual barracks that had doors, windows, cement floors and a tin roof. It needed some work but compared to the 2-month continuous camp-out with the Herd, this was a four-star hotel. We were advised that we were now all part of 1st Platoon of Company F, LRP. We made our bunks and relaxed as we were told to do, without any harassment from officers or NCOs. It was during this time that we got acquainted with each other and we learned that not all of us had actually volunteered for the LRPs. Some of the personnel had been selectively volunteered for the LRPs by brass and NCOs of the various companies comprising all four Battalions of the 173rd Airborne Brigade. Primarily, they were selected because they were considered discipline problems. In actuality, most were not discipline problems in the standard definition of "discipline." They, both NCOs and privates, were the ones that refused to follow uninformed and stupid orders that would have gotten men killed or wounded. Most of these "discipline problems" were in fact just smart troopers who had been in combat in the jungle for a while and had developed skills that saved their lives and the lives of men of their individual squads. I don't know if the entire company was made up of these discipline problems, but we all quickly learned that you wanted to be on a LRP Team with experienced combat troopers that could think on their feet. As Lurps, we always had a Plan B, C, etc. If Plan A didn't work out, which happened a lot on Lurp missions, we adjusted the plan to what would work. We also learned that it was expected of every member of a team to be able to adjust to the circumstances and pick up the slack if a member of your team was wounded or killed while on a recon patrol. Individual failure was not an option, because with only 6 men on a team, your failure would most likely lead to death and destruction of more team members or maybe even the whole team.

Company F not only had all of these outstanding NCOs and private misfits from the line units, but also most of the original senior NCOs and Officers were hand selected by someone. It appeared that someone, probably at the rank of general, had carefully developed a plan and then executed it with precision. This allowed Company F to start off with very competent leadership to make the transition from regular line company operations to LRP Team operations in a safe and competent manner. Probably the most surprising of all was that this appeared to have occurred in actual time in a little over several months, which is an amazing short period even in a war zone. Company F from the 173rd Abn Brigade and Company E from the 101st Abn Division were the first two Lurp companies to be stood up and eventually in 1969, the original members of the newly formed 75th Ranger Regiment.

Chapter 6

MACV Recondo School

Recondo School was developed and taught by 5th Special Forces, in NHA TRANG, South Vietnam. The entire cadre were Special Forces (Green Beret) personnel who had extensive combat experience running Long Range Patrols, both in Vietnam and rumored to have been in both Cambodia and Laos. They were the cream of the crop and what they said and taught you was Gospel.

In early November of 1967, first Platoon was sent to Recondo School shortly after the entire complement of Company F personnel were finally assembled at Bien Hoa. All of us had been through various Army training programs, but this one was different. You were expected to keep your shit packed tight at all times, but you weren't harassed and treated like a trainee if you made a mistake, unless it was a stupid mistake then hell descended on you! The 5th Special Forces Cadre were there to train you and to make sure you understood each specific piece of the *Recondo Puzzle*. All the assembled pieces made up the complete picture of what is required of you to become a successful long-range-recon patrol member. They discussed the subtle things, like individual hygiene and the obvious things like camouflage, how it could make or break an operation.

There was also a lot of time spent on learning how to call in helicopter gunships, artillery and air strikes by fighter/bombers. The obvious point being that they were used as what is now called a "Force Multiplier", whereby you used all the tools of war to exact a terrific cost to the enemy in death and destruction of their units, equipment and supplies. What we quickly learned on LRP Patrols was that it was also the means used to extract your ass from a bad situation in which you were out numbered and out gunned. It did not take long for a 6 man recon team or even a 12 man Heavy Team (aka Hatchet Team) to be in deep ca-ca after you made contact with what you thought was several enemy troops when in fact they were a point element for maybe a platoon or even a larger unit. To say the natives were pissed off after you had just blown up some of their fellow troops would be an understatement! They were hell bent on your death and destruction. They would bring a maximum effort to complete their deadly task. The Team usually had two choices, stay and fight or Di Di Mow (run like hell in a somewhat organized manner) or combination of the two. It was very common to have helicopter gunships making gun runs parallel and sometimes perpendicular to your route of escape, to keep the enemy soldiers from catching up to your team and taking them under fire.

The first two weeks were packed with class room activities with training such as recognizing and interpreting various signs of enemy activity, their superb jungle camouflage methods, their weapons, tactics and their operational methods. We also spent hours upon hours on radio procedures, map reading and medical training. We had very detailed medical training especially about how to treat various wounds. We were taught how put an IV in the arm of a wounded trooper, then we had to place an IV in each other to see if we actually could do it. This was primarily for injecting albumin into a Lurp that had been wounded and had lost a lot of blood. Albumin was a blood expander. The intent was to expand the blood to slow the bleeding from a serious wound. We each carried a bottle of albumin protected inside an OD metal can about the size of a small bottle of milk. It was taped to our gear. Our medical training was well above the level of first aid training and was a condensed version of the actual Army Medic training. The primary purpose for all of the training was to keep the trooper alive until he could get transported to a field hospital where doctors would perform the necessary medical treatments.

We spent a lot of time hands on training with all types of weapons, especially captured enemy weapons, including Second World War

American weapons, Chinese, Russian and even a few German and Japanese weapons. We were allowed to test fire them and some liked the AK 47 we actually broke down and cleaned.

Of all of the weapons and gear we had available to us, the Claymore mine was the premium weapon of the LRP Teams. It was an arched, directional mine that had one and a half pounds of C-4 explosive behind a matrix material that held 800 plus ball bearings about the size of a 25 caliber round. Think of it as about 80, twelve Gauge Magnum Shotgun Rounds pointing in the same direction and capable of simultaneously firing all 80 rounds. It was a devastating weapon and LURPs were taught to deploy them in groups, which created a kill zone that nothing, neither man nor beast could escape.

We also had daily PT. There was a special kind of physical hurt that was projected on us by the 5th SF Cadre. It was called the fast walk. It was described as slower than a run but faster than the airborne shuffle. It basically required that you extend each of your steps to the maximum length of your stride and at a fast pace. This allowed you to move reasonably fast through the jungle, while carrying a heavy load of gear. It was, however, designed to be executed at a sustainable rate which was fast, but not so fast that you quickly tired, had to stop and rest. It allowed you to travel great distances, especially away from your LZ once you were inserted for a mission. The required passage of that physical test was to walk 7 miles in 1.5 hours carrying a 30 pound sand bag in your pack, plus your weapon and all of your other gear you were expected to carry on a LRP mission. All of us passed the test, albeit some by a few seconds, but we all made it.

The third week was to be water borne insertions; however, someone somewhere, probably at the Corp Level, decided that we didn't need that particular training since we would be working in III Corp Area of South Vietnam. The geographical description of that territory mainly consisted of mountains, lowlands, swamps and rice paddies. The decisions makers forgot that some of the major rivers, like the Song Be, passed directly through our AOs. They also never thought about all of the small rivers and canals that came directly out of Cambodia into

23

South Vietnam and were basically unrestricted paths of movement for the VC and NVA. This was our first introduction into Vietnam War politics by which we were immediately affected. We would pay a price down the road for that decision and other political decisions.

The final test was literally a trial by fire in which a Special Forces NCO took out a six man, newly trained, LRP team on an actual recon mission. We conducted a couple of days of recon in a specific area and practiced the true ins and outs of what it took to function as a LRP Team in a combat zone. None of the teams from 1st Platoon had any contacts. After everyone was back in the SF Compound, we had a brief graduation ceremony and were sent on our way back to Bien Hoa. Of course there was one caveat they didn't tell us until after we were on our way back to Company F. We were told that since we didn't complete all three weeks of training of the 5th Special Forces MACV Recondo School, per regs, we could not wear the coveted Recondo Pin/Patch that all graduates received; however, we were now recognized as trained LURPS. This revelation went over like shit on a doorknob and most of us purchased the Recondo Pin at a PX and wore it on our uniforms during R&R and other transits that caused us to be in a Class A Uniform. If you check the 5th Special Forces Recondo Book, written by Special Forces personnel, you will see that there were approximately 350 personnel that went through the two-week course instead of the three-week course and graduated but were not given full recognition as having graduated (did not receive an individual LRRP ID #) from the MACV Recondo School. Xin Loi, GI! (Translation; Tough Shit, GI)

Definition: LRRP – Long Range Recon Patrol was executed by 4 to 6 men and their sole purpose was to gather Intel and send it via radio back to their Headquarters Intelligence Unit (HQ). They used stealth as their primary weapon and were the eyes and ears of larger combat units such as a company, battalion, regiment or brigade.

Definition: LRP – Long Range Patrol was normally executed by 6 men and up to 12 men (Heavy Team). Their dual purpose was to gather Intel and execute ambushes on trails and locations that enemy soldiers were traveling through. They were specifically detailed with disrupting or destroying enemy supply routes, couriers, caches and capturing prisoners when possible. They operated by being extremely stealthy, hitting the enemy with maximum firepower in a surprise attack and then disappearing back into the jungle. The LRP Teams were as much a psychological factor of war as they were a physical factor of war.

In captured documents taken by one of Company F LRP Teams on the border with Cambodia, the enemy referred to LRPs as "special forces with painted faces" and at one point there was a ($5,000) reward for a live, captured LRP. Later in the war, the NVA developed specially trained units including dogs that were deployed with the sole purpose of tracking and destroying LRP/Recon Teams. This was an especially dangerous fact for the crossborder patrols of Special Forces/SOG Teams, who went into Cambodia, Laos and North Vietnam.

Chapter 7

The First Mission as a Lurp

I was assigned to Team 1-5 when we formed Company F, LRP in October of 1967. A Lurp Company's TO&E (Table of Organization and Equipment) is different from a regular line company. Team 1-5 indicates that it is from 1st Platoon and the fifth team of the 1st Platoon.

The Lurp company has four platoons that are manned by seven 6 man teams. They also have a large Communications Platoon, because of the vital need for communications between teams conducting missions and their HQ. The HQ could send helicopters and aircraft to assist them when they got in trouble. The radio, PRC-25 (aka Prick 25), was also the life-line to artillery and helicopter gunships that were effectively used by Lurp Teams to call in ordnance on enemy troops, equipment and camouflaged bunker complexes.

Our team leader was Sergeant Lavender, aka Mississippi, and he was probably one of the best suited American troopers to conduct LRP missions, simply because he was at home in the jungle. He lived in Mississippi and had fished and hunted in the swamps from a very young age. Vietnam was just a change of AO (Area of Operation) for him. The other five team members, including myself, were troopers that had some jungle experience from being in the Herd, but it was not a natural transition for us and we needed to up our game to safely stay in the hunt.

Our first mission for our team was in late November 1967 and in an area southeast of Bien Hoa, and not surprisingly called Operation Virgin for all of the Lurp Teams from Company F. It had some enemy activity, but was not considered a hot bed! I assume that this area was chosen to break in the new Lurp Teams, because Long Range Patrols were a fundamentally different way of conducting combat patrols compared to an infantry line unit of equal size. It gave us a chance to mature as a team. We were inserted in the afternoon and our mission was to recon a specific area, stay one night and then move on to another LZ where we would be extracted. What I remembered about the first mission as we were moving through our AO, was that it was covered in double and single canopy. There was a lot of vegetation on the floor and it made for good cover, but also difficulty in moving through the area. The one thing that stands out was when we found a large trail that had been basically pushed through the dense vegetation. It looked like some smaller military vehicle like a jeep or a ¾ ton powered through the area; however, there weren't any tire tracks. At that point Mississippi was walking point so he hand motioned us to set up a quick defensive perimeter while he checked things out. It is one of the things that separated a line Squad Leader from a Lurp team leader. When a Lurp team leader observed something that they didn't understand, they took the time to investigate it further to see if it was caused by enemy activity or was some natural phenomena. In fairness to the line squad leader, they usually had marching orders to move from point A to point B and the sooner they got there the sooner they could rest and set up a large security perimeter for the 100 plus troopers in the line company. Sgt Lavender took the time and after about five minutes he came back with one other team member he took with him as security to tell us that it was an elephant trail, because up the trail a short distance they found elephant foot prints in the soft soil and the clincher was a large pile of elephant crap. Sgt. Lavender estimated that it was at least a day old. So the Intel that he had gathered was that there were elephants in the area, but it was unknown if the enemy was using them as pack animals. In later patrols we would again find elephant trails and in one instant a pissed-off elephant. Our first night in a RON (Rest Over Night) was in dense jungle that we could hide in, but the sounds were unbelievable. The night-time insects and animal

27

sounds were something that we all knew we would have to learn to contend with and to recognize some of the singers of the sounds. We had already been taught that if you understood them, you could use them to your advantage. The problem was that in the beginning everything you heard, you thought it was Charlie (Victor Charles), so your ass was puckered up pretty much the whole night.

Once the team settled in and the guard schedule was established, several team members at a time were allowed to eat a Lurp ration. The Lurp rations were sealed in a waterproof bag about 6 inches wide by 7 inches long that was made of a clothlike material on the outside with a thin aluminum covering on the inside. Each ration contained a main course that was freeze-dried inside a plastic bag. All you had to do was add water and mix it up. There were six different kinds of meals, with one of my favorites being chili con carne. Also in the ration was some kind of desert, one of my favorites being an orange flavored, small oblong bar that was sweet to the taste and provided some carbs. There was a small piece of folded toilet paper, an OD Green pack of "strike on the cover" matches, a pack of 4 cigarettes, usually some type of crackers and peanut butter package and of course an OD Green set of plastic eating utensils; spoon, knife and fork. The advantage of the Lurp ration was that it was light in weight and it didn't make noise as you prepared it to eat, since everything was packaged in a waterproof type of soft material, not metal cans as in C-Rats. The disadvantage was that it required at least a cup of water to bring the freeze-dried meal to paste like mixture that you could eat. In the dry season water was at a premium for each team member and in one instance it became a matter of Life & Death for my team. We were taught at *Recondo School* to adapt to new problems, so in this instant what most team members did was to add water to their first Lurp Ration and bring it with them already prepared. That saved at least a cup of water and the extra weight of one prepared ration was negligible.

Another difference for a LRP company from a line company was that a Lurp company had a dedicated helicopter unit for each company.

In Company F, we had three Bell UH-1D Iroquois Helicopters known to everyone by the nicknames of Hueys, Slicks or Ships. They sat on pads next to the company area. Two slicks were lift shifts for the teams to be used to insert and extract Lurp Teams. The third was the C&C ship. In addition to the slicks there were originally a pair Bell UH-1 Model B Huey helicopters that had been converted to gunships. Later we received the Bell Cobra gunships.

The B Models had one M-60 machine gun mounted on each side of the fuselage pointing forward and usually two 18-round 2.75 rocket pods mounted next to them. They also had two door gunners who were armed with M-60 machine guns.

Later we got the Bell UH-1 Cobra gunships (aka Huey Cobra or Snakes) who sat at our pads. They were armed with a nose turret containing a more powerful automated 40 mm grenade launcher and a 7.62 cal short barreled mini gun. On the two wing pylons – one on each side of the ship – they had a 7.62 long barreled mini gun and a 2.75 rocket pod with either 12 or 18 rockets. They were extremely fast, deadly accurate, rugged and could bring an extreme amount of firepower from the sky to a firefight. Later on in the war they were also armed with Hellfire missiles and became deadly tank killers.

The gunships, both UH1Bs and the Cobras were normally already in-flight and orbiting, waiting to escort the slicks for an insertion or an extraction. Company F had a second set of Cobras on a 10-minute stand-by, a third set on a 20-minute standby and more if needed that were on 24 hour standby for immediate response for a team in contact.

Having the slicks and their crews located with the company created very fast responses by the slicks when a team was in trouble. It also made for very tight team camaraderie between the slick crews and the Lurp team members. They literally ate and slept with us and there was a high level of mutual respect amongst all involved personnel.

For a team on the ground conducting a mission their vital communication lifeline was the PRC-25 and tied into that communications system were the helicopter crews. UH-1D Iroquois Helicopters were the primary delivery system for Lurp teams, because they were relatively fast, could insert the team into a very specific location and could extract a team from very small LZs or in some cases no LZs. Of all of the external equipment that Lurps used, helicopters were the number one "go to" machine that literally saved the Lurps' asses on many occasions. I personally would not be alive, writing this book if it weren't for helicopters and the very brave crews that operated them.

Of the three slicks one was designated as the C&C (Command and Control) Ship. The slick normally flew with its crew of four, plus one of the Company F Officers, from the commanding officer to a Platoon Lt, Artillery liaison Officer and an Air Force liaison officer. The concept behind the C&C ship was that it would fly high above the two insertion/extraction slicks as an "eye in the sky" and would control the overall operation. The C&C senior pilot (left seat) was in charge of the helicopters that were conducting the operation and closely coordinated with the Company F officer that was on board and talking to the team. If a team was in contact then the eye in the sky could literally be the controller of death and destruction on the enemy and the team savior!

Each LRP company also had a FAC (Forward Air Controller), a US Airforce aircraft and pilot assigned to it. The officer normally flew a Cessna OE1(aka Bird Dog) a single engine tail dragger with a pilot and sometimes an observer, call sign, ALOFT. The primary reason they were there was to provide aerial radio relay for the teams that were out of range for direct radio contact with HQ. The FACs also directed the fighter/bombers on strikes that were requested by Lurp teams. One of the problems was that all of the Air Force aircraft radios operated on VHF(Very High Frequencies) the teams' radios worked on UHF (Ultra High Frequencies) so they could not directly communicate. The second problem was that the jet fighter/bomber aircraft (aka fast movers) made quick decisions on what they were being told by the liaison officers or FAC. Once the bombs were released there was no calling them back. Or they were making 20 mm cannon strafing runs and there was no room for error. If the team on the ground gave bad coordinates or their smoke from a smoke grenade drifted after rising through double or triple canopies they could be in big trouble and on the receiving end of the deadly firepower from the fast movers. The primary fast movers that assisted us were the McDonnell Douglas F-4 Phantom. It had awesome firepower and the distinctive whistle sound of the wings passing through the air. It was such a beautiful sound when you were up to your ass in angry alligators, who wanted nothing more than to kill you and/or fuck up your entire day! If you needed fast movers then you were definitely into some deep shit, either pinned down and unable to move or observing multiple targets that warranted some big bombs to cause a lot of damage and/or destruction.

The one support element that the Lurp team probably used the most after identifying a target such as a manned bunker complex, enemy troops in the open, was artillery. Artillery units claim to be the "Kings of the Battlefield," and maybe they were when the enemy had our artillery rounds exploding amongst their personnel. The reason Lurp teams liked using artillery was because it was somewhat anonymous, since the enemy had no idea who or how the artillery was being directed at them; however, if you kept moving the rounds as the enemy moved then they quickly figured out that they had "eyes on their position" so they would attempt to find and eliminate those eyes!

It was pretty much a sleepless night for most of us on Team 1-5, because it was our first night out with only a six man team, deep in the jungle in enemy territory. Sleeping while on a mission was an individual thing and everyone had to adjust to the team mentality (trust your team members). That came with time and more experience. Eventually when I became a team leader, I developed an ability to wake up every hour on the hour to make sure that a team member was setting up, awake and on guard duty. Because of our close proximity to trails, while conducting ambushes, the average being 15 feet or less, it would have been a death nail to have everyone on the team sleeping. The VC and NVA were very adept at quickly moving through the jungle terrain while making the minimum amount of noise. On a trail they were deadly silent and could be on top of your position before you even noticed them. Later with more experience I developed my sense of smell and that became my number one "go to" when the enemy was near.

Early the next morning, just before first light, we set out on a route that would take us to an LZ and an extraction. In 1967 we did not have any night vision equipment that could be worn on your head or helmet; therefore, we were just as blind as the enemy at night. We also did not have GPS equipment, so we navigated by using a compass and a pace count. Being under double or triple canopy, there was virtually no light filtering down from the stars or moon. You couldn't see your hand more then a couple inches in front of your face and it was just a blur. Your best sense at night was sound because it traveled along the jungle floor, especially if it was man made. The trick was learning to differentiate between a "natural sound" and a man-made sound. There was many a night when I and other team members were on "high alert" because of a sound we could not identify and believed it was the enemy trying to sneak into our position to kill us. Normally in a situation like that, our hearts with a kick from adrenalin were pounding so loud in our chests that you were certain the enemy would here it.

The other problem with moving at night was that the jungle provided a perfect "all natural" obstacle course and it was a very frustrating one, at the least and could also be very deadly. It is the primary reason why a Lurp team never wanted to do an extraction at night, unless it was absolutely necessary and then only when you were in contact and the enemy was trying to finish you off. You couldn't see where you were going, you were probably even more night blind by the fact that you had fired your weapon, ruining even the minimal night vision you might have had. The real killer was that you were making so much damn noise stumbling and falling as you tried to move through the bush, so the enemy knew exactly where you were and the direction you were moving. The two essential requirements to establish a hasty ambush and kill your whole team in one swift assault!

We probably moved half a click or so when we reached the LZ. We used a small handheld Air Force issue strobe light (used by downed pilots) to direct our extraction ship in. As soon as it touched down, we moved toward the right side of the helicopter, which was closest to our position. We were trained to move in a semi arc backing toward the ship if we were under fire so that we could put down a lot of firepower in the direction of the enemy as we maneuvered toward the ship. The first three to reach the helicopter would crawl in and immediately slide to the opposite door of the helicopter so that the rest of the team could quickly climb in and one of the door gunners could give the "clear to lift off" voice command to the pilots. Normally the team leader was the first off the ship on insertion and the last on in an extraction, so that he had complete control over these situations. We did a reasonable job of executing a hasty "load up." I was one of the first three to enter the chopper from the right door and slid across the floor, ending up sitting next to the left door gunner with my feet dangling out the side between the belly and the struts on the helicopter. This was the standard position that most combat soldier's road while on a Huey, because it allowed for a very quick exit from the bird, sometimes at a height that was not conducive to a gentle landing!

The helicopter quickly lifted off from the LZ. Just as we cleared the tree line I saw several campfires with gooks standing around them on a small ridgeline to our west. I yelled "Gooks" at the team and started to bring up my M-16 to take them under fire. The left door gunner grabbed me and told me they were friendlies! I was surprised because we had not heard, seen or smelled their campfires. We later learned that they were ARVN troops and had heard us plowing our way through the bush. The only reason they didn't fire us up was because we were making so damn much noise that they knew we had to be Americans and not the enemy.

The team and the command staff both learned some valuable lessons from that first mission. First of all it is critically important to know the location of all "Friendly Troops" that are in your AO. It was a problem that persisted for us in Company F (LRP) and I'm quite certain with other Lurp units. In fact I developed the following prioritized List: "How to get Killed in Vietnam while patrolling as a Lurp"; # 1 American or Allied aircraft, primarily helicopters; # 2 American or Allied Artillery; #3; American or Allied Troops and last #4; Enemy Troops with AK 47s and RPGs along with various forms of mines, trip wire bombs, homemade claymore mines, etc.!

The second lesson was that there wasn't a good reason to push a team to an extraction point unless it was an emergency. Night movement put the team in danger of being ambushed by the enemy or worse by "friendly troops"! If we had to be extracted at night we usually had some form of aircraft or artillery dropping parachute flares, which lit up the entire area like it was almost day time. This, coincidently, gave the enemy the same visual abilities as us so it was a crapshoot! The only time it wasn't on even grounds with the enemy troops was when Spooky or Puff the Magic Dragon (aka a C-47 Gunship or C-130 Combat Talon gunship) were dropping those flares. In those cases, only the really hard core NVA or pinned down enemy troops stayed around to be blown to bits by a 105 Howitzer, 40 MM Boffers anti aircraft guns, 20 mm Gatling guns, or 7.62 mini-guns. A computer-controlled targeting system that proved to be deadly accurate directed all of those weapons. When gunships fired their 20 mm Vulcan Canon Gatling Gun or the 7.62 mini-guns you would see a steady stream of red tracers arching toward the ground, like a water hose spraying red water in the night sky. The bitch was that the tracers were only every 5th round, so you were only seeing one out of the five rounds that had been fired. The noise emitted by the guns sounded like an evil, metallic growl. When you're lying on the ground, seeing and hearing it above you, you said your prayers to some god for the gunships being there to bale your ass out of some deep shit. You also hoped like hell that the pilot was dead on target with his aiming of the guns. It was said that when the mini-guns fired a long burst there were at least one 7.62 round in every square foot of a football field size target that moved forward at the speed of the aircraft. It was fucking bitching and it made you damn glad that the enemy didn't have such a weapon.

Chapter 8

In the Rear Routine

Team 1-5 had several other non-event missions in the area south of Bien Hoa, but then the company got assigned AOs in the notorious War Zone D. A normal mission was scheduled for 4 nights and 5 days, primarily because of the need to resupply food and water if you patrolled longer than that time period. If you got compromised or shot out then you came back to the company and your team went to the bottom of the list of teams available for a mission. With 7 six man teams assigned to each of the four patrol platoons, you normally had around 25 plus available teams that were on the active patrol list. During normal operations you usually had three to five days before you rotated back up to the top of the list and were assigned a new mission. In really hot AOs I had my team turn around in 24 hours, especially just prior to the 1968 Tet Offensive.

Of course, this "in the rear time" was not slack time. We usually had some type of training occurring in the company area, guard duty on the perimeter or filling sand bags. We had taken over an area once used by E Troop, 17th Cavalry of the 173rd Abn. Brigade and they had not completely finished the protective sand bag revetments. The sand bags were used to help bring the company area up to a higher standard of protection for the barracks and bomb/rocket shelters located between each barracks. The sandbags around the barracks were stacked six high and two wide around the perimeter of every barracks to protect the troops inside if they were asleep and a rocket attack came in to the company area, which did happen on a limited basis. The theory was that if a barracks took a "near hit", you would have some protection. If your barracks took a direct hit, you were pretty much fucked and if it was your day to "Get Your Ticket Punched" you died.

The bomb/rocket shelters were approximately 4 foot wide by 5 foot deep by 30 feet long, a trench that had been dug into the ground and covered with wooden beams and plywood or semi-circle corrugated steel. The steel was often half of a 12-foot diameter culvert that got converted to overhead cover on a bunker. Either way they each had about four to six layers of sand bags on top of them and the protection was somewhat better for near hits, but "same, same" as the barracks protection for a direct hit!

Bien Hoa Airbase was approximately three miles directly south of our company area and we occasionally got 107 mm or 122 mm rockets short rounds or near misses that were aimed at the airbase but missed. Twice we had some 82 mm mortar rounds fired by the enemy from north of the perimeter. The perimeter on the north side of the base was flat and open and then a mile or more of rice paddies before the thick jungle began. Most of the smaller caliber enemy mortars like the 82 mm didn't have the range to make it to the base. The 107 mm and 122 mm rockets did have the range: 8,300 meters and 11,000 meters respectively. The 122mm made really big holes and you did not want to be anywhere near one of those when they dropped in and exploded.

Chapter 9

Training for LURPS, Repelling and McQuire Rigs

Training for a Lurp was continuous, even when we were fully operational. The simple reason was that you "trained as you fought" to the point that most things became second nature and you really didn't have to consciously think about doing it. More importantly for a Lurp team was that the entire 6 man team was in synch with each other so there weren't a lot of intra-team surprises while on a recon or ambush mission.

Insertions and extractions were how a Lurp team began and ended a mission. Kind of like a modern day commute to the office with a Huey instead of car, train or subway. The difference being that each ride to the office ended at a different location and sometimes the reception at the office was very unfriendly at the least or deadly if things went to shit!

We had been trained at MACV Recondo School to repel out of Hueys and how to use McQuire Rigs for an emergency extraction. We used the standard 125-foot green US Army repelling ropes for repelling out of a Huey. The ropes were tied into the floor of the Huey and that is where the Lurp would hook into the rope with his carbineer that was secured to body through the use of a Swiss Seat. A Swiss Seat was nothing more then a short piece of a repelling rope that was cut to length for your particular body style. When it was tied properly around your legs and waist, you could think of it as diaper made out of a rope. Each Lurp tied on their own Swiss Seat so if you screwed up you paid for it in pain or death.

Repelling was taught and sparingly used for insertions into an AO where there simply wasn't any room for a helicopter to land within a reasonable distance to your AO. It was sparingly used because a Lurp repelling out of a helicopter was very vulnerable to enemy fire as was the rest of the Lurp team waiting to repel and the helicopter and its crew. Normally only two Lurps repelled out of the helicopter at one time. One out each door, because of the balance of the helicopter and the shift in weight from side to side. Secondly, while a Lurp was on repel he was attached to the helicopter and whatever the helicopter did the Lurp was along for the ride! It also meant that if the helicopter had moved even a few feet, for whatever reason (pilot having a hard time holding it in a hover, wind, enemy fire) the Lurp was on a pendlum and could swing into the trees next to the designated landing zone of sparsely populated trees on the jungle floor. It was agreed (by his action of hooking into the repelling rope) by the Lurp that if he got hung up in a tree and couldn't easily get loose, the crew would cut the rope and he was on his own to figure out a way to get to the floor of the jungle. The problem was that the repelling ropes had enough strength to hold the helicopter in place and it was more or less stranded there in the hover position. At least by cutting the rope the Lurp had a chance of surviving instead of being jerked up into the air by the force of the helicopter snapping the rope with the Lurp still attached. Only bad shit could occur for the helicopter, its crew and the Lurp, if that was what had occurred!

Even if the repel occurred without a problem the Lurp had to unhook from the repelling rope, normally by just walking to the end of the rope and then pulling it through the carabineer. This took time and you had at least 6 Lurps to repel and unhook. Later the Fast Rope Technique was developed for Special Operations Troops so that they could quickly repel/slide down the rope and they didn't have to unhook from the rope when they hit the ground hopefully feet first.

We conducted training for repelling every couple of months, depending on the operational tempo of the company and of course the Hueys and their crews. It was just as important for the helicopter crews as it was for the Lurps. Normally we would have one Huey and its crew hovering over an open area in the company area. The helicopter would take off with six Lurps on board and the crew. It would lift off essentially straight up to approximately 100 feet above the ground. There would be two safety men on the ground holding the ends of the repelling rope as a brakeman and also to control the ropes so they didn't get fouled in the blades of the main rotor or even worse the tail rotor. Once every thing was in place and the brakemen signaled the helicopter crew that they were ready, the first two Lurps would hook into the repelling ropes via their carabineers and then turn and back out the door, stand on the strut with the repelling rope tight between the Lurp and the rope tied into the floor. Each Lurp would then lean out past the vertical while standing on the strut so that when they pushed off their head would not strike the strut they had been standing on. It was literally a "leap of faith" because once you pushed off the strut you were going one direction, DOWN!

We learned the hard way about some mistakes made as we trained. For example you had to have your brake hand and arm behind your back so that you were already braking when you stepped/pushed off the strut of the hovering helicopter. Gravity took over as soon as you stepped off and if you couldn't break your slide down the rope, you would logger into the ground at bone breaking speed. Of course that is why we had the brakemen on the ground because they could pull hard on the repelling rope and hopefully slow down your speed so that you could land at a relatively safe speed. My first time out on the struts for a repel I did not have my pack straps pulled tight to my body so when I tried to break with my right hand by pulling into my hip and tighten the rope in the carabiner I couldn't get my hand/arm in position to tighten the repelling rope in the carabiner and I steadily gained speed as I fell toward the ground. Thankfully the brakeman saw what was happening and pulled hard on the bottom of the repelling rope which causes friction between the rope and the metal carabineer and thus brakes your fall. I hit with a relative safe speed, kind of like doing a PLF in jump school.

We had another Lurp who had his M-16 on his chest with the barrel facing up and as he came in at a relatively fast speed the butt of the M-16 struck the ground as his legs partially collapsed. The front blade of the rifle hit his face and cut a groove from his upper lip, nose and the left side of his face up to just below his eyes. Probably at least 4 inches long and deep to the bone. He was immediately taken to the field hospital for surgery and then on to Japan. He never returned to the company.

A lot of us also got rope burns even with leather gloves on, from gripping the repelling rope too tight trying, incorrectly, to use that as the break. Xin Loi GI.

The McQuire Rig was used for the opposite reason with a Lurp team. This technique was developed by Special Forces Sergeant Major McGuire when their recon teams were in trouble, in a firefight, and possibly with wounded members and they needed to be extracted, but didn't have any LZs that they could easily walk or fight their way to. It was three Army repelling ropes that were tied to a 4 x 4 post that was attached to the floor of the helicopter, all on the same side. Each rope was coiled and sitting on the floor with a small ammo can filled with sand attached to the end of the rig. On the end of each rig that was dropped out of the door of the Huey was a loop of a heavy-duty strap material, like those used to secure a load on an aircraft. The loop was probably 4 feet long and both ends were permanently attached to the repelling rope. It was essentially a flexible swing seat that you just sat in and the helicopter lifted you and two Lurps straight up (hopefully). It also had a small hand loop that you placed one hand through past the wrist. It was there so if you got shot while riding in the rig the hand loop would hopefully tighten around your wrist and you wouldn't completely fall to your death out of the rig. MACV Recondo School Cadre taught us to interlock our arms to make like a flying wedge with the three Lurps. It was done to prevent the Lurps from individually spinning around and tangling the three ropes/Lurps. Plus, it was important to have some stability for the Huey as it flew through the air.

Once the Lurps had been taken a safe distance from their extraction point, the Huey would slowly lower the Lurps onto the ground and then land to pick them up, because they most likely had to fly back and pick up the remaining three Lurps if the other Huey had not conducted the extraction.

Again this was a learning experience/training for both the Lurps and the helicopter crew. The critical thing here was that the Huey lifted straight up with the three Lurps suspended on end of the 110 + feet of rope below the helicopter as it flew through the air around 80 + mph and 2-3,000 feet above the ground. A real damn E Ticket Ride!

Once again, the Lurps were attached to the Huey by the repelling ropes, so if the Huey didn't get high enough it would drag the Lurps along the ground and into whatever was in front of them. Worst yet was if this was an actual emergency extraction with trees around the site, the Lurps could get hung up in the trees and so it was the same unwritten code of; chopping the rope in the helicopter to free the Huey and its crew. This actually happened on one particular emergency extraction where one of the three Lurps got hung up on a tree, while he and the helicopter were being fired on by the enemy. The crew cut him loose and fortunately he was still hung up on the tree and didn't fall to the ground. He was actually able to cut himself loose and make it to the ground where he was met by the three other Lurps still waiting to be lifted out by the McQuire rigs. It was decided that they would hump some distance to an LZ because it was too hazardous for the Huey and its crew to attempt another McQuire Rig extraction. Of course, they got air support in the form of helicopter gun ships, so Charlie backed off to live and fight another day.

We also did training with other Lurp units, one being the 101st Airborne Lurps. Everything was going as planned until one of the three Lurps in the McQuire Rigs had a problem at about 2,000 feet in the air. Once all three Lurps cleared the ground and the helicopter flew to a safe altitude it would then cruise at a forward speed of approximately 80+ mph. The three Lurps would interlock their respective arms and the two outside Lurps would extend their right or left arms to prevent the three Lurps from spinning in the air due to the air rushing past them.

They were about half way through sending their platoon of Lurps on the training ride when the Huey came back and landed instead of dropping the three Lurps while it hovered and picking up three more Lurps. We also noticed that one Lurp appeared to be very shaken up so we inquired what had occurred.

The three Lurps were riding at 100+ feet below the helicopter at around 3,000 feet and at approximately 80 miles per hour. They were following proper procedures and had their adjoining arms interlocked so that they were sailing through the air as one group to prevent the spinning and tangling of the three ropes. All of a sudden the rope of the right outside Lurp came untied. The Lurp started to fall away from his interlocked Lurp to his left, but made one desperate grab with his left arm and was able to grasp the lower leg/upper boot area of the middle Lurp. That desperate grab saved his life, because he would have fallen around 3,000 feet to his death. The helicopter crew slowly lowered the Lurps to the ground and they had to literally peel the fallen Lurp's arms off the boot of the other Lurp. They then flew back to Company F's Helipad and landed.

What had occurred is that the repelling rope that had been wrapped around and tied to the 4 x 4 post had simply come untied and gravity took over. That was a mistake made by the crew chief for not checking the tie down of the ropes each time they loaded three more Lurps into the McQuire Rigs. We also had a belly man on-board who should have also double checked the ropes.

Needless to say the training continued, but none of us were quite as excited as we had been before the rope/safety crew failed in their duties. I don't know what happened with the one Lurp that had almost fallen to his death, but I would think that down the road and years later he would need some excellent psychological counseling at the very least! Murphy was a dangerous bitch in the war zone!

Chapter 10

A Lurp Team's Mission Preparations

After a little over a week of what we considered "training missions" in areas that were not very "active" with enemy troops, we got our "real" assignment to War Zone D. It was a hot area about 25 miles northwest of Bien Hoa and all of the various combat units including the 173rd Abn Brigade had had some major firefights in those AOs. Two of the first teams inserted into War Zone D (a large area north and east of Tay Ninh) had contact with enemy forces, including Team 1-2 who had contact with a platoon of VC. They actually killed two VC and captured an M-1 Garand Rifle. This is a testament to the effectiveness of a small well-armed and superbly trained Lurp team that used stealth, surprise and shock to their advantage. Another team from Second Platoon had contact, had a man KIA (killed in action), sadly our first trooper killed (Specialist Fourth Class Lindsey) and unfortunately not our last. We had no doubts about the area being hot, so the nerves and the pucker factors were up.

I'm not sure how long it had been since any friendly troops had been in the AOs assigned to Company F, LRP, but it was not unusual to have AOs assigned to our company that had not been patrolled in 4 months or more! Vietnam encompassed large areas of uninhabited jungle that were not patrolled even when there were half a million US Troops "In Country" to prosecute the war. This of course gave the enemy free rein and they acted like they owned those AOs. Surprise, surprise for them when they got their asses killed or wounded in a Lurp team ambush/contact.

We got our "warning order", which is given to the team leader (TL) and assistant team leader(ATL). It tells them the who, what, when, where and how of the mission for the team. Once they receive that information the team leader/s do a high altitude over-flight (usually around 3,000 ft altitude) of the AO so as not to compromise the LZs. The TLs pick their primary LZ and the secondary LZ. In the meantime the assistant team leader is getting the team squared away with the right gear for each of their assignments. Each individual member of the team has a specific assignment and specific equipment for that assignment in addition to his personal equipment such as food, water, etc. The specific equipment included things such as the M-60 machine gun, the M-79 grenade launcher, LAW anti-tank weapon, the PRC-25 UHF Radio and possible other equipment specific to the mission. Even though each team member had a specific assignment, everyone was expected to "share the load" because some team members, like the M-60 gunner had the heavy gun plus some ammo, but he couldn't carry all of the ammo. The combined weight of the machine gun, ammo and personal gear would load the gunner down to the point that he would be overloaded and susceptible to injury or heat exhaustion from the excess weight. It is important to note that like a chain, the team is only as strong/efficient as the weakest member of the team.

The average weight of the gear each team member carried was around 80 lbs. That included his weapon and magazines (usually 10 to 20/20 round mags), grenades (2-4/M-26), smoke grenades (2 of different colors), E&E equipment (signal mirror, strobe light, pen flair gun, etc.) Lurp rations and water for a 5 day mission, poncho liner, some type of combat knife, and of course all of this was contained and carried in either his LBE (Load Bearing Equipment) or his pack. All of that gear was considered his personal gear, but he still had to carry M-79 ammo (usually one bandolier of 6 grenades) for the grenadier, M-60 ammo (usually one cardboard box of a 100 rounds), one claymore mine per team member except for the M-60 gunner who only carried his personal gear and approximate 500-800 rounds of ammo. Someone, normally the ATL carried a LAW and usually the TL carried the radio, but some TLs had a RTO (Radio Telephone

Operator) that carried the PRC-25 with extra batteries. The RTO normally carried his personal gear, the radio, extra batteries and maybe a claymore mine, but no M-60 ammo or M-79 ammo. It was up to the individual team member to carry the basic load, plus whatever extra he wanted to carry as long as he could handle the load and not slow down the team. Also the TL or ATL carried some det-cord (detonation cord), a pound or two of C-4 (Composition 4 explosives and some times pencils (chemically timed detonators to explode the C-4 and the det-cord). As a TL, I also carried one willi-peter grenade (white phosphorous grenade) which was great for "breaking contact" or marking your location in the dense jungle for air assets. It should be noted, however, that during the dry season the willi-peter grenades also started a lot of fires with all of the dry brush. You had better know which way the wind was blowing, if there was a wind, because you might also be running from a brush fire you started.

It was a hell of a load of gear, but the last thing you wanted was to run out of ammo during a firefight with no friendlies arriving for what seemed an eternity. We tended to over-load ourselves at first, but with experience we got the weight down to the average of 60-80 pounds per team member. This of course varied somewhat for the seasons, because you carried more water in the "dry-season" and you carried more ammo and explosives in really hot areas.

On a light team, which is what a 5–6-man recon team was classified as, the team was configured/equipped to travel quietly and efficiently through its patrolling area with the stated probability of no contact with enemy troops. The light team was there to "snoop and poop!" They were to gather intel such as new trails, their direction and amount of use, possible troop concentrations/base camps and any weapons or food caches they may locate and identify. This is not to say that the light team wouldn't initiate contact with enemy troops if the opportunity presented itself and was advantageous for the team. It is important to realize that with only six men it did not take long for a compromised team to be surrounded and in serious trouble. The Lurp teams were operating long distances (20-60 miles) from friendly troops and their 911 call was via the PRC-25 radio, which could be used to call in artillery, helicopter gunships, air-strikes by fast movers or helicopter lift ships to extract the team. The problem was that all of that support took time to respond to assist the team. During that response time, the team was on its own and had to fight and/or maneuver to keep the enemy from pinning them down and eliminating them by superior numbers of troops and weapons. If Murphy was around, which he seemed to be a lot of the times, you could have more than one team in-contact at the same time. If you were the second team waiting/fighting while the first team was being extracted from a hot LZ, you might be in contact for a long time (30 to 60 minutes) and have to E&E (Escape and Evade) which was a nice term for running like hell with the enemy pursuing you in an on-going firefight. Thankfully, most of the time the C&C ship could bring up another pair of Cobras and they could assist you to keep the enemy off of your tail. It got real dicey when the two teams in contact were fairly close (not by design) to each other. Coordination of the air assets was extremely important to prevent mid-air collisions or worst, collateral damage to the second team because the gunship's mini-guns and rockets were also impacting in the second team's area.

When the TL received the warning order, he was also given the approximate date and time that the team would be inserted. This could be moved forward or backward depending on the activity and/or number of contacts the already inserted teams had with the enemy. Usually the day stayed the same, but the time could be moved up or down, because it was best to insert the team around first light or not later than a couple of hours before dusk so that the team had time to leave the LZ and find a safe location to rest overnight (RON) without being compromised.

Once the team had completed assembling their gear and loading it on-board their individual pieces of LBE and pack, they all walked to the weapons test area and fired a few rounds from their weapons. This was to ascertain that they worked properly after disassembling them to clean and then re-assembling them. It also included the M-60.

Once they were test fired, they were unloaded, for safety reasons, because even in a war zone, AD (accidental discharges) occurred, most with deadly consequences as we were to learn later in 1968.

Approximately one hour prior to the insertion time and after the Lurp team had assembled all of their gear, been inspected and approved by the TL and ATL, test fired their weapon, they moved to the TOC (Tactical Operations Command). The TOC was located in an underground bunker and also housed communications. The team received the mission brief from S-2 (Combat Intelligence) and S-3 (Operations and Plans) which were dedicated positions with company officers assigned to those particular positions. This gave every team member all of the up to date Intel about what was occurring in the AO they were going to be inserted into. The briefing also confirmed their call signs, coded map coordinates, primary and secondary radio frequencies for the team radio and for all of their support units, i.e., Artillery, FAC, etc. The TL carried a small waterproof code book known as the SOI (Standard Operating Information) that listed all of the frequencies and other confidential information pertaining to **All Of The Teams in the Field**. It was the one piece of equipment that you never wanted to fall into the hands of the enemy, because it could compromise all of the teams and be a disaster in the making.

The mission brief was one of the major differences between a Lurp unit and a line unit. Everyone on the team knew specifically what was happening in the AO they were going to be patrolling through. If necessary, each team member could take over the team if both the TL and the ATL were wounded or killed and couldn't function as the team's leader. It also gave each team member the buy-in that they were a major part of the operation and their input mattered. Compare this to a line unit, where the Platoon Lt. and maybe the Platoon Sgt. got the briefing from the Captain and they in-turn gave it to the squad leaders who then briefed each individual squad. By the time it got down to the individual troopers in the individual squads you got something like; "this is the route of march, this is our position in the march, load-up and get ready to move out, and don't ask any questions!" It made you feel like you were an insignificant little wheel in the big machine and you could be replaced without a problem if you fucked up and got yourself wounded or killed. I thought it was a shitty way of doing business and it sure as hell didn't make you feel like a member of the team!

Once the mission brief was completed the team usually loaded up and walked to the heliport to load on-board the slicks for insertion. The final two very important checks occurred: every team member jumped up and down to see if anything made noise or they had loose equipment and at the revetments they jacked a round into the weapons chamber and put it on safe. Even the M-60 gunner loaded his machine gun with what we called an "assault belt" which consisted of approximately 30 linked 7.62 machine gun rounds placed in the firing tray of the gun. This allowed the M-60 gunner to be able to immediately put out some rounds if the LZ was hot or if the team had contact as they ran off the LZ. It was all about putting out the maximum amount of rounds (fire superiority) if contact was initiated. It gave the team time to maneuver and take the enemy under fire. When the M-60 talked everyone listen, especially the enemy, because they respected and feared that gun. It also gave the team a brief psychological advantage, because the enemy was aware that normally the M-60 was used in conjunction with larger units such as a 30 man platoon. This kept them guessing regarding what type of unit and how many American troops they were actually in contact with. The Australians also used a machine gun very effectively at the squad level.

As the final checks were completed, the helicopter crew chief and gunner unhooked the tie downs of the rotor blades and the pilots fired up the turbine on the Huey. As the whining turbine spun up with the normal smell of JP-4 jet fuel emitting from the exhaust of the engine, the team climbed on board and put their game faces on. Three team members in the left door, sitting on the floor with their legs hanging out the door and the other three team members, same-same in the right door.

When I became a TL and as we lifted off and over the berm of our base camp, Ed the nice guy became Ed the hard ass TL whose entire focus was on completing the mission, while protecting every member of the team. It was a very heavy psych load, but it came with the territory!

Chapter 11

First Contact for Team 1-5

We received a warning order on January 2, 1968 as a heavy team to establish an ambush on an identified crossroads of two trails. I would be walking point and Spec 4 Renolet (aka Dicky Gross) would be carrying the M-60. The heavy team would consist of our team, 1-5 and team members from two other teams to bring us up to the necessary number of 12 men.

We inserted at around 1230 hours on January 3, with it being a sunny and hot day. Of course, Murphy was there and screwed up the insertion. Since we were a heavy team, it required two helicopters to carry all of the men, so somehow the second Huey got separated from the lead insertion Huey with our team on it. Fortunately neither team had a Hot LZ, so after a nerve racking 30 minutes we finally hooked up. The hook up is especially dangerous because you have two completely covert teams moving toward each other with everyone on high alert and your finger very close to the trigger. In this instance it took a lot of radio communications between the two team leaders, to coordinate their movements and finally join back together as one team. It also created additional helicopter activity in the area, which is exactly what you don't want if you're trying to be covert and move through the jungle without bringing a lot of enemy attention to the area. This is especially true for right after you have been inserted and once you're fairly certain you weren't spotted or compromised on the LZ.

Once we got everyone in their appropriate positions for the line of march, Sgt. Lavender gave me an azimuth to follow. We slowly headed out, primarily on a northern route with the LZ to our left approximately 50 meters, but with plenty of cover to move through. I was walking point and on high alert. I had walked a lot of point in the two months I was with the 173rd and I liked doing it. Partially because I knew exactly what was happening and probably for the adrenalin rush that came with that position. Sgt. Lavender was usually three positions back from point which meant I had Spec 4 Schmidt behind me and then Gross with the M-60, Sgt. Lavender, Spec. Johnson, as his RTO, and then Sgt. Rock, the Assistant Team Leader who was rear guard followed by a similar arrangement with the second team.

We were in somewhat of a hurry to get away from the LZ because of the problem with the second helicopter inserting the other team in the wrong part of the LZ. That little problem delayed our movement away from the LZ. *It had been instilled in us by the Cadre at MACV Recondo School to clear the LZ as soon as possible, because that was one of the most compromising and dangerous locations to be for a Lurp Team.* Once you moved away from the LZ, you became a truly covert team and could move to your target area with relative safety, if you were following the training and protocol of Recondo School. However, there had to be a compromise between speed and safety while moving through the jungle. I had a feel for that and I would adjust accordingly to the terrain and keeping in mind that I had 11 other team members behind me that needed to also move quietly, but safely through the jungle. We had only moved approximately 200 meters when I realized the LZ had curved in toward our route of march and worse yet I hit a high speed trail. I slowly raised my right hand in a fist to indicate I was stopping and had seen something. I did a hand signal by pointing at my eyes and making a walking motion with my index and middle finger on my right hand, that I was observing a trail. I also indicated by pointing at Sgt. Lavender that I wanted him to come up and take a look. All of these hand signals had been silently passed on to each member of the heavy team so they knew what was happening. It was amazing to observe that all twelve men could silently receive semi-detailed information about what was occurring on point, adjust to the situation and set up security while in a patrol line march. The team members immediately squatted down and covered their area of responsibility as they had been trained to do. Sgt. Lavender came up along with Spec 4 Johnson, because he carried the radio and was always within arm reach of the TL should the shit hit the fan. Spec 4 Eric Johnson was one of our "discipline problems" who had made it all the way through Special Forces Communications School but did not graduate because of a minor problem with him and the SF Commander's daughter being in bed together the night before graduation. Special Forces loss and our gain because he was an excellent radio operator and would automatically transmit a radio call when we were in contact. He usually handled the coordination of gunships and slicks if Sgt Lavender was busy with controlling our fight against the enemy we were in contact with.

I had moved back from the trail by a meter or so, as taught by SF. The reason was that you didn't want to be seen by anyone on the trail, but you had to be close enough to see and or at least hear what was happening on the trail. Again this was a "do it by feel" type of situation. Depending on the foliage alongside the trail, you might be closer or further from the trail.

Sgt. Lavender slowly moved up to the trail, then moved into the low crawl position and by spreading some bushes that were next to the trail he took a cautious look up and down the trail and also at the trail itself. Sgt. Lavender was over 6 ft tall, but he moved like a shadow and you rarely ever heard him make more noise then just a whisper of movement. He crawled back to mine and Spec 4 Johnson's position where we covered his back by watching up and down the trail. After a moment, TL Lavender decided that we were going to cross over the trail and set up an ambush. This is pretty remarkable because he had assembled all of the possibilities in his mind and came up with a plan, which although controversial in concept, proved to be a brilliant idea. The controversial part was that we were up against a "High Speed" trail, had unknowingly been moving toward the LZ on our left and were now at a pinch point. We had the open area/LZ on our left, the trail to our front and worst yet the trail ran perpendicular to our line

53

of march and had another open area to the right front of the trail. I had unknowingly marched us right into what basically looked like the tip of a pyramid with everything around us, except to the rear, being an open area, *which is one of the "don't ever do this" situations that we were warned about in Recondo School, but "shit happens", so you adjust and go forward with a plan.* Secondly, the minutes are ticking off when you are at a trail, especially a "High Speed" trail, since the enemy could come walking down the trail at any time and you probably wouldn't hear or see them until they were right on top of you. That means that it would be who was the most alert or who had the fastest reflexes would probably win the "shoot or die" scenario. Also with the heavy team being in a straight patrol line of march, they were spread out and couldn't bring full fire power to the trail where it would be most needed in a firefight.

The other controversial thing about Sgt Lavender's decision to move across the trail and set up an ambush, was that *it was a second "don't ever do this" lesson we had been taught at Recondo School.* The reason was that if you crossed a trail especially with 12 men there was a very high likelihood that the enemy would see the trail you had made and would send someone to follow it. You have to realize that the VC and the NVA lived in the jungle, it was their home 24/7 and they were in-tune with it. Something like a man-made trail coming out of the heavy bush and crossing a trail was an immediate indication that enemy troops were in the area. Their own personnel would have used the trail when they bumped into it and would not have crossed over it. Secondly, they knew that most of their personnel would have been on the trail in the first place, since it would be like someone walking down a street with sidewalks in a suburb, but instead of using the sidewalks, that person would be walking on the lawns of all the houses on the street.

Sgt Lavender moved back to rear of our team after whispering to me what he wanted us to do. He talked with Sgt Rock and also with Sgt McCavee the TL for the other team. It was decided that we would cross the trail one team at a time, as we had been taught in Recondo

School. The basic principle being that there was always at least two team members watching the trail, one to the right and one to the left as the other team members crossed over, one person at a time. Then the last two team members would individually cross over. We had practiced this at Recondo School and back in our company area, but this would our first time of actually doing it in combat situation and on a high speed trail!

For someone that has never been in combat, it may seem like a trivial thing to cross a trail, but it was anything but trivial, because it was dangerous and could ultimately lead to injury or death of a team member. I was first to cross since I was walking point and I have to tell you that my heart was pounding as I took one final look both ways and then rapidly stepped almost across the trail. It was a little too wide to make it in one step so another half step and I was across and in the brush on the other side of the trail. I immediately moved to a position near the trail and was looking east down the trail, which I could see skirted the south side of the open area for approximately 50 meters. As soon as I crossed over and established security, Spec 4 Schmidt came across and took the security position to the west looking toward the LZ which the trail also skirted on the northern side of the LZ. I had glanced in that direction and observed that the trail was visible for approximately 25 meters in that direction, so I knew we had good observations on the trail and would be able to immediately react if the enemy came walking down the trail. We completed the cross-over without incident, but now the two teams were reversed in order with the second team actually setting up rear security on our position and the trail. The most important thing was that Sgt Lee, the ATL for the second team and the rear security person for his team and the entire Heavy Team, was the last one to cross over the trail. As he crossed over, he put the bushes back in place as best he could so that it didn't look like it had been a trail and he also brushed out with a dead branch our Vietnam jungle boot prints we had left at the edge of the trail. Again these may seem like minor things, but to the enemy if they observed these signs on the trail, it would be like a large, red, neon, flashing sign with an arrow pointing in the direction the US soldiers had taken. After a brief wait to make sure we hadn't been compromised while crossing over I again headed out in a northerly direction as ordered by Sgt Lavender. We had moved approximately 50 meters north of the trail and took a hard left for about 20 meters, then another hard left heading back toward the trail. This info had been whispered to me by Sgt Lavender, while we were at the trail and before we crossed over. Again this is a lesson taught at Recondo School to give misdirection to the enemy. If they found our trail at the crossover point they would see that we had headed north or south from their trail and they would think that we were moving through the area and away from the trail. Unless they followed the trail we made, they wouldn't know with all of the heavy vegetation that we had made a turn and had other ideas other then leaving the area.

Jungle warfare, guerilla warfare and now asymmetrical warfare are consequently as much about "getting into the heads of the enemy" as they are of a physical nature or an outright firefight!

I had moved another 30 meters when I stopped once I could see that the vegetation was thinning out at least in the overhead cover area, because I could tell that the light was brighter to my front. I signaled a halt with my raised fist as I had been told to do by Sgt Lavender. We sat up a hasty 360 degree perimeter with Dicky Gross and his M-60 covering the majority of the trail to our front. Sgt Lavender and Spec 4 Johnson moved forward to check out the area and find a good position for us to establish an ambush on the trail we had crossed over. Earlier I had said that Sgt Lavender's decisions were controversial for various reasons, but now his "smart as a swamp fox" decisions started to appear. What TL Lavender had decided to do was establish an ambush with our crossover point on the trail being in the "kill zone." If our crossover trail was discovered by the enemy while moving down their trail, we would know we had been compromised and better still the enemy wouldn't know that they were in a kill zone until it was too late.

Sgt Lavender and Spec 4 Johnson returned and Sgt Lavender started issuing orders, via hand signals where he wanted everyone to position themselves in a linear ambush parallel to the trail. *It is important to understand that the TL makes the ultimate decision on every aspect of the team while on a combat patrol. You may disagree and even tell him why you disagree, but he has the final say on everything. This was one of the Golden Rules taught to us by the Cadre at Recondo School.* Once everyone knew the general area they were to cover at the ambush site, we began the complicated and time sensitive operation of physically establishing an ambush on a trail. Setting up an ambush on an active trail is time sensitive because the team is at risk during the time the claymore mines are being placed in position. The enemy could come walking down the trail, not making any noise and they would be on top of your positions before you even noticed them. The positioning of the claymores can be complicated because each ambush site was different and was dictated by the trail and the foliage along the trail. The ambush always included a kill zone, flank and rear security positions. Supporting those offensive and defensive positions were numerous claymores placed for interlocking fields of fire in the kill zone and pointed outwards in the flank and rear security positions. Of course the team members and their individual weapons such as the M-16, M-79 or the M-60 provided the additional firepower after the claymores were detonated in the kill zone. There could be, depending on the nature of the ambush, a firefight immediately after the ambush was executed, between any enemy soldiers that were not killed or wounded in the kill zone and the team members.

It is probably a good time to explain the claymore mine and how significant a weapon it was for a Lurp team. The M18 Claymore mine, affectionately known just as "the claymore" by Lurps, was our "go to" weapon and we used it in various ways. The main feature of the claymore mine was that it was directional and had a 60 degree arc/kill zone in front of the mine with an affective range of 100 meters in an open environment. In the dense jungle environment it was probably only 20 meters, but then we normally used multiple claymores in the kill zone so death was almost always achieved. The real business end of the mine was that it contained 700, 1/8 inch steel ball bearings molded into an epoxy resin inside the front of the mine. What pushed those steel balls out at over a 1,000 feet per second was 1.5 pounds of C-4 and that is what made it so deadly and effective when used in an ambush. If you think of a twelve gauge shotgun with #4 Buckshot in a 2 3/4 shotgun shell that contains 27 pellets (.24 inches in diameter for #4 buckshot and .125 inches in diameter for the claymore ball bearings) you would have approximately 26, 12 gauge shotguns simultaneously firing and in the same direction for each claymore mine.

When I became a team leader and was leading a heavy team, I usually had between 5 to 7 Claymore mines set in the ambush/kill zone plus additional claymores on the flank and for rear security. Hypothetically, this would be approximately 182/12 gauge shotguns pointing into the kill zone. It was almost always fatal to anyone standing within 10 meters of the mine and most of the time the enemy was only feet from the mine when it was detonated. The way we were taught to deploy them by SF personnel was to aim them so that every other claymore in the kill zone was interlocked with the next claymore to its right or left. In other words if you had set up a linear ambush on trail that was parallel to your position the first claymore in the center could be pointed to the right and the next one to the right of that claymore would be pointed to the left so that the individual claymores kill zones made a hypothetical X on the trail. This was continued down the ambush site with normally two claymores being deployed as a pair; however, the trail and the terrain dictated how the claymores were actually set in an ambush. The most important thing about the claymores was that the last one on the left and right of the ambush kill zone was always pointing down the trail and away from the actual kill zone. This placement was necessary so that if the enemy troops were spread out in a line of march along the trail, not every enemy soldier would be in the kill zone. The last two claymores normally wounded any enemy soldiers that had not been wounded or killed in the kill zone. It also devastated their ability to immediately flank your position, because even though those additional soldiers were not killed they were either wounded or so psychologically stunned that they normally fell back to a position they felt safe from the direct fire from our ambush sight.

Sgt Lavender assigned each of the 12 men of the heavy team a position either on the line to front and in the kill zone offensive positions, the flank or rear security defensive positions with all positions overlapping to create a 360 degree secure perimeter.

The following list shows the positions from right to left and weapons used by each team member, who were up front on the line in the kill zone, as the ambush was established. Sgt Lavender the TL (M-16 & M18 claymore mine) took the extreme right position on the line of the ambush site; Spec. 4 Johnson the RTO, (PRC-25 Radio & M-16) was the first position to his left; Spec 4 Renolet, machine gunner, (M-60 machine gun with 500 rounds of military ball & tracer ammunition) was to Johnson's left; Private Schmidt (M-16 & M18) next position; Private Britton (M-16 & M18) next position; Private Cunningham (M-16 & M18) next position; Spec 4 Dvorak (M-16 & M18); Private Kozak, Grenadier (M-16 & M-79 & M18); Sgt McCavee (M-16 & 2/M18's). Because of the terrain and front cover, Sgt McCavee and Private Kozak were positioned to my left approximately 10 feet away, but I had a clear view of them. They were responsible not only for the left end of the kill zone, but also the flank security to our left of the ambush site. It was for that reason that Sgt McCavee placed two Claymore mines to his left front area. One mine covered the east end of the trail as it disappeared into the tree line and the other mine covered the open area that was to the left of his position and to the north side of where the trail disappeared into the tree line.

To the rear of the front line positions were the three personnel that made up the rear security of the ambush sight. Spec 4 Market (M-16 & M18) was to the left rear; Sgt Lee, Grenadier (M-16 & M-79 & M18), was in the next position to the right; and finally Sgt Riggs

(M-16 & LAW & M18) was in the final position to the right rear of the ambush sight.

There were 6 claymores positioned in the kill zone and 4 claymores used as flank and rear security for a total of 10/M18 claymore mines; however, as shown by the what occurred with this ambush, sometimes a claymore placed for flank or rear security actually is used as an offensive weapon instead of its intended use as a defensive weapon. You should also note that in additions to the 10 claymore mines, the heavy team had 11/M-16 Rifles; 2/M-79 Grenade Launchers; 1/M-60 Machine Gun & 1 LAW anti-tank weapon at its disposal. The collection of weapons as a whole constitutes enough firepower to easily attack and sustain a firefight with a larger force of enemy soldiers. The other advantage is the surprise/shock of the attack and the viciousness of the Claymore mines when combined with the small arms firepower, a machine gun and grenade launchers.

It had taken the team approximately 20 minutes to place all of the claymores in the kill zone, flank and rear security. The placement of the mines was the first and premiere activity that the team had to complete. Once the claymores were in place and armed then the team had established good offensive and defensive positions, relative to the ambush sight in general and to the kill zone in particular.

The second priority that the team must complete is making each individual position as quiet and comfortable as possible, given the fact that you should be making minimal noise and movement while you're completing this task. This usually involves placing your pack to your front as both some cover and concealment and later as back support/pillow depending if you're "on guard" or "off guard". You would also clean the ground you're laying on by brushing and or moving any leaves or other vegetation that could cause noise or discomfort and in that order. *It is a necessary process, but you can't do a clear out of your position, because when you leave, you are expected to put everything back like it originally was. The reason being that if the enemy was to walk into your old position they wouldn't know that the team had ever been there and in an ambush position. This was another lesson taught to us by the Cadre at Recondo School. It was a necessary practice so that the enemy did not first of all even know that you had been in the area and secondly how and where you had established an ambush or Rest Over Night (RON) position. I guess in today's Army they would call it counter-intelligence of Lurp Teams Method of Operations. We just called it Covering Your Ass for future patrols of all Lurp Teams in the Area of Operations (AO)!*

Team 1-5 got settled in for the wait *(this was the Patience Card that the Cadre at Recondo School pounded into our heads)* to see what would come down the trail. It could be a long wait of days or maybe not very long, like minutes after you established the ambush. You never really knew how long you would be there, but the waiting was normally directly proportional to what you observed about the trail itself. If it was well used, clear of vegetation, approximately 2-3 feet wide, had overhead cover in the form of bent & tied branches or cut branches and with the dirt on the trail packed down by numerous enemy soldiers/persons walking on it, then it was what we called a "High Speed Trail" These were all indicators that there was a high probability that you would see some activity on that trail within a day or less. It should be noted that these trails were normally in areas that were called "free fire zones", which meant there probably weren't any friendly villagers living in the area and so whoever came down the trail was considered "an enemy combatant." Also, the trails were not something that villagers would normally use unless they were close to the village or a small town. The South Vietnamese farmers, who grew rice, vegetables and fruit, tended to live in small family groups/villages probably for mutual protection and to help each other in the fields. Unless they were close to some larger town or provincial capitol there weren't a lot of secondary roads like you would find in rural areas of the US. The Vietnamese would use streams, canals and rivers as their primary means of transportation. There were of course major highways that had been in place for years but these were normally used to connect major populated areas such as Bien Hoa with Saigon, etc.

Myself and Spec 4 Cunningham were clearing out the leaves and branches near our feet to prevent any noise if we moved while lying in the ambush mode. This site was rather unique because there wasn't a lot of growth to the rear of our position even though there was only a single layer of canopy above our heads. It was like a cave within the overhead and frontal growth of vegetation. We continued to sweep away the leaves and it was at that time that we discovered a sheet of metal approximately 4 feet square that was covered with a thin layer of dirt and the fallen leaves. It appeared to be made of tin, because it had some corrosion on its surface and was double over around the edge. This immediately put Cunningham and me on alert, because this was not a normal place for a piece of cheap sheet metal to be hidden or where it could have accidently fallen from possibly an aircraft or vehicle. It felt like it was supported across its length and width by some kind of frame beneath it and possibly hollow below the frame. This could only mean one thing. It was a cache, which also usually meant that it was probably booby-trapped to prevent anyone from breaking into the cache to take whatever it was holding. I immediately got Sgt. Lavender's attention by snapping my fingers and when he looked in our direction, I indicated with hand signals that I wanted him to come to our position. When he arrived we showed him the metal sheet. I whispered to him that we thought it was a cache. He examined it with his eyes and then felt the slight give in the metal sheet as he pushed on the top center area of the sheet of metal. He agreed with our assessment and told Cunningham and I via hand signals and a whisper, not to disturb it. He indicated that we would deal with it when we were ready to leave the ambush site. Sgt. Lavender crawled back to his position and started a whispered message along the line of Lurps about the cache and his decision to leave it until later. This may seem like a mistake, because we were now essentially sitting on top of probably some kind of explosive booby-trap protecting a cache. If it was rigged with enough explosives, it could literally blow up the whole team. The fact that Sgt. Lavender, as Team Leader, made what could be a life or death decision for team members, shows the intelligence, experience and pure intestinal fortitude (aka Huevos/ Balls) he possessed to make that split second decision. Secondly, it reflected the professionalism of the entire team to accept the TL's decision and get on with our "lie in wait" to ambush what ever would come down the trail. It did of course add some tension to the already semi-intense team, because of how and why we had picked this ambush site and the fact that we were in a very active combat area.

I had previously mentioned that the clock is always ticking as soon as you are inserted into an LZ. Essentially there are two clocks, the first one records the amount of time you have been on the ground conducting your LRP Patrol. That clock is set to expire, without having contact with the enemy, approximately four nights and five days after you touch down on the LZ. The primary reasons being your team would be nearly out of food and more importantly low on water, low on batteries for the PRC-25 and near the end of their stamina. There is also the physical stress of patrolling through the tough jungle terrain and the mental stress of being only six men deep in enemy territory, essentially "always behind the enemy lines."

The second clock is more like a stop-watch and is activated as soon as you find a trail or enemy facility such as a bunker complex. If the TL decides to establish an observation post, an ambush site or more likely a combination of the two, the team needs to accomplish that maneuver with speed but safely and silently. As I previously explained it takes time, especially to set up an ambush and during that time the team is at risk of getting into a firefight or being observed, which compromises the team's existence and position.

We had been taught by the Recondo School Cadre that normally the enemy moves at first light and just before or just after sun set in the twilight hour. One of the reasons being they were the coolest parts of the day in the tough jungle environment and also the enemy, like us, did not have night vision equipment, so they needed light to see where they were going.

Only a few minutes after Sgt. Lavender made the timely and important decision to stay in the ambush site with the cache in the middle of us, we heard sounds like equipment bouncing against other equipment and Vietnamese voices. This immediately got the attention of everyone on the team, especially since it was only around 1430 hours and in the heat of the afternoon sun. Secondly, they were making so much noise and talking loudly that we believed it could be a South Vietnamese Army Unit that was on a patrol and where they were not suppose to be. That alone could be a real problem and cause a friendly fire incident. Or it was a large group of enemy soldiers, who believed that they had sufficient numbers of fighters to ward off any attack and were in a "safe area", so that their operational security was lax!

Within a minute of originally hearing the sounds, we observed that it was in fact a large Viet Cong formation moving down the trail. By now everyone was spun up and we were on a 100 percent alert. Most of us had already moved the safety off our claymore mines in anticipation of executing an ambush in the kill zone. That was everyone except for Sgt. McElwee (aka Mac), who was a skinny guy of average height and build and no external indications of his intestinal fortitude. Mac was calmly sitting up and eating a Lurp ration. I hand signaled him to get his claymores ready to fire. He simply gave me a short hand wave and took another bite of his Lurp ration. What you need to know about Mac is that he had a set of balls (figuratively) so big that we wondered how he could even walk with them and he was calm as a cloud floating through the sky in even the most hair-raising combat situations. That is until the shit actually hit the fan, then Mac was Hell on Wheels!

Everyone looked over at TL Lavender as we let the first seven heavily armed VC (3/Ak 47s; 3/M-2 carbines; 1 Thompson sub-machinegun) move through our kill zone. We all wanted to blow our claymores, but TL Lavender just slowly moved his head from side to side indicating a No! The probable reason for the "Don't Fire" was that there was another group of seven heavily armed (primarily M-2 carbines) VC following that group and not quite in the kill zone. That was a total of 14 armed VC as a point element. There was a high probability that this was a VC Company of somewhere between 50 to 100 personnel marching down the trail and acting like they owned the world or at least this little piece of Vietnam.

After the entire point element passed by the next group of six VC walked into the kill zone; they consisted of two women, two teenage boys and two men, who were armed with SKSs. All of them were carrying large packs that appeared to be very heavy. As they walked threw the kill zone one of the men briefly stopped, squatted down and looked under the brush along the trail. He was looking back toward Mac, and he said something in Vietnamese in a rather quick phrase and I knew we had been compromised. In this instant I knew I had to blow my claymore, because I was concerned that he was going to shoot Mac, who was now down on the ground, but looking up the trail where more VC were moving toward our ambush site. Due to our excellent training we had restrained from firing on the point element as ordered by TL Lavender, but we also had the individual responsibility to initiate an ambush if we thought we were compromised. What I didn't know, until later, was that two of the VC had left the trail and walked over to where Mac had placed the claymore that was facing out onto the open area north of the trail. Mac had crawled out in the semi-tall grass and had found a small piece of poncho that had probably fallen out of a helicopter as it flew overhead in some distant past. He had placed this on top of the claymore that was facing east to give it some additional camouflage and apparently one of the VC had spotted this piece of poncho and two of them went out to recover it for whatever purpose they thought to use it. Just as the front VC bent over and picked up the piece of poncho, Mac blew that claymore and the other one facing down the trail. His two claymores detonated simultaneously with my claymore and milliseconds later the other four claymores in the kill zone were detonated. That was a total of seven claymores which equaled 10.5 pounds of C-4 exploding along an approximate 25 meters of kill zone. It was one hell of a big bang and we saw it, felt it and heard it all at the same time! The sky turned black and temporarily blocked out the sun with the black smoke and all of the back blast dust and debris that was blown out and up into the air. Five of the claymores were within 15 feet or less of the Lurps lying on the front line of our ambush. We all got a hell of a concussion/shock wave and a lot of debris blasted into the line. It also caused all of us to temporarily loose the majority of our hearing because the claymores are designed to be detonated 75 feet away from the back of the claymore and with some kind of cover between the soldier firing the claymore and the claymore itself. Of course we couldn't deploy the claymores that far away because we wouldn't be able to see the trail or the claymores when it got dark. *As per our training at Recondo School we each fired (on full auto) a partial magazine from our M-16s and Gross fired a burst from the M-60 into the kill zone. This was standard operating procedure to ensure that whoever had been in the kill zone and might still be alive, could not return fire or throw a grenade into your position!*

There was an immediate silence that followed the large explosion and our burst of automatic fire. The primary reason for the silence was because no one could hear anything and the enemy was in obvious shock with the explosions that had just ripped through the middle of their formation. That did not last very long, because what we didn't know was that the trail to the west of the ambush site made a right turn towards the north approximately 30 meters from the ambush. Most of the point element of the 14 heavily armed VC had made the turn so they were not hit by the claymore that TL Lavender had placed facing west down the trail. After the initial explosion, they quickly recovered and started flanking us. From somewhere to our right flank, we got two grenades thrown into and near our west perimeter and when they exploded, two of the Lurps got hit with some shrapnel. At this time TL Lavender got up on his knees and let out this blood curtailing Rebel Yell and immediately started firing his M-16 toward our right flank where the grenades had been thrown. That was the release button for everyone's anxiety and fear. We all opened up with return fire in the direction of where we were now receiving fire, which was to our left and right flank along with some fire coming in to our rear. Of course our rear security was putting down suppressive fire with their M-16s and the M-79. Just before the two enemy grenades came into our perimeter, I heard what sounded like moaning coming from the kill zone, it was probably pretty loud but with our temporarily damaged hearing it sounded like I was hearing it come through a small pipe from a long distance away. I also saw that one of the two males that was in the group of six in front of my claymore, had a red rooster chicken tied to the front of his pack. It was still alive, missing the leg not tied to the pack, but kind of flopping around like it had also been hit by the claymores or our automatic weapons fire. It continued to flop around like it was trying to escape, but I thought it was rather ironic that that was the only thing I could see moving in the whole damn kill zone!

I noticed some movement to my left and saw that Mac was up on his knees and was about to throw a White Phosphorus grenade. He pulled the pin and lobbed the grenade toward the center of and just to the south side of the trail and the kill zone. I was thinking, "what the hell was Mac doing?" Later, I learned that he saw an enemy soldier crawl out of the kill zone and into the area he had thrown the willie peter grenade. I watched the grenade sail through the air and land about 10 meters to our front. It blew with just a slight popping noise, but sent a large mushroom cloud of white smoke into the air and quarter size chunks of burning white phosphorous in a 360 degree pattern. We were all in our "kill or be killed mode" and we returned fire in all directions trying to suppress the incoming enemy fire. Our biggest concern was that the point element would come on line and try to overrun our position from the rear while the remaining enemy pinned us down with fire coming from our left front and left flank.

During this entire time, Spec 4 Johnson had been on the radio and put out the info that we were in "Heavy Contact" with a large enemy force and that we had some wounded in action (WIA) Lurps. Spec 4 Johnson was also our go-to medic. He handed off the radio to TL Lavender and moved over to Spec 4 Schmidt. It was at that time that I noticed he was wounded with a metal leg from one of the claymores sticking in his left upper chest, just to the left of his left front breast pocket. He was bleeding, but from the angle of the leg it appeared that it had bounced on the ground and then hit him in the chest in an upward movement. That probably saved his life, because the leg had only penetrated his chest for approximately an inch and was just under his skin. Spec 4 Johnson pulled out the leg and put a bandage on the hole in Schmidt's chest. He was in pain but not down and out. Once Spec 4 Johnson was finished administering first aid to Schmidt, Schmidt started firing his M-16.

We were in the firefight for approximately another 10 minutes, which is a long time when you're taking a lot of enemy fire from three different directions. Most of us were putting out short 3-4 round bursts from our M-16s and Gross with the M-60 on "Rock and Roll" was hosing down the area with approximately 10 round bursts to our left front and left flank where the enemy had taken refuge in the tree line. They were firing a lot of rounds into and around our position. During that time, none of us even thought about the cache we were lying on top of. Even with our temporary loss of our hearing, it was still damn loud with all of those weapons firing, along with the M-79 rounds exploding in various locations as determined by the gunners.

Finally, the gunships arrived overhead and after TL Lavender threw a smoke grenade to our front they started making gun runs on the enemy positions. They first made 7.62 mm mini-gun runs and 2.5 rocket launches to the west of our position where the 14 armed VC point element was down in the trees and bushes, firing on us. We could hear them firing back at the helicopters as they made their gun runs, which was pretty ballsy, because they had to have known that there was a lot of death raining down on them. Kind of like taking a knife to a gunfight! The gunships also made several runs to our left front and east side of the open area, after which time TL Lavender indicated that we should saddle up and prepare for a "Hot LZ" extraction. Earlier I had mentioned about the LZ to our right front approximately 50 meters away. This was to be the location for our extraction and since it required two Hueys to lift out the whole team the pilots needed extra room to get both helicopters to land simultaneously and pick up the whole team on one extraction. It is imperative that this occurs because you are cutting your firepower in half when you lift out one light team, leaving the other light team on the ground.

For some of us, especially me, this was my first firefight (finally busted my cherry) and as firefights go it was pretty damn serious. Of course all firefights are serious because it only takes one bullet or one piece of shrapnel for you to have a "bad day", or maybe even your last day on Planet Earth! I wasn't thinking about that though, because we were about to pick up from our ambush site and move to the LZ, while still taking fire from the enemy. We would move out in two teams, so that when we got to the LZ each light team would be ready to load onto their individual Hueys. TL Lavender actually took point with Spec 4 Johnson right behind him and me behind both of them. As we crossed over the trail where the dead bodies of the VC lay, I reached down and pulled a pair of Ho Chi Minh Sandals off of one of the bodies and took them with me. I also noticed that the damn "VC Chicken" was dead! All of my senses were on "overload" but I could smell death emitting from the dead VC. It is a combination of body odor, blood, shit and maybe just fear in addition to the smell of expended gunpowder and heated gun oil from the hot barrels of our weapons! It is a smell you never forget and for some, the last thing they ever smelled!

We could see various weapons lying on the trail to our left where numerous VC had been killed by Sgt. Mc Elwee's and Spec 4 Kozak's claymores. To get to the weapons you would have had to expose yourself to a lot of incoming enemy fire, so we left them where they were lying next to the VC bodies. We knew that an infantry platoon or a larger formation would be dropped into the area to clean up the enemy weapons and gear. Eventually, I took over point and we moved out onto the LZ in two separate Light Teams with everyone firing into the jungle to our right/north where the VC point element was hiding and still firing at us. Although the VC were a lot less enthusiastic now, probably from being shot up by the gunships!

The extraction of a Lurp team on a LZ is somewhat of a deadly dance, especially on a Hot LZ! You have the slicks (Huey Lift Helicopters) coming in fast and then flaring to rapidly decrease speed and sometimes landing hard on the LZ. At the same time, two gunships are behind and parallel to the two Hueys. As the Hueys touch down the two gunships in staggered formation fly overhead with their mini-guns firing on parallel strafing runs. Each strafing run is to left or right side of the landed Hueys and then forward to the front of the Hueys extraction flight route. Depending on the circumstances the rounds could be striking 10 meters or less from the Hueys. The Lurps on the ground are also firing into their flank positions to keep the enemy down while they board the Huey. At this point, you are not trying to conserve ammo so everyone is firing on full automatic, especially the M-60 which was putting out long bursts of fire into the possible enemy positions. In this instance the Hueys landed facing to the east, so both teams entered the choppers on their left side. The way that maneuver is completed is that when each team is even with a landing helicopter, they turn their backs to the helicopter and with the team on line, walk backwards while firing their weapons into the bush. The team stays on line until just before reaching the helicopter and normally the TL and the M-60 gunner are the last two to get into the helicopter. Also at this point the two door gunners on each Huey are also again firing their M-60 machine guns into the brush for more suppressive firepower. It is one hell of lot of firepower being thrown at the enemy positions for the sole purpose of preventing the Lurp team members, helicopter crew or the helicopters themselves from being hit by incoming enemy rounds. It is also loud as hell and is the "Ultimate Rush" if you're into a lot of weapons firing on full auto!

As we reached the second helicopter in line, Cunningham and I were the first two in and *as dictated by training we stopped firing, turned and climbed aboard, sliding across to the opposite door way and looking for targets to fire at.* The whole team boarded in less then 20 seconds and per protocol, TL Lavender and Gross with his M-60 blazing away were the last two to enter the helicopter. The second team had simultaneously entered the lead Huey. On command from the flight crews, both helicopters simultaneously lifted off and started to pickup altitude and speed. Also *per protocol, unless you have visual enemy personnel/targets firing at you once you board the helicopter, you are to stop firing your weapons because in the excitement of the Hot LZ Extraction, non-flight crew members might hit the helicopter's main rotor or tail rotor.*

Our flight path took us directly over the ambush site. I looked down and counted 14 dead enemy troops lying on the trail. The door gunners were still firing their M-60s into the tree lines, so I don't know if the enemy was firing at us, but I would guess they were. Once we reached some altitude and away from the LZ, the door gunners stopped firing and everything got very quiet! It started to cool off, both emotionally and physically from the lack of enemy fire and from the cool air at higher altitude. It is the moment when you look around to see that your team members and the helicopter crew members are all ok, then you develop this big smile or your face. It is also the most pleasurable moment of your "Lurp life", because you know you and your buddies are safe, you just kicked some premium ass on the enemy and your headed back to base camp for some hot chow and a cold beer! Life doesn't get any better than that and the adrenalin high is about as high as it gets! Non-combat veterans and civilians may never feel that moment and understand what it means to be "brothers in combat."

When we landed back at our helicopter pads next to the company area, we were greeted by our fellow Lurps, who came out to welcome us back and to congratulate us on a successful ambush, with the killing of a large number of enemy combatants and of course with none of the team being Killed in Action (KIA)! Up to that point I think it was the largest body count by any team in the young life of Company F, LRP!

We all dropped our gear at the front gate of the TOC and filed down into the underground bunker to get debriefed. Normally it was done by the Officer on duty (OD) probably one of the lieutenants and the

Intel Sgt Today we were debriefed by Major Maus, our Commanding Officer, and several lieutenants. Most of the other company officers were also at the debrief. This was because we were all part of the Lurp team concept/experiment. Every successful mission proved Special Forces/MACV Recondo School had been correct in their assessments of how to train and deploy Lurp teams to gather fresh and usable enemy intelligence at the brigade or division level. Once the debrief was over, Major Maus took TL Lavender to II Field Force Headquarters, because the general wanted to personally meet TL Lavender and congratulate him on a very successful mission! Eventually TL Lavender was recommended for a Silver Star and received it while in Japan where he had been med-evaced for hepatitis, several months after this ambush.

The mission for all intents and purposes had been a success; however, all of the weapons and any useable intelligence had to be recovered to complete the mission. Usually a reaction force of a platoon size group would be immediately sent back into the area to recover any and everything they could. This ambush was different because our S-2 believed this was probably a VC Company of 100 personnel or more (minus the 14 we killed plus an unknown number of wounded from the firefight and the gunships strafing runs) so they wanted to send a larger unit into the ambush site. This led to delays and the reaction force was not landed until the next morning. In the meantime it was decided to intermittently drop artillery all night long into and near the ambush site to prevent the enemy from recovering their dead and their equipment. Our artillery liaison had called fire missions onto the ambush site once we were extracted. We were advised at the debriefing that they got a fairly significant secondary explosion at the ambush site, which we all believed was the cache we had been lying on top of! That was never confirmed but it is the only possible explanation for a significant secondary explosion. When the reaction force actually got inserted the next morning, at the ambush site all of the gear and weapons were gone, along with all of the bodies except for one. That body was found in the brush to the south

72

of the ambush site, with an SKS basically melted into the VC's body. That was of course compliments of Sgt McElwee and his willie peter grenade he had thrown right after the execution of the ambush.

Apparently the enemy had crawled in during the night, while the artillery barrage was being randomly dropped in on them, and recovered their dead, wounded and all of the gear. A hell of a feat for the enemy and something that you had to respect even if the enemy had completed the mission under our noses! The one thing we all knew for damn sure was that particular VC Company would never go strolling down a jungle trail again, making a lot of noise and believing they owned the jungle. You can bet your ass the survivors, from that day on, were always half stepping down those trails, keeping their eyes open for an ambush and hoping like hell it wasn't their day to run into a Lurp team ambush! Sat Cong! (Kill Communist)

There was one other downside to the ambush and that was that the reaction force recovered two of the heavy team's own personnel packs and several un-fired claymores. They were from one of our light teams, and I'll leave it at that! As I said before, this was the first big firefight for some of the team members and obviously not everyone had performed to the highest standards of our training. We would learn from these mistakes and we would make a lot fewer in the future. Of course the enemy also learned from their mistakes, so it was a continuous learning scenario and a modifying of tactics almost every time we conducted a Lurp mission! You learned to play the cards you were dealt and just rolled with the punches. The Lurp translation being, "shit happens, so stop crying in your beer and get on with the mission!"

Chapter 12

Top of Lurp Pride, Bottom of the Patrol List

The following day our heavy team was back to the normal routine and most of us either had guard duty or sand bag detail, so reality slapped you in the face and you got on with your Lurp life. Of course, all of us were very elated with the results of the ambush, but we all knew that this time "Lady Luck" had been on our side, but the next time out everything was back to zero on the scoreboard. We knew we had better have our shit together, because Murphy was alive and well and out there every time we executed a mission!

As I had previously mentioned, each team when they returned from a mission, got placed on the bottom of the list of teams ready to be inserted on a mission. There were normally about 15 or more teams on that list. The company had the potential of 28 light teams (6 man recon teams), but shortly after we became combat ready, the numbers significantly dropped. This significantly cut the number of days that you were in the rear as compared to out in the jungle on a mission. The initial average for a team to be in the rear was around 5-7 days, but it was also directly proportional to the combat tempo for a specific area (AO – Area of Operation) the company had been assigned to recon.

One cause of the drop in team members/teams was because of normal rotation of troopers back to state side duty after a year in-country (DEROS). All of our original personnel had come from the 173rd Brigade. Depending on how long they had been with the Herd, we started seeing a lot of Lurps leaving the company, unless they extended their tour for six months. This caused shortages in team member numbers and so some teams had to be consolidated. Of course now that we were in combat and making a lot of contact, we were also loosing a number of Lurps to wounds, and depending on how serious their wounds were, they might be gone for days, weeks or never returned because they were transferred to medical facilities in Japan and then home to the states. Of course substitutions or new team members interrupted the individual teams' fitness and their ability to perform at their highest level. Even the top professionals of any sports team know that you have to train together to maintain that "edge" you need as a team to always come out as the winner. This was especially true of a Lurp team, because if the team didn't perform in near perfect sync, there was always the potential for things to go to shit in a hurry and in those instances you lost the game. At the minimum, your team was compromised and got their asses chased out of the jungle by some really pissed off enemy troops hell bent on killing our young asses! If you were lucky, that was all that happened, but potential WIAs and KIAs were always in the back of your mind.

Because of the constant rotation of new team members into teams, most teams did individual training in the company area or we had organized training by the company officers. A lot of the individual team training involved going to the old jungle school training area of the 173rd, south of the company that still had some thick vegetation. It involved just having the team walk in their normal Lurp patrol formation. We did that to keep the team functioning almost as one body with six individual extensions to that body. It also ingrained into each team member's memory, how his other five team members moved through the jungle. It caused you to develop a sixth sense when something was not right with the way a particular team member was acting while on a Lurp mission. For example, if I was walking point and I just stopped and stood very rigid, without moving, usually the number two man in the patrol would pick up on that immediately, because of my body language. Even though I had not made any overt motions, given any hand signals or made a sound. He would know that something was not right and he would send a signal back to the rest of the team, at the very least indicating a halt in the line of march. Why I had stopped could have been something as simple as sighting a trail or enemy fortification to my front or flanks, or it could be that I observed enemy movement or just observed a booby trap that appeared out of nowhere and I was very close to tripping it. This kind of intuition only came with a lot of training and/or a lot of missions with the same team members being intimately involved with each other. It could be a truly "life or death" scenario in which the team was involved. Some times it went well and some times it went to shit; however, training and the number of "same team-member missions" definitely put the results in favor of the "in sync team" being the winner of whatever combat scenario developed.

After nine days of in-the-rear activities including everything from guard duty in a bunker on the perimeter berm, guard duty at the KP Gate checking the Vietnamese workers in and out of the base, numerous hours of filling sand bags and general work parties, several get-up-and-get-ready-to-move-out response team notifications, we finally got a Warning Order in the afternoon of January 12. Team 1-5 was going to be inserted into an area approximately 5 miles from where there was a suspected regimental headquarters for a VC Regiment, or at least that was the intel at the time of our warning order. Originally we were going to set up on a trail, but TL Lavender, while doing the flyover for the LZs, didn't think that it looked that active, so they were suggesting we set up on a fairly large stream that would allow small sampan traffic to use it.

We finally got inserted in the late afternoon and moved off from the LZ without incident. We located the trail after moving less then a klick and set up an over-watch/mini ambush of the trail. The trail, as the TL had seen from the air, had not been used in a long time. You could tell that by the vegetation that was starting to grow in the trail and no recent foot prints or Ho Chi Minh sandal prints in the dirt of the trail. We set up on it anyway, because it was late in the day and we needed to be in a position and set up before it got dark. Getting dark in the jungle happened very quickly so one minute it was fairly light and the next minute you couldn't see your hand in front of your face. At that point your sense of hearing and smell became your primary tools for warning you that the enemy was coming.

Just because the trail did not look like it had been used in a while, didn't mean that no enemy would ever use it again. They had trails all over the jungle and it appeared that depending on where their units were and what activity they were involved with, determined whether a particular trail got used a lot or was a reserve trail that was only used occasionally. The absence of use of a trail was just as important, sometimes, to intel as a heavily used trail. If you had enough intel over a large AO you would be able to calculate what was the general enemy tempo for that AO and for specific areas within the AO. From that intel you could develop an overall plan on where the enemy was generally located, what units and how large the units were in the area. Then, hopefully, the officers could design a plan of attack to kill, wound or capture a significant number of enemy troops.

The US Army never had a problem getting into a fight with enemy troops once they were found and fixed. This was especially true with the advent of the helicopter assault companies, that could lift an entire company of grunts/infantrymen (100+ troops) into an area in a matter of an hour or two. Then followed the insertion of combat troops with artillery support and supply drops with heavy lift helicopters like the CH 47 (aka the Shit Hook). The problem was locating the enemy, because Vietnam was a really large area of thick jungles that hid almost everything unless someone was there on the ground to get a first hand look. Of course that someone was us, a six man Lurp team (light team) who were dropped in to snoop and poop and send back real time intel to our company HQ. Ultimately that intel moved up the chain of command to the big boss at the Brigade, Division or in Company F's situation, II Field Force.

This type of low-level enemy activity situation was a test of the team's professionalism and also a test of the team leader's abilities. *Recondo School Cadre drummed into our heads that "Patience" was*

77

a primary tool for a Lurp Team in conjunction with staying alert and not becoming complacent! Some teams fell into that trap and they paid dearly for their loss of focus and just doing stupid things, like smoking or cooking a hot meal!

What you don't read about in most true war books is about the boredom before and after combat. This is especially true for a Lurp team. They are given a mission and are dropped on an LZ to carry out that mission; however, there are no guarantees. The mission may be really exciting with lots of sightings, contact or an ambush and some dead gooks who paid the price for bumping into a Lurp team on the hunt. The real truth is that even with a Lurp team deep in enemy territory, sometimes nothing happens but the sun rising, it getting really hot, cooling off in the evening, relentless attacks by the local insect population and then darkness. Of course this was directly proportional to how hot the AO was that you were patrolling in. It was also a documented fact that the closer you got to the Cambodian border in the south and west areas of South Vietnam, Laotian Border in the northwest or the DMZ at the very north end of South Vietnam, your operational tempo increased exponentially.

The difference with a Lurp team is that once the team hits the ground the TL is in charge and he decided where and how long they would set on a trail. If it was a dead trail and nothing happening for hours or days then he may decide to move on and see what the team could find. Some times it also hinged on the fact of the actual site the team was in. If it had everything you wanted for a site such as good overhead cover, good cover and concealment especially to the front, was situated so that the team had good views of the trail and general area around it and it was comfortable for the team to stay in that position because of all the above, then the TL may decide to stick it out longer. If a site had just about everything wrong with it then he may have decided to move on. Sometimes, the only reason he had set the team up in a crappy site was because it was late or there were other problems that made him decide to RON (Rest Over Night) at this shitty location rather then push on to find a better site. In that case, normally the team just pulled back from a trail or active area to set up in whatever they could find that offered the best cover and concealment for the team for that particular time period. I liked to use a very thick growth of bamboo. It normally provided good concealment, sometimes if the bamboo was really large it also provided good cover especially if there was a termite mound in it. It also offered something better than concertina wire for your perimeter, because live and growing bamboo had small hooklike barbs where the leaves grew and it could stop almost anything from crawling in on you. Of course there was a downside to bamboo trees. They attracted a particular kind of small leech that just showed up and on a very quiet day you actually hear them and see them crawling toward you over the dead bamboo leaves with their inchworm type movements. The bug juice usually killed or dissuaded most of them, but if you stayed all night there was a good chance that you would have to remove a couple of them in the morning that had attached to your skin. Also there was a small light green snake they called a Bamboo Viper that was suppose to be very deadly if one of them bit you. Fortunately they were relatively meek and usually stayed in the trees and off the ground where you were lying. I had seen more then one crawling around in the bamboo above our heads, but it was one of those situations where you didn't bother them and they didn't bother you. It was also during these semi-safe RONs that you learned to listen to the jungle and what it was telling you. Everything that lived in the jungle, regardless if it was large or small and lived on the ground or in the trees, had its little nitch and survival techniques. There were so many different insects that I don't think even an entomologist could have ever identified all of them in just your little given area of jungle. What you could identify was when things were not right and something was out of sync with the insects in your area. It was especially telling at night when there was almost no movement of the day animals and the nocturnal animals were not out yet or were not in your little particular area. There were of course always insects out there and they all had their particular noises that they made, especially at night. It was the best damn burglar alarm or in our case, "Charlie Alarm". The enemy

79

was known as Victor Charlie, phonetic pronunciation for Viet Cong or just Charlie or Mr Charles! When the insects stopped chirping or doing their calls, you knew something had disturbed them and they were looking out for themselves/self preservation, we just used their instincts to assist us. Most of the time it was just some nocturnal animal out there moving around looking for dinner, but some times Mr Charles was out there trying to mess up your quiet evening in your little jungle paradise! During the day time, monkeys were probably the best alarm system around, but of course they started screeching if they saw a GI or Mr Charles so it was a two sided sword; however, if you settled into a RON they would normally settle down themselves and then they could be used as a premium Charlie Alarm, but not always.

As a team member and as a TL I have used both types of patrolling situations. Some times we sat for days on a trail and nothing happened, so I would advise the TOC that we were moving out to find better hunting grounds. Some times the TOC would send out new orders to move out and see what else the team could find. Either way, the TL decided if and when they were moving and where they were going to move to. It was probably one of the primary reasons why Lurp teams were so successful. Our initial commanders, who were back in the rear, had also been properly trained, had combat experience and knew what their roles were. They understood that ultimately it was the TL's decision even when he was given orders to move out. Later with our company and from information obtained from other Lurp company team members, we all had commanders who wanted to micro manage the Lurp team. They made decisions that were based on anything but what the team was telling them about the particular AO they were in. It led to the death or wounding of Lurps, and the loss of a team until they rebuilt with new Lurp team members. This problem was compounded when Lurp companies were attached to brigade or divisions and some of those commanders were clueless as to how to correctly use a Lurp company in conjunction with large line unit operations such as company to battalion search and destroy missions. Sometimes, it appeared that those field grade officers purposely put Lurp units in harms way because they disliked or distrusted the units and basically used and abused them. As with our company and other Lurp companies that got assigned to their parent division, they usually fared OK with that command structure. It was when a company or part of a company got "loaned to" some other unit at the battalion or brigade level that bad things started happening to Lurp teams in general and Lurp team members in particular.

Our over watch of this particular trail continued to be a very boring mission. The only exciting thing was that for the first two nights Sgt Gonzaga and I would have to move back a couple of feet from where we were during the day time. This was because we had the misfortune of setting up over a black ant (ants that both bite and sting you) trail that they used exclusively at night. We tried using insect repellant (AKA: Bug Juice) but that only seemed to piss them off more and they would swarm either me or Sgt Gonzaga, so at night we would move our gear back just a couple of feet and we didn't have a problem with them. More importantly they didn't then have a problem with us. The next morning we would move back into our day positions and the ants were OK with that, since that was their nocturnal trail.

It probably would seem to a civilian that our move away from the black ants was a rather stupid thing to do, since they were just small little ants! If there had been maybe a dozen or even a couple of dozen I would agree, but when you have hundreds, probably thousands of those little black ants crawling down this trail on a nightly basis, you would understand the magnitude of the problem. Also, I think I mentioned before that their bite and sting hurt like hell and each bite/sting stayed with you for a while. *Again as taught in Recondo School you learned to adapt to the jungle and all of the plants, animals and insects that lived there. It was not the other way around and the quicker you adopted this philosophy, the sooner you made the transition into the "jungle mode", where you were part of the jungle environment, at least for the time you were on a mission.*

The Viet Cong and the NVA were excellent at living/blending into the jungle and being part of it, because they didn't have a choice. This was their home 24/7. They did have R&R areas where they could go to and somewhat relax, but most of those areas were across the border in Cambodia or Laos. They were there because, for the most part, there weren't any GIs or Allied troops looking for them and aircraft over-flights were limited to secret mission operations.

By the beginning of the third day we were all pretty antsy and wanting to move on to something more exciting. Around 0900 hours a helicopter circled over our general area and TL Lavender contacted them via PRC 25 radio. The helicopter was our C&C ship. They advised TL Lavender that we were being extracted and to move the team on 350 degree azimuth for approximately 200 meters where there was a small LZ. It did not take us long to roll up our claymore mine wires and we were ready to move out. It was a sign of a good team, because they should always be prepared to quickly move out, taking only a few minutes to be saddled up. Sometimes you got orders to move out and other times you got pushed out by the enemy, so it was very important for the team to be prepared and not have gear laid out like you were on a BBQ at the beach. In fact when I was the TL and we were in a really hot area, most of the time I never took off my web gear, I just unbuckled and let it hang loose on my shoulder straps. I also never had my M-16 not touching some part of my body 24/7. During the rainy season I slept with it under my poncho liner to keep it from getting soaked in the rain. During the dry season it was usually leaning, barrel up, against left side of my chest (I shot long guns left-handed) when I slept on my back and in the cradle of my arm when I was sleeping on my side. This was another lesson drummed in our heads by Recondo School Cadre. *NEVER leave your rifle further than an arm's reach from your body. When you went to the toilet, which was usually a short distance away from where the team was located, you always took your rifle with you and kept it in your hands, regardless if you were standing to take a pee on a tree trunk or squatting to take a dump in a hole you dug to conceal your droppings. Covering your excrement' was two fold: first to prevent the odor from compromising your ambush/ over watch position on a trail or other point of interest; secondly to prevent the enemy from knowing you were ever in the position in the first place.*

We quickly moved out toward the LZ and I was walking point. I moved fairly fast toward the LZ, partly from having laid in one position for two and half days and partly from the excitement of being extracted with hot food and cold beer on the menu! Apparently it was a little too fast and I got my ass chewed out by TL Lavender, because he thought I was moving too fast. Maybe I was, but I didn't think it was an unsafe speed, but he was the TL and his word was THE LAW on a mission. That was another good sign of an excellent TL. He was always looking out for the team regardless of the situation and down the road it did help me when I became a Team Leader.

We extracted with only a few problems, one being that the first chopper came in and tried to land but the LZ was small and he chopped up some small trees with his main rotor, so he lifted out and the second one was able to land and pick up the team. For whatever reason, Gross fired the M-60 on lift off and scared the shit out of everyone. He was chastised by TL Lavender and it should have stuck in his brain to "follow orders", but unfortunately it didn't. Spec 4 Rennolet was the youngest person in Company F, having just turned 18 years old when he arrived in Vietnam and sometimes he didn't think like an adult. It would come back to haunt him in the near future.

We learned upon going to our debriefing that our company had been assigned to or loaned to the 101st Airborne Division because they were having some difficulties in their AOs. The intel was that they lost contact with two of their Lurp teams and only one man made it back from a third team. We never learned if they just had a bad run of luck or the area was really hot and a lot of enemy troops were occupying the area. Either way we were going to be running some missions in their AOs.

The "in-the-rear" routine was something that was very different between the line troops and the Lurps. When a line unit came in from the field it was normally at a fire support base and not back in the rear at a base where you had some of the state side amenities, like a PX, EM & NCO Clubs and maybe passes to go into the local town. The entire time I was with the Herd we only moved to an actual military base one time and that was when we moved from the mountains around Dak To to the coast at Tuy Hoa to protect the rice harvest. The rest of the time we would walk into a fire support base and if we were lucky we might get hot chow and a warm beer. Of course it was still better then lying out there in fox holes that were the perimeter for the entire unit as compared to concertina wire, bunkers with machine guns and of course some kind of arty. Usually a fire support base had 105 mm howitzers and sometimes 4 deuce mortars (4.2 in). Of course nothing was for free and we still had to man the bunkers on whatever side of the base we were on. Usually they put us near the damn artillery and until you got use to being real close to the guns, you damn near had a heart attack when they fired off salvos for arty fire support missions, day and night! This was especially true of the 4-deuce mortars. The crew did not make a lot of noise and the first thing you heard was a giant bang and a whoosh noise as a round was fired out of the short barrel of the mortar tube. There was an even more dark side to this artillery. All of the guns had to have ammo resupply brought in by heavy lift helicopters, mainly the CH 47, twin rotor, Chinook Helicopter. They normally would sling load part of their lift under the Chinook and they would fly directly to the area where the ammo was stored for the big guns, hover and then slowly descend until they were low enough to drop the sling load of ammo. The sling load probably weighed several tons, so it took a lot of lift to keep the Chinook in the air as it was hovering to slowly descend and drop its load. This translated into extreme down draft created by those huge, two x four bladed rotors spinning in opposite directions. We're talking about over a hundred miles an hour downdraft and anything and everything that wasn't tied down was blown to shit and scattered about. Thus the nickname of "Shit Hook" evolved from troopers who had been blasted by the downdrafts and had everything including their personal gear blown all over hell with fine dirt, sand and small rocks sandblasting the trooper, his weapon and other war gear. It was not a pleasant thing and on some occasions the downdraft even tore up and sent flying our hooches that were made by snapping two ponchos together and then using some made up frame to drape it over, thus making a small two man tent. They were our only portable overhead cover in the rainy season to keep you semi-dry and to protect you from the sun in dry season. So between getting the shit scared out of you by late night fire mission or having your body and your gear sandblasted by the Shit Hook, after a few days most of the troopers were ready to saddle up and head back into the boonies.

There was one other favorite "Night Sport" that the Herd troopers enjoyed during their short stay at a fire support base and this was the process of "reallocating equipment" that belonged primarily to the arty troops. Arty troops got resupplied on a daily basis by air, so they had a lot of extra equipment, especially cases of C-Rat that were normally stacked outside of their ammo bunkers and for the most part weren't guarded. This was the primary target for reallocation of equipment by the Herd Troopers. As a trooper in a line unit you carried everything you owned on your back. When you were prepping to return to the patrol mode, C-Rats would be brought in and divided up amongst all of the troops and that was your food supply until the next resupply came along. That was normally around 7 days, but a lot of time it was longer than that, because it depended on the tempo of the unit and the terrain they were in. Thus, when the C-Rats got handed out and I might add a Cherry got what was left over, you always broke down your C-Rats and took only what you needed to survive out there, everything else was discarded or traded for something you wanted. The bottom line was all about the weight and C-Rats weighed up if you took a lot of them. Of course there were some rats that almost no one wanted such as ham & motherfuckers (ham and lima beans) or the powdered eggs that sometimes were green when you opened the can or even a slight shade of blue. There were some C-Rats that everyone wanted like pound cake and peaches.

Everyone always took their cocoa powder, coffee, sugar, cheese and crackers, 4-pack of cigarettes and the toilet paper. It was the reason why GIs in the field came up with all of these strange concoctions for food, because you ate what you carried and that was it, no snack food. If you were lucky and got a "care package from the world" (canned food, hot sauce, candy and maybe a magazine), you were living large, but you always shared it with your buddy or buddies and they normally did the same when they got a care package. Of course those were few and far between because the Army in general and the 173rd in particular didn't have the means to transport all of that extra material to the field from the base camps. A lot of it got destroyed or was just thrown out after things inside the package spoiled because of the high temperatures and humidity. You did get mail but that would normally be in the form of a letter and that was about it.

The Lurps usually came back from a mission aboard a helicopter and that bird sat down at your company area, which was normally at base of some size. Thus we had access to some of the better amenities that were in-country and I often wondered why the troopers I left behind in Dog Company, 4th Battalion of the 173rd Airborne Brigade, thought being a Lurp was bad duty. Of course you hung your ass out when you were on a mission, but your down time was excellent compared to a line dog (in-the-field trooper). Being a young, gung-ho paratrooper in a war zone tended to make your mind wander to the better things in life, like hot food, cold beer and lots of boom boom girls (prostitutes) to fulfill all of your sexual needs.

Since Company F had a permanent area assigned to them, we slowly developed the area with our own amenities, such as showers, shitters and eventually an outdoor movie theater. This was all done with material we either traded for, stole or in some cases actually got allocated to us through Army supply. It was all built by the muscles and sweat of Lurp team members when they were not out on missions. It became part of the routine when you came back in to continue to upgrade our company area. Along with the standard operations such as guard duty and shit burning detail!

Chapter 13

New Year, a Festive and Dangerous Holiday

Most holidays in Vietnam went by without much fanfare, even Christmas, probably because most GIs didn't want to go there in their minds. This was especially true for a Lurp, because your head needed to be in the game at all times, not wondering about what everyone was doing for the holidays at home!

One holiday, actually one night did standout. New Year's Eve was very festive and dangerous! We happened to get lucky and our team was in for the festivities. We had a great dinner, hot turkey, sitting down in the mess hall. For some teams they drew the short straw and were out on missions. War doesn't have any holidays, so it was "take two salt tablets and drive on" for the teams in the field.

Sgt Bill Schmidt and I decided to have our own party. We got a cooler from the mess hall and filled it with crushed ice (a rarity in Vietnam but Bill being the company clerk had some pull). We had a preplan as good Lurps would and had bought a fifth of vodka at the PX, via a 21-year-old trooper since we weren't old enough to buy it. It was one of those stupid rules probably carried over from the Second World War. Anyway, we also bought a case of Wink soda, so we were set. We dumped the entire fifth of vodaka in the cooler over the ice and then added the case of Wink, stirred profusely and then closed the lid to let it chill. Around 1600 hours we decided to taste the "Panther Piss", as it was called in Vietnam. Of course it was very hot and sunny so when we took our first taste it was like drinking lemonade in the states. It was ice cold, had an excellent taste and went down very smoothly.

Bill also had a taste for anchovies so he had bought numerous tins of it. It wasn't my favorite appetizer, but what the hell we were on our third glass of Panther Piss by then and feeling no pain. Since we had already eaten it didn't take long to fill up on Panther Piss and anchovies; however, not to be light-weights we just kept drinking. Around 1800 hours we were totally shit faced and I was beginning to feel a little sick. Within about 15 minutes we were both puking our guts out from the combo drink and hors d'oeuvres. Nothing worse then salty anchovies coming back up with used vodka and Wink to wash out the throat. After an extended period, we finally stopped puking but both of us felt like shit and we were still drunk. It was now dark and the festivities along the berm were beginning. I'm not sure if this happened every New Year's Eve, because it was my first time, but it was one hell of a show. As soon as it got dark, there were all kinds of explosions and firing of weapons all along the north berm at the Bien Hoa Army base. There was everything from M-16s, M-60 machine guns and then later on M-79 grenade launchers along with an occasional captured weapon also being fired. At one minute to midnight all hell broke loose in our company area. By this time the entire company compound was engulfed in various colored smoke from smoke grenades being thrown in the company area, muffled explosions from concussion grenades being thrown into the bunkers alongside our hooches. It was from that activity that we got our first three casualties of the night. Three of our OG Lurps were short and paranoid about getting killed before they left Vietnam, probably in a few days, so they all hid out in one of the bunkers between the barracks. Two had nothing on but Infantry helmets and some flip flops and the third was partially clothed. Some drunk idiot threw a concussion grenade in the front of the long narrow bunker, not knowing that there were Lurps hunkered down inside. The resulting explosion gave all three of them a mild concussion and wiped out their hearing for hours. What probably saved them was the fact that both ends of those bunkers were open so the pressure wave and sound wave was able to partially escape, but it had to still be one hell of body hit for the three Lurps. I would guess that years later they probably all developed hearing problems as result of that concussion grenade blowing up next to them and of course all their other exposures to loud explosions and rifle fire from previous firefights.

Things just got crazier after that. Our helicopter gun crews had linked together around 500 rounds each of tracer ammo and they started firing the guns up over the berm in a long, loud stream of red tracers. They very rarely used a full belt of tracer ammo in combat, because they produced so much heat in the barrels of the M-60s that the barrels would turn red then white hot and eventually start to droop from being so hot that they were deforming. This caused the guns to cook off rounds in the barrel and was very dangerous for the GI firing the gun. It also caused the tracer rounds to come out of the barrels with a slight wobble and some would even tumble in the air. Of course they were using barrels that had already been shot out on various missions so it wasn't like they were destroying a new M-60 barrel. It was still dangerous as hell but a great sound and light affect. By now it sounded like the MAD MINUTE, which is what the GIs called it when every weapon in the arsenal was fired for one minute. We also had drunk Lurps throwing hand grenades over the berm and the finale was several artillery pieces actually firing artillery rounds out to the north of the base.

I wondered what the enemy thought of all of this, because it had to be an impressive light show from a distance. They never responded so I guess they just thought it was a bunch of stupid GIs wasting ammo, in the millions of rounds. They never did that of course, because most of their ammo was either carried down from North Vietnam on some soldiers back or on a truck down the Ho Chi Minh Trail.

Well, actually they did respond about 28 days later when they executed the Tet Offensive; however, all of their rounds of ammunition were aimed at GIs, their vehicles or their fortifications.

The next morning everything was back to "normal" with a bunch of hung over GIs on police call picking up all the spent ammo cases, burned out smoke grenades and a few empty cans of beer and some whiskey bottles. The three Lurps from the bunker incident didn't mention a word to the brass and just marked off another day on their short timers' calendar. One less day to survive in Vietnam and one day closer to that "Freedom Bird" taking them away from Vietnam on a permanent basis. Xin Loi GI

Chapter 14

Continuing Pre-TET Missions

Of course, II Field Force wanted more intelligence on the enemy activities and in identifying the particular enemy units. Team 1-5 was combined with Team 1-6 to form a Heavy Team. SFC Carter would be the TL for the Heavy Team, while SSG Lavender would be the ATL (Assistant Team Leader). This was the normal procedure when a heavy team was sent out. One of the two TL would be designated as the TL for the entire Heavy Team and the other TL would be designated the ATL. This eliminated any command problems prior to being inserted and usually the TL with the highest rank/most experience would be designated as the overall TL.

We were inserted on January 25, 1968, at 1600 hours in War Zone D. Things went bad right away because the choppers set us down on the wrong side of the LZ so we had to cross the LZ to get to where we needed to be. That was bad enough because of the extended exposure time, but also the other side of the LZ had water on it and by the time we made it across we had all been in water and mud up to our waist. Not that the water was that bad, it just slowed you down, but the mud in the water has an unpleasant habit of getting into your equipment, especially your magazines and your rifle. Once across the LZ we moved into the jungle for about 50 meters and set up a RON. We didn't have any enemy activity that night and at our sit rep in the morning we were told that they wanted us to move 1,000 meters north to set up an ambush on trail junction. A thousand meters is a long way to move and realistically it would take at least several days to move that far and may take longer depending on the terrain. It's not like you're out for an evening stroll and you can just step out at a given pace. A Heavy Lurp Team means 12 men moving through the jungle in a very slow and deliberate pace with 100 per cent security around the team as they move. It is a slow process and if done correctly can be a very quiet and secure process, but nevertheless still a dangerous ordeal.

Just prior to moving out Spec 4 Bass thought he heard Vietnamese voices. TL SSG Carter, Bass, Diers and me did a recon of the area to see if anything was out there. We didn't find anything so the heavy team moved out. We only moved a few hundred meters when we hit a trail and TL Carter decided to establish an ambush on the trail. It was one of those sites that had everything we need, good front cover and concealment, good overhead cover and the terrain gave us a good view of the trail. We spent the entire night in this ambush position, but of course nobody showed up to "dance in our kill zone."

We moved out the next morning and after moving approximately 300 meters we stopped for an extended break, because it was hot and we had all drank a lot of water to stay hydrated. After the long break we moved out again for another approximate 100 meters and ran into a large open area, which supposedly contained the trail junctions that could be seen from the air. The problem was that we couldn't see the trail and secondly we were all low on water. Most of us carried several canteens and one large soft plastic bag/container called a Fat Rat that held approximately 2.5 quarts of water. During the dry season, which runs from November through April, you could not carry enough water to sustain you for a 5 day mission, so you had to plan on resupplying yourself with water from the jungle. That meant that you might take a side trip to a water source and then resume your march through the jungle to your destination. During the dry season you were always looking on your map for the blue line that designated a stream, river or some other water source. During the raining season it was the last thing you wanted to see, because you were up to your ass in water every day and normally wet 24/7.

Based on the map and what TL Carter and ATL Lavender could see they believed that there was water on the opposite side of the open area, so it was decided to make a water run to get water for the entire team. This means that a small group – in this case four troopers – would move out to the water source with all of the canteens from the entire team, fill the canteens and then move back to the team and distribute the water. ATL Lavender, Sgt Lee from Team 1-6, Spec 4 Bass and myself were selected to make the water run. Once we had collected several canteens from each team member we moved out toward the water source.

When I say an open area, it is basically an area devoid of trees, but it is not open like a golf course. The area would have elephant grass and other forms of bushes and fauna growing on it. It is possible to move through an open area and not be seen by the enemy, but it is more challenging than moving through the jungle with trees of all sizes around you to give you cover and concealment.

We made the crossing without incident and collected the water. The canteens are filled by two troopers while the other two troopers cover the area. The upside was that the water detail usually fills their canteens first, puts in the disinfection tablet, vigorously shook the canteen and then took a long drink of semi-delicious and sometimes cold water. Of course you're suppose to wait 30 minutes before drinking the water, but that never happened. I guess we thought that some of the decontamination would happen in our stomachs. I never got sick from drinking the water after adding a disinfection pill, but that didn't mean that some of the jungle water was very dangerous.

We crossed back to the Heavy Team without any problems and distributed the water to all of the team members. TL Carter decided to move a short distance and set up an ambush towards the open area. It was not the best site but it did have some overhead cover but not much cover to the front. A lot of the site was elephant grass approximately 4 feet tall so you could hide in it, but it didn't allow for much air movement so you usually just cooked while laying in it. Also if you moved around in your position it made a noise like rustling grass so you had to clear out, or at least bend over the grass to make it semi-habitual. Of course elephant grass is sharp on the edge like a razor so all of us had cuts on our arms and hands from making a position to lie in.

Once we had settled into the position TL Carter called in our position and was advised that we would be there two more days. We had expected to be extracted tomorrow morning as that was our fifth day, which was a normal Lurp mission time frame. Because of the change in the mission, TL Carter decided to send another water detail across the open area and the four troopers completed the resupply without incident. That was now twice that we had resupplied from the same location and it was apparent to everyone that this was going to be a problem.

As I previously mentioned, patience is one of the primary factors that separates an excellent team of Lurps from a not-so-great team. It involves not only individual team members but also the team as a whole. Some of the team members were impatient and started to stand and move around, this really pissed me off, because it compromises the entire team not just the individual team member who wants to be stupid. It also distracts from the continuity of the team and could cause deadly consequences. Some of those same team members paid for their mistakes in the future with a lot of pain and suffering!

Miraculously, we made it through the night without incident, but the planned Tet Holiday Cease-Fire was to begin at 0400 on the morning of January 29, 1968. Our orders were not to fire on the enemy unless they first fired on us. I'm not sure who came up with this plan, probably some dick head from the State Department and of course all of our ball-less politicians agreed with it. It left our asses hanging out, because one of our most effective tools was the element of surprise.

Around 1600 hours we started hearing a lot of noise, like banging on metal sheets and other noises coming from the south end of the clearing. Around 1900 hours, four gooks came walking parallel to and through our kill zone and except for the Cease Fire, they would have been dead meat. True to the professionalism of the team members, we let them pass through and never executed the ambush. The last gook appeared to have seen my claymore, which was concealed in the elephant grass, but I wasn't certain. After they cleared our ambush site and had walked some distance they fired four shots, which we believed were signals to the rest of the gooks in the area. Between the enemy patrol and our two water resupply missions we all believed that we were compromised and that shit was going to fall on our heads when it got dark. True to our suspicions around 2100 hours we could see four flashlights approaching our positions from across the open area. They were spread apart approximately 10 meters between each position/flashlight. When they got close to our position and approached us from the front, the four flashlights went out and they started tapping two sticks (probably bamboo) together as they moved directly at us. Based on the noise, we could tell that they had other enemy troops following them, most likely covering their asses as they moved through our ambush site. It was nerve racking as hell and I would guess my heart along with everyone else heart was hitting the 150 beats a minute or more. One of the gooks walked within three feet of my position and I could see his outline only because I was looking up and he was outlined against the stars. They moved at a deliberate pace for maybe ten steps, would stop and tap the sticks together and then move ten more steps and repeat the process. They slowly passed through our ambush site without actually stepping on any of the Lurps, which would have led to a deadly point blank firefight. The second group appeared to wait at the edge of the clearing and did not walk through our ambush site. Apparently they thought if they walked into the high elephant grass and bushes that they might mistake each other for one of us and end up shooting each other. It was a good decision on their part, because I had straightened the pin on a frag grenade and was prepared to throw it if the second group started to move into our position. It would have been a shitty situation at best, because we would have had the enemy intermixed with us and there wouldn't have been any guarantees on who came out on top.

It took probably 30 minutes for the whole scenario to play out, but it felt like hours. After the noise making/recon group passed by us they apparently circled to the south and went back to their camp. The other group that had been in front of our positions had slowly faded away and within the same time period we could no longer hear movement to our front. We were never sure if the enemy knew where we were and were trying to provoke an incident or if just by plain dumb luck they missed us and we all lived to fight another day. Needless to say, none of us slept the rest of the night and we were all on a hundred percent alert.

At the 0700 sit-rep we were advised that we would be extracted and would use the open area in front of our ambush site. As the helicopters landed and we loaded on board, Bass spotted a gook across from us, but he never fired on the helicopters and we never fired back at him. So much for the fucking cease fire, because it would shortly go to shit in a very big way!

Chapter 15

1968 TET Offensive, Phase 1

There had been a lot of increased activity/contact with our teams and we all knew something was happening. It was rumored that there was going to be a large-scale enemy attack during the TET Lunar Year Celebrations, which is like Christmas, the Fourth of July and New Year's Eve all combined into one big celebration for the Vietnamese. It is also the period when probably 90 per cent of the Vietnamese soldiers and sailors go on leave. It would be the perfect time to plan an attack.

The enemy activity dramatically increased just prior to the Tet Offensive in the month of December, 1967 and early January of 1968. You didn't have to be a military scholar to know that things were spinning up and the ca ca was about to hit the fan. In five missions that were assigned to Team 1-5 we were only able to stay on the ground overnight on one recon mission, the rest of the time we were extracted because we were in contact with the enemy. Of the four other missions we either hit a hot LZ or encountered enemy troops very soon after leaving the LZ. I liken it to trying to step on an active red-ant hill and not get ants on your boots. It was statistically and physically impossible!

Because of the increased enemy activity most missions were assigned to a heavy team to give added firepower when the teams made contact with the enemy. This caused the rotation of teams from the base camp in to the field to speed up because a heavy team was actually two light teams combined. The combination of the two light teams to a heavy team caused less teams per platoon to actually be available to conduct missions. Added to this was the fact that the number of contacts with the enemy sharply increased, so most teams only got a day or two back at the company area before they were assigned another mission. Realistically you needed 24 plus hours to get your gear cleaned and resupply what you used in the last firefight; however, the critical need was for each team member to get some actual sleep and not be sleeping with one eye open!

The dramatically increased tempo of the Lurp teams also made II Field Force S-2 (Intelligence Unit) concerned as to what was occurring. They wanted to have more intelligence on the enemy movements, so more teams were sent out to conduct the recons and intelligence gathering missions. It was also obvious that the closer you got to the Cambodian border, the more enemy you encountered and the majority of the contacts were with the NVA.

Team 1-5 and 1-7 were combined as a heavy team and we were given a mission in War Zone C, fairly close to the Cambodian border. Other teams had conducted missions in the area and most had contact with the NVA. We actually inserted around 1400 hours in a small LZ and made it off without contact. We only moved several hundred meters when we hit a high speed trail running north to south. SSG Lavender decided to set up an ambush on the trail, so the heavy team proceeded to install their claymores in the kill zone and on our flanks and rear security position. The entire process only took about 20 plus minutes and then everyone began the process of cleaning out a position so as not to make noise and to be semi-comfortable. The perimeter of the ambush site was in low brush and some smaller trees, primarily double canopy. It provided good concealment but not much cover to use as a position that could stop enemy fire from hitting you. As always, the terrain dictated how you set up your ambush or observation point and you didn't always get to pick a prime location.

We had been in the site for less than an hour when we heard Vietnamese voices close to our position and approaching from the north on the trail. I'm not sure what the point man heard or saw as he walked into the kill zone, but he abruptly stopped. He turned to look into our position and he started calling out as if he was asking us who was in there (later we learned from Tony Thu that is exactly what he was asking). Most of us couldn't see the enemy soldier, but we could all certainly hear him. He called out several times and threw something, possibly a rock into our position to see if he could make anything move. All of us hunkered down behind our packs for cover because we thought he had thrown a grenade into our perimeter. This was very concerning because we had been compromised and there was obviously more then one enemy soldier close by on the trail. Nothing happened from whatever the enemy threw into our perimeter, so he called out again. This was too much stress for Tony and he blew his claymore which was located about in the center of the kill zone. Tony fired some rounds from his M-16 and then threw a M-26 frag grenade in the direction of where the enemy soldier had been standing. Tony was a very excitable Chu Hoi and we had to control his actions because of this. The grenade he threw only went about 10 meters when it hit a tree and bounced back toward our perimeter. Most everyone saw what had happened and everyone tried to become a ground hog and dig a hole to hide in. The grenade exploded and luckily no one on the team was hit. By this time we were receiving enemy AK-47 fire from the north and northeast sides and probably 50 meters out from our perimeter. Some of the team members on our north flank returned fire. It was a very short firefight, but we were obviously compromised and had to move or get extracted. SSG Lavender called in the contact and we were advised to move back to our insertion LZ and prepare for an extraction. We recovered all of our claymores except for two, one pointing north up the trail and one pointing north from our perimeter. Once we were all packed up and ready to move, SSG Lavender had those two claymores detonated to cover our initial movement from the ambush site.

I was carrying the M-6o machine gun so as we moved out I put some rounds in the direction of the enemy fire, which was now sporadic and not very accurate. It was a short march to the LZ and by now the enemy fire was almost down to nil. The two lift ships arrived in less then five minutes and they landed in a left echelon formation facing north and approximately 30 meters apart. As we headed toward the two ships and separated into two light teams, SSG Lavender headed toward the trailing helicopter. Our team turned their backs to the helicopter and fired some M-16 rounds in the direction of the last known location of the enemy troops. I also fired several bursts from the M-60 as we reached the left side of the helicopter. Three of our team members jumped on the helicopter and slid through to sit in the other door. SSG Lavender, myself and one other Lurp just backed up and sat down in the left door of the Huey.

We had radioed to the C&C ship that it would be a hot LZ, so as the helicopters started to land and the helicopter crews had the team in sight, the door gunners opened fire out the respective sides of each ship. There were 4 x M-60s firing from the door gunners along with numerous M-16s and my M-60 firing. It was one hell of a noise added to the loud noises made by the spinning main rotors of the two UH1D Hueys. The gunships were also making mini-gun strafing runs on both sides of the LZ to further dissuade the enemy from firing on the helicopters and their crews as they lifted off from the LZ!

The front Huey lifted off first just as I was firing the final burst from my M-60. It flew directly over the top of my M-60 rounds. I was later told that the chief pilot of that helicopter was pissed about me firing under his ship. It wasn't intentional on my part and sometimes things don't go exactly as planned. I had full control of my M-60 and was not haphazardly firing the machine gun. I had seen the helicopter lift off and had purposely lowered my target area and then immediately stopped firing. We lifted off without taking any hits to the ships, the crews or the Lurp Team members. It was always a great feeling to have a cool and relaxing flight back to our company area. We landed and headed to our debriefing. It didn't take that long. We were notified in the briefing that the gunships that had been making gun runs along the perimeter, observed one dead enemy soldier lying on the trail. Apparently, Tony's claymore had hit and killed the enemy soldier, because it sure as hell wasn't from his misdirected grenade and probably not from his M-16.

In future missions Tony was not allowed to carry hand grenades because his throwing strength and accuracy were unpredictable! The last thing a team needed was to have members killed or wounded by one of their own.

Chapter 16

The E-Ticket Ride: Pre-Tet, 1968

II Field Force gave Company F new orders to check on enemy concentrations and movement from the Cambodian border to areas west of Saigon. II Field Force was certain if there was a major attack, Saigon would be on the top of the target list, not so much for strategic significance but for psychological and political strategy. If Saigon could be attacked in-force by the enemy, then all of Vietnam was theoretically vulnerable! Of course, it would also play right into the hands of the left wing anti-war media and the bleeding heart politicians that lubricated the whole process!

The problem with a lot of the area west of Saigon was that it was flat with miles and miles of open rice patties. There might be little islands of vegetation in the middle of this sea of rice paddies, but they were few and far between. Also it was the dry season so there was a lot of activity in the rice paddies during the day and the farmers were not far from their fields at night, either in small compounds or villages. Since we normally only inserted at first light or last light it would be impossible to insert without being seen by someone, either the enemy or the farmers or a combination of the two!

Of all of the areas that II Field Force wanted intel on, Team 1-5 drew one of the shitty ends of the stick. To make things worse we would be inserted around 0900 hours, which for the local rice farmers was probably their first break of the day, since they started work at first light. The second problem was that the only LZ/insertion point that had any cover at all was an island-like raised area that had been an old French fort when they occupied Vietnam. It was approximately half a football field in size and raised above the rice

102

paddies by probably 15-20 feet. It was dead in the middle of the rice paddies with miles of open fields on every point of the compass. It did have a lot of overgrowth including elephant grass on it with some palm trees growing on the west end of the island. There were allegedly some old fortifications on the island but from the air you couldn't see them because the elephant grass and other bushes and small trees had everything covered up! Trusting TL Lavender's intuition and experience we loaded up with extra ammo and grenades because we knew that we would probably be in contact as soon as it got dark as the enemy started moving across the rice paddies toward their pre-attack positions. Also we didn't think we would be moving very far so the added weight, which usually played a larger role in the decision making process of the equipment you took with you on a mission, didn't play such a large role. Of course, believing that you were probably going to be in a fire-fight with NVA also tended to make you load up on ammo. We also took an M-60 machine gun, which gave us added firepower for just a six man team.

We had to pre-stage for insertion at a South Vietnamese airbase located west and south of Saigon, because of the distance (in excess of 75 miles) from our base at Bien Hoa, to the designated LZ. We would have the two insertion slicks, the C&C ship plus a set of Cobra Gunships for the insertions. Once everything was coordinated, which took longer then anticipated, we lifted off from the airbase probably closer to 1000 hours to be inserted into our LZ.

Normally TL Lavender would ride in the right front position of the helicopter and by leaning out the door, while sitting on the floor with his feet on the strut, he could see what the pilots were seeing as they headed into the LZ. For some reason, probably because of his over-flight of the LZ, he elected to ride in the left front position of the helicopter and he along with two other Lurps would exit the left side of the helicopter while I, the M-60 gunner and one other Lurp would exit the right side of the helicopter. We would all meet at the front of the helicopter once it lifted off. Part of the reasoning was that the helicopter might not be able to land because of unknown obstacles hidden in the four feet plus high elephant grass, so we might have to jump off the helicopter. This had to be somewhat coordinated so that one side of the helicopter didn't lose the weight of three men heavily loaded men (well over 250 pounds each with his weight and gear = 750 pounds off one side and 750 pounds still on the other side) and cause the helicopter to be seriously out of balance.

I, as the point man, chose the right front position, which I liked for the same reasons the team leader normally chose that position. The other factor was that the frame of the helicopter on the front leading edge of the door frame just to the right and behind the pilot's seat had three large approximately 5 inch holes in that frame work to reduce the overall weight of the frame. The second hole, which was probably 3 feet from the floor of the helicopter, was the prefect hand hold as you sat on the floor of the helicopter, so the Lurp in that position had the best observation point and the best means of staying in the helicopter if it made sudden evasive moves. The Lurp to his right only had the strut for his feet and leaning back on his pack to keep him in the helicopter and the Lurp next to him had the base of the machine mount that he could grab onto if things went bad. The Lurp in the middle on either side of the helicopter would probably grab the Lurp to his left to hold on since he was carrying his rifle in his right hand, so only his left hand was free to try to grab a hold of something. Of course there were grommets and ropes on the floor of the helicopter where the McGuire Rigs were tied in; however, with all of your gear on and the pack on your back it was nearly impossible to be able to twist around and grab something in a split second.

It was a hot, beautiful, sunny day and getting hotter as we lined up for the LZ, which I could clearly see from my vantage point. I could also see numerous Vietnamese rice farmers out in the rice paddies, some less then a quarter of a mile from our position. So basically we were compromised before we even got on the LZ and I had a shitty feeling about this insertion, but what the hell we were Lurps and we played the hand we were dealt. We came in really fast and fairly low so that all the helicopter pilots had to do was flair at the right moment and drop down on the LZ. Of all the shitty LZs they had dropped Lurp teams into, this one, from the pilots' point of view, would be a piece of cake, not so much so for the Lurp team! It was a perfect landing or at least a quick flair and then a hover just above the elephant grass. The crew chief on the right side and the door gunner on the left side of the helicopter scanned the LZ for any hidden obstructions the helicopter, especially the tail rotor, might strike causing the helicopter to basically crash land with all of the Lurps standing on the struts! There were some stumps to the right rear of the helicopter but the actual landing spot looked to be clear.

As the helicopter started to flair, I stood up with both feet on the strut and a hell of strong grip with my left hand on the helicopter frame. It is at that time that the helicopter and its crew and of course the Lurps are at their most vulnerable point of the entire mission. Everything below and around the helicopter is an unknown and your heart-beat starts to rise in anticipation of the possibility of things going to shit very quickly. The noise is also increased because when you're flying in a helicopter on a level flight a lot of the noise is just air rushing by and the whine of the turbine, but when you come in to land everything speeds up and you now hear the noise of the main rotor blades biting into the air, the rush of downwash as the air from the rotor blades strikes the surface of the LZ and pushes upwards. Depending what is on the ground some of that can be dust, dead leaves or even small branches and pieces of grass. You are also hit with a sudden blast of hot air, since flying in altitude can be cool to damn cold some times, but not on the ground.

Just as the helicopter started to settle onto the ground, I stepped off with my right foot and it just touched the ground. I still had my left foot on the strut and the grip on the frame. It was decision time and I had already decided that it was a go for the mission, but the TL was still on the helicopter so we waited for his movement as a go signal. In that slight second or two, I took one more look around. To my right front and probably about 10 feet away the elephant grass separated because of the down draft and what appeared to be the aperture of an old bunker revealed itself like a bad dream. I was just starting to think that this was not good when up popped a NVA with pith helmet on and an AK-47 in his hand. He had this very surprised look on his face! I instantly fired my M-16 at the NVA who was less then 10 feet from me and the rest of the crew. The M-60 gunner next to me also fired a burst and the crew chief fired his M-60. I think the other Lurp fired also but everything happened so quick I wasn't sure. The NVA, who I think was probably sleeping and woke up to the sound of the helicopter landing in his front yard, fired on full auto directly at me, the other Lurps, crew chief and the helicopter. This firing instantly alerted the pilots and they pulled maximum torque for the helicopter, in fact they pulled past the red line for safe torque on main rotor of the Huey. The results were almost instantaneous and the helicopter lifted straight up, it felt like about 5 gs. We were probably about 40 feet above the bunker with me having only my left foot on the strut, my right foot dangling in open air, a death grip on the frame of the helicopter and firing my M-16 with my right hand. I was looking straight down just as we reached that maximum lifting point and observed a flash and then a loud explosion as one of the Cobra Gunships (loved those Snakes) put a 2.75 rocket directly in the aperture of the bunker which the NVA had been firing out of. It was a shitty day for us, but a deadly day for that NVA!. The helicopter transitioned over into forward flight and we got the hell out of Dodge as fast as we could. The crew chief reported to the pilots that the ship had been hit and told all of us that we were heading back to the Vietnamese airbase to see how bad the helicopter had been shot up. I along with the rest of the Lurps and the helicopter crew checked each other out to see if we had any hits on us or our gear. We were amazed that none of us were hit by the full automatic fire from AK 47 from the very surprised NVA. We were all very happy to fly back to the airbase most riki tiki because Hueys with holes shot in them have a tendency to leak hydraulic fluids and make unscheduled landings! We all also needed to take a piss and the smokers needed to bum a cigarette from someone. Once we landed, the team exited the helicopter and let the crew check out their bird. It had eight holes in it, one in the right strut and then holes in the cowling of the engine, the skin covering the power shaft to the tail rotor and one hole in one of the main rotor blades. The AK 47 bullets had not, by some miracle, hit any major hydraulic lines or critical equipment on the engine. I did not want to think about what would have happened if the pilots had set the Huey down just five feet to the right and in front of the bunker, Hell, Ray Charles could not have missed the pilots and critical parts of the helicopter at that point. We were damn lucky to get out of the hot LZ with nothing more then some holes in the Huey. It's one of those experiences you think about years later when you're safe and sound at home and the question always comes up why it hadn't been your day to "get your ticket punched"? Every combat soldier asks himself that question, but no one has the answer!

Years later when I finally visited Disneyland and they had the E-Ticket rides, I just laughed at that because I already had done my E-Ride and I damn sure didn't want to repeat it! Xin Loi GI!

The helicopter, which happened to be brand new, now had to be flown back to Long Bien, for a major inspection and repair. Once the torque meter showed that it had been taken past the red line/safe operating setting, it was required to be torn down and inspected to make sure that nothing had been damaged and eventually showed up in the form of a mechanical failure, which could be catastrophic for the crew and the ship.

We on the other hand had to "take two salt tablets and drive on" with our mission. It was decided that since we would be compromised anyway on any insertion in that general area, we would just be inserted in the open onto a rice paddy to get a look at the trails we could see from the air and make an assessment of who and how many had made this trail. We got into insertion helicopter #2 and headed back to the same area, but further east of our last insertion point. We actually had to stay clear of the immediate area of our hot LZ because a FAC was calling air strikes on that particular island of grass and I'm quite sure that it ended up being a really bad day, even in the old French fort, for the NVA that were most likely hiding inside.

The good news was that once we photographed and made an assessment of the trails across the rice paddies, we would be extracted and taken back to our base camp to rest and clean our gear at least for that day. The insertion was non-eventful except that every rice farmer and NVA within 5 miles could see us. We set up in a basic wagon wheel formation right on top of the main trail. Even though it was the dry season the rice paddies still had moisture in them from the monsoon rains so they were damp to muddy in some areas. The first thing we noticed is that the trail was very fresh, approximately 18 inches wide and 6 inches deep in the soft soil of the rice paddy. The second thing was that all of the marking on the trail indicated that they were made by people wearing Ho Chi Minh Sandals, as indicated by the cross tire treads of the sandals. The C&C ship was flying overhead and Major Maus, the CO, wanted us to give an estimate of the numbers of troops that had made this trail. Hell, all we knew for sure is that is that it took a hell of a lot of troops to tromp down a 6 in trail in damp rice paddy. It made the hairs on the back of my neck stand up knowing that within seeing distance there was probably a lot of NVA just itching for a fight. We would have been prime meat except for the fact that they were all trying to keep a low profile so as not to draw attention to their numbers and location, preceding the Tet Offensive. The other interesting observation was that all of the sandals were indicating that they were heading east toward Saigon and we estimated that it had taken hundreds of troops if not thousands to make a trail like that. None of us had ever seen such a high speed trail as this! Fortunately and mainly because of our air power no enemy or rice farmers came near us and after about a half an hour on the ground we extracted and headed back to base, to fight another day!

Chapter 17

The Tet Offensive; Phase II, The Attack

After returning to our base camp and cleaning our gear, we were all restricted to the company area. II Field Force and most of the Senior Command Structure of Vietnam believed we were going to get attacked and they started restricting individual US units and spinning up for the assault. The attacks themselves were not a surprise but size of the attack was certainly a surprise to the US Command staff. All of South Vietnam's major cities, district sights and ports were attacked by the Communist Forces.

The world press later made it look like the entire US Command in South Vietnam were completely surprised by the attacks. I say bullshit with a capital B! It wasn't the first or the last lie or misquote the news media used to vilify the War in Vietnam.

Several light teams were placed in observation positions east of Bien Hoa. They were along several of the actual paved roads that were used by US Military and Vietnamese civilians to enter and leave the general area of Bien Hoa and Long Binh. At 0200 hours we were alerted by one of our Lurp teams that they were seeing large groups of VC and NVA carrying every conceivable weapon and double timing down the roads toward Bien Hoa. There were so many gooks that they lost count on the numbers, but it was in the hundreds per group. Needless to say that team had to become one with the earth and burrowed in. If they were compromised they would have been over-run and dead in minutes. After the initial attack on the bases the NVA and VC were frantic about leaving the area and some of them actually walked into the perimeter of one of the teams. There was a hell of a firefight with a lot of enemy troops being killed and wounded by the team, but also several of the team members were wounded. Additional enemy troops were joining the firefight as they tried to Escape and Evade from their original attacks and this created a very dangerous situation for the 6 man Light Team. Eventually the C&C helicopter with Major Maus onboard landed under heavy enemy fire and physically extracted the shot up team. The results of the desperate extraction being that Major Maus was awarded the Army Cross of Gallantry for his valorous actions. It also showed the true metal of our company commander, Major Maus, whose Lurps would follow him to hell and back after his valorous rescue of the team. Of course there were other soldiers involved like the helicopter crew, but it was Major Maus's decision to have the C&C helicopter land. It shouldn't have landed in the middle of the firefight to extract the team, because of the significance of the persons on board and all of the secret radio equipment, but truly gallant leaders in times of war make hard decisions for the betterment of their troops!

At 0300, Bien Hoa Air Base was hit with rockets and mortars followed by a ground attack. By this time we were all geared up and each platoon took a section of the north berm of the company area, which ran along the entire length of Bien Hoa Army Base. At 0400 they hit Long Bien and there was one hell of a firefight occurring all along the south berm of Long Bien and the east perimeter of Bien Hoa Airbase. At 0630 the ammo dump at Long Bien was hit and there was a large, bright flash, a large mushroom cloud like an A Bomb had exploded, followed by a rolling cloud of a shock wave coming out from the explosion. Several seconds later the sound hit us and it was massive. They had apparently either used rockets or detonated with explosives the large aircraft bombs and the artillery rounds at the Long Bien ammo dump. It was a fat target because the ammo dump was over a square mile, so it was a target rich environment.

We sat on the north berm all ready for a firefight, but nothing happened. Most likely because the area outside the north berm was flat and open with very little vegetation. The area on the south side of Bien Hoa Army and Airbase had trees, including a rubber tree plantation and lots of brush almost up to the perimeter of the fences. In addition all of the primary targets such as the airbase and the Long Binh Supply Depot were located on the south perimeter, so it made tactical sense to attack that side for the above listed reasons.

At some point the NVA and VC actually breached the east perimeter fence to Bien Hoa Air Base, but they were too late to capitalize on the their brief success. It was later learned by Intel that the VC guides that were escorting the NVA attack units got lost in the dark. The coordination of the attack by multiple units was affected and so the attack was piecemeal instead of one large push. It didn't allow time before daylight came, for the units to attack their targets and then hold those positions. The results being that the American Army units had time to establish solid defense positions in addition to what was already permanently in place like bunkers, concertina wire perimeters and some minefields. It also gave the Army helicopter units time to coordinate their operations and resulted in the killing of hundreds of VC and NVA soldiers that were caught out in the open at sunrise. The Cobra gunships had a field day attacking retreating units in the open with nowhere to hide. As we watched from the north perimeter we could see that the helicopters were circling in a formation reminiscent of the wagon trains circling to protect their members from an Indian attack, the difference being that each helicopter had at least two M-60 machine guns firing down on the main points of attack. You would see hundreds of red tracers firing down into that circle of death and occasionally green tracers would come flying up at the helicopters, but those were quickly suppressed by the massive firepower from above. In addition to the helicopters, Bien Hoa Air Base and some of the south perimeter of Bien Hoa Army Base had armor that was referred to as "Dusters". They were Second World War twin 40 mm Boffer anti-aircraft guns mounted on the M-48 Tank frames and they were mobile. They could fire the guns from flat to high angles and they put out a tremendous amount of fire. They were devastating to troops on the ground and lightly armored vehicles such as jeeps and trucks. Wherever there were concentrations of enemy troops they would move in to bolster the defensive positions and suppress the enemy attack. By the next morning the attacks on Long Binh, Bien Hoa Army Base and Bien Hoa Air Force base were substantially over and it was more of a clean up operation with Special Forces Mike Units sweeping the area around the perimeters to catch any enemy stragglers or small units that still had fighting capabilities. It was also a field day for collecting numerous enemy weapons including up to 37 MM anti-aircraft guns that the NVA had brought in to suppress air power. Needless to say that SF had an abundance of captured enemy weapons the day after the beginning of Tet. There were still fierce battles occurring in Bien Hoa, the city, and in neighboring and outlying districts, but the attacks on the primary bases of Bien Hoa and Long Bien were over. Of course there were still major battles occurring throughout South Vietnam especially around major cities like Hue, and it would take weeks of very deadly and costly combat actions to finally remove the enemy from positions they had captured during the initial attacks.

Chapter 18

Shit Burning Detail

I don't think most people understand what shit burning detail was all about. It is exactly what it sounds like with some very important minor details! In Vietnam and also in future wars, the military didn't have a human waste management system in place except maybe in the VIP locations where the generals and their staff worked and lived. Everyone else had to take a dump in an old fashion shit house with some modifications. I guess someone with computer skills could figure out how much human waste was generated on a daily basis by just the 500,000 US troops on the ground in South Vietnam. It would probably be in the hundreds of tons per day, so that created a very dangerous health situation at the bases in South Vietnam. The US Army's method of solving that problem was to burn the shit until it was reduced to only ash.

Naturally, that job transitioned down the rank ladder to the bottom row of privates, spec 4s and on some occasions for Sgts in our company we originally had a 4-hole shitter for the enlisted men and a separate 2-hole shitter for the officers. If you looked at a normal 1-hole shitter that was used back in the home country locations as opposed to the cities, that would be it, multiplied by 4, but with only one door in and out. It was built off the ground with the floor being about 4 feet high. The front of the building had screen where you might think windows should be. Those weren't for observation purposes, but were for letting the repugnant odor allegedly escape, that had developed by the fecal matter decaying inside the metal barrels of the latrine/shit house. The venting of the odors out of the shitter was also allegedly assisted by having a slanted roof, sloping up toward the top of the open screened-in area. During the dry season, when the temperatures were at their max, you normally held out until night time if you could, because the smells inside the very hot day time shitter would truly "gag a maggot" and about as bad as you ever wanted to smell if it involved human wastes.

The real technical part of the design was at the outside rear of the latrine. Below and perpendicular to each hole in the shitter seat was a trap door that hinged from the top. Behind each of the four doors was a "no surprise there" approximately half a 55 gallon drum filled with liquid wastes and urine. If you were lucky, it had two handles welded to it. It was of the utmost simple design with gravity being the primary tool to make each human defecation function properly. Basically, one GI would sit on the bench/shit hole and deposit their bodily excretions into the metal drum, wipe same and leave the location as soon as possible.

The inside were just several planks laid side by side lengthwise and faced with four more 2 x 8 planks that gave it some height. There were four semi-circular holes cut about 3 feet on center. Basically a 10' x 12" bench with four holes cut in it. A very standard design.

Two GIs would open the trap door and each would grab one of the handles. Hopefully, you were able to find the leather gloves that were suppose to be inside one of the doors. As a team, you would slowly and carefully slide the full drum of very liquid fecal matter out on its built-in floor and out of the trap door to a location where you would slowly lower it to the ground. You always wanted a very steady-handed partner, because if the drums were full as they usually were, the slightest uncoordinated movement would cause the liquid shit to flow over the side and onto your gloved hand! The problem was made worse by the fact that most Lurps in our company had diarrhea, primarily because of the malaria pills we had to take on a daily/weekly basis. Also because no one wanted to do this dirty deed, the mission was not completed on a daily basis, which led to the liquid shit having hundreds of white maggots squirming around on top of the liquid shit. More then one Lurp left his meal in the drum or on the ground especially those that were hot, sick and hung-over! Xin Loi GI!

After all four of the drums from the enlisted men's shitter were on the ground sitting in a parallel line, then we next had to pull out the officers' three drums and stack them on top of the four other drums. Contrary to some officers' beliefs, their shit did stink just like the enlisted men's did! This was followed by two drums from the Vietnamese shitter. The reason the Vietnamese workers had their own shitter was because they would squat on the bench over the hole and they were notorious for being off target. Again, more then one Lurp lost his lunch when he went in to take a dump and found a pile of shit prominently displayed on top of the bench seat and near the hole! It didn't take long to find enough volunteers to build a separate shitter for the Vietnamese.

Once the stacking process was completed, you had a nice pyramid made up of usually 9 half-drums of liquid and very smelly shit along with the swimming maggots! (4 on the base; 3 in the middle stack; 2 on the top stack). Depending on the style of the team you either poured into each drum about a gallon of diesel fuel before you stacked them or after you stacked them. You had to stir each drum to get the diesel thoroughly mixed in with the liquid shit so that it would actually burn. The primary method of lighting this liquid concoction was by throwing a trip flare in the bottom center drum and once it caught on fire it would normally spread to the other drums as the flames rose and the next row of drums heated up! Along with the great smell and black smoke you had the snapping sound of the maggots cooking off and exploding in the burning shit. You've probably seen the iconic pictures of various bases in Vietnam with black smoke rising all over the base. This was not normally caused by an enemy artillery, rocket or mortar attack on the base, it was a whole lot of shit burning details doing the ugly deed! The smell of burning shit is locked in the memory of most GIs who had that duty! The actual quote for a GI in Vietnam would be more like, "I hate the smell of burning shit in the morning!" Xin Loi GI!

Chapter 19

Post-Tet, February 4, 1968

Immediately after the Tet Offensive began and while it was still raging in various places throughout Vietnam, Company F started inserting teams. Their mission was to ambush enemy soldiers that were still in the area and to disrupt any concerted efforts for them to regroup. We were also to gather intel on the units that were involved with the Tet Offensive. My team, Team 1-5, was inserted near the Song Dong Nai river to ambush enemy soldiers coming down a well used trail. Because of all the combat occurring in the area, TL Lavender decided to take an M-60 machine gun on this mission. I was assigned to carry the gun and since they weren't individually issued I had to draw one from the armory. The first one was filthy and I refused to take it and the second one wasn't much better, but I was able to clean it up, since this was a short notice of only hours from when we received the warning order to when we were actually inserted. I did give the assigned armorer some shit though, because the guns were suppose to come back in cleaned and ready to be re-issued out to the next team needing a M-60. It was him and his crew that should not have accepted a gun back into the inventory if it was not properly cleaned. Xin Loi GI!

We were inserted at 1830 hours, which was late to be inserted in an active area and so we only moved about 50 meters before finding the trail and setting up an observation and or ambush position. We were not far from the river and also had a village probably a click away from our position. It was not the ideal location but you had to make duo with what you were given in those types of situations. The night got exciting when friendly artillery started landing near our position.

This was of course a mistake by an artillery Fire Direction Control Officer because our A/Os were not to receive H&I rounds and the only artillery was suppose to be if we called for a fire mission. As I had previously mentioned, friendly artillery was one of the major dangers for a Lurp Team on a mission. There was so damn much artillery fire occurring throughout Vietnam and it seemed to be always near a Lurp Team. After getting the artillery shut down we then heard a firefight erupt from the village. It may have been an enemy attack or just some nervous guards of the village and it didn't last long.

We survived the night but did not have any enemy sightings. After the 100 percent alert at sunrise for the team, *per Recondo School SOP,* we settled into the normal routine of having one person on guard and the rest just relaxing or sleeping. At approximately 1300 hours we heard noises of someone approaching our position and using an old road that was next to the trail. It was unusual for the enemy to be using the road instead of the trail and they were making a lot of noise, but after the Tet Offensive anything was possible. As the enemy came into view we knew we were in big trouble because the enemy was actually a squad of American Infantry Troops obviously on combat patrol with their fingers on the triggers and primed for action. We on the other hand were wearing camouflaged uniforms like enemy troops and hidden in the bush. They were not supposed to be in our AO, furthermore it was obvious that they didn't know there were friendly troops in the area. They now call it Blue on Blue, but we just called it Friendly Fire, which was an oxymoron. It had the potential for a lot of troops to be killed or wounded during an exchange of gunfire with each side thinking enemy troops were firing at them.

This was the second time I saw TL Lavender do a very brave thing and that was to just stand up and say "How are y'all doing!" TL Lavender had allowed the first four Infantrymen to walk through the ambush zone so that the point man, who was usually the fastest shooter had passed by our position. The slack came out of every trigger from the Infantrymen in the patrol, but fortunately they did not fire, probably because of Lavender's Southern drawl and his

117

6 foot 4 stature. I'm not sure whose hearts were beating the fastest, the Infantry patrol or the Lurp team's, because if the firing started we wouldn't be able to fire back and they would have hosed down the area with M-16 automatic fire, thinking they were being ambushed by the enemy. After everyone took a long breathe SSG Lavender advised them of who we were and that they had just walked into our ambush site. He showed them the claymore mines they had missed and we each stood up to reveal our positions. They were all shocked at how they had completely missed everything and they would have been dead men if the ambush had been set up by the enemy. We learned from the patrol leader, a young second Lieutenant, that they were from a Company of the 199th Light Infantry Brigade and there were numerous other patrols out from the company and in our AO. After reporting all of this via our radio and their radio, our TOC sent everything up the chain of command and the infantry company was pulled out of the area. We never learned where the screw-up had occurred, but it was obviously at a level higher than the company. It was not the last time these type of Friendly Fire Incidents would occur between our Lurps and other US or Allied Troops who were in our designated AOs.

What civilians don't understand is that in a war zone, especially one where there are no front lines, it is easy for friendly units to get lost or be assigned to an area without knowing that other friendly troops were also in the area. The problem was partially mitigated by having specific areas assigned to specifically large units such as a battalion or brigade so they had tactical control of that area and would know who within their internal organization was assigned to which area of their AO. The problems arose when units like a Lurp company, who were independent of any large unit and usually worked for a Division or Field Force, didn't have specific AOs until they were assigned missions in that area. If the info was not immediately passed on to commands in that AO, then one unit never knew another unit was also operating in the area. It was doubly dangerous and confusing for air units especially helicopter units because they pretty much

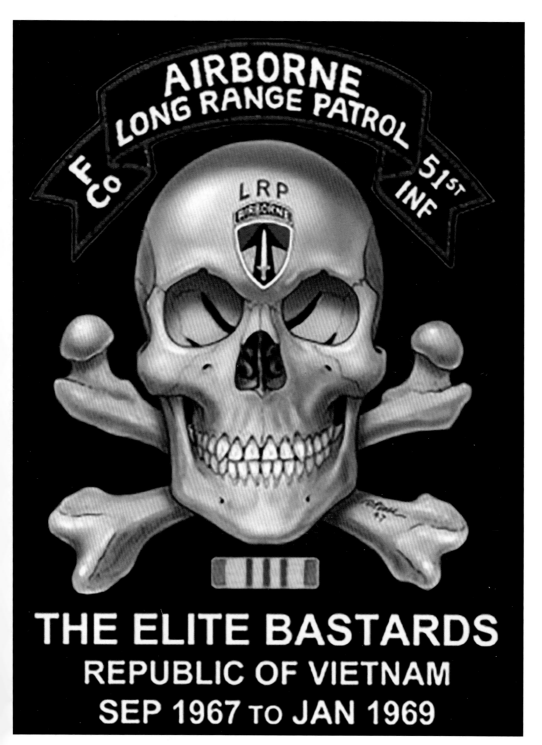

Elite Bastards Emblem. Artist: Sgt. Dave Peace.

ARTIST – Mark Eastman; Hot LZ extraction of a Lurp Team.

ARTIST Mark Eastman – Up close and personal ambush of VC on an active trail.

Author and Myron Anderson (remained in Army and retired as full Bird Colonel).

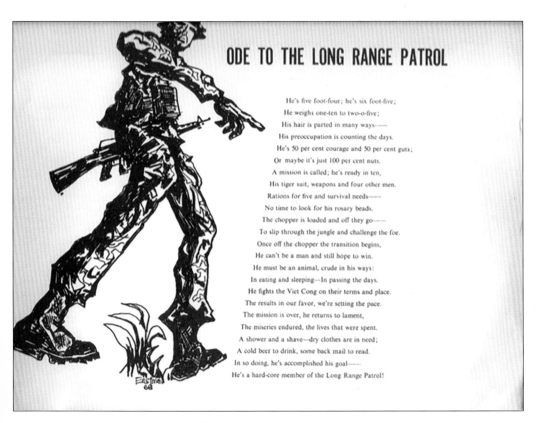

Author: Sgt. Berrow and additional Lurps.

CH 47 AKA Shit Hook.

Early UH1B Heuy Helicopter converted to a gunship.

Hien Van Tua (AKA Tony) Chieu Hoey who was force-drafted as a VC and repatriated to the South Vietnamese Army as a scout.

Jungle looking west to Cambodia; My backseat ride in a Cessna tail dragger, forced to fly in Cambodia

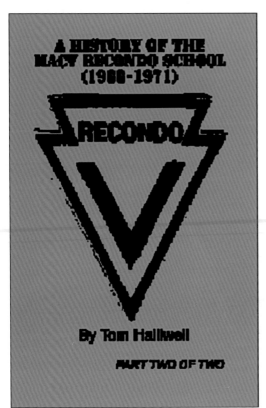

A HISTORY OF THE MACV RECONDO SCHOOL (1968-1971)

RECONDO

By Tom Halliwell

PART TWO OF TWO

Left: MACV RECONDO SCHOOL HISTORY.

Below: MACV Recondo School Mcquire Rig Training.

Right: MACV Recondo
School NHA Trang South
Vietnam and the school's
emblem on the water
tower.

Below: MACV Recondo
School Training jungle
penetrator evacuation for
wounded Lurp.

MACV Recondo School: Actual lift and transport on a McQuire Rig. (Author's Photo)

Right: MACV Recondo
School Foreign Weapons
Training.

Below: MACV Recondo
School repelling training
from a Huey.

Left: Several of the UH1D Hueys (AKA Slicks) from Company F, LRP, with different configurations for different purposes. Hurry Sundown was the C&C ship and was in control of all air operations for insertions and extractions of Lurp Teams.

Below: Sgt Eric Johnson eating a lurp ration; SF qualified medic and communications specialist.

Practicing a McQuire Rig extraction; helicopter altitude was between 2,000 to 3,000 feet and around 80 knots to safely remove the Lurp Team members from a Hot LZ!

Sgt Ralph Bolt (Assistant Team Leader for 1-3) collecting intel.

Sgt. McElwee (AKA Mac with Mucho Huevos Silver Star Recipient) with captured RPD.

SSG Dvorak on a mission in the bush.

Team 1-5 (Heavy Team Hatchet Team for ambushes). Author standing 3rd from left with the M-60 Machine Gun!

Team 1-5 (Light Team for recon and hit and run attacks).

Team 1-5 in-bound for insertion on an LZ. A Lurp's "Hole of Life" which was the cutout in the Huey's frame that the first Lurp sitting on the floor held onto so as not to fall out of the helicopter on a really fast insertion!

Above: Live Fire training. Practicing a "Break Contact Drill" with a Willi Peter (AKA White Phosphorus) grenade thrown to delay the enemy as the team evacuates the area!

Right: Inserted Team headed out on a recon mission.

Why camo was necessary.

ranged over all areas of Vietnam and would attack any target they could identify as an enemy unit. Of course a six man Lurp team all camouflaged up and moving like an enemy patrol was a prime target for misidentification and they usually shot first and asked questions later! It was one of the reasons that Lurp teams tried not to operate in single canopy environments, because it was possible to be spotted and attacked from the air. My team almost became a victim of one of those friendly fire attacks.

That incident happened in the area of War Zone D in 1968 and it was about as close as you wanted to get to being killed by US Forces. By that time, mid 1968, Co F had been given Chou Hois who were VC and North Vietnamese that had been captured and persuaded to fight on our side. A lot of the Lurps in Company F were hesitant about using them, believing that in the middle of a firefight they might decide to rejoin the enemy and turn on us. SSG Lavender was one of the few that from the beginning loved the Chou Hois and spent time with them in the rear at our base camp. It was rather comical to see 6 foot 4 SSG Lavender with 5 or 6, four and a half to maybe five feet tall, Chou Hois following him around and having great fun with him. He was like the pied piper and the Chou Hois were his children. They of course knew of his abilities in the jungle and they all wanted to be on SSG Lavender's Team.

Chapter 20

Death from Above (Almost)

Rockets Red Glare: February 9, 1968

Two nights later after I had been the belly man on an insertion with nothing happening at all, I got drunk with some of the other team members from 1st Platoon. SSG Edwards had a bottle of vodka and Sgt Wade was making popcorn using some C-4 and a mess kit pan. We partied until the booze ran out and everyone went to bed around 2300 hours. By 0030 hours I was sick from all of the vodka and popcorn and I deposited all of it out back of the hooch in one of the drainage ditches. I got back into bed after about 15 minutes of puking my guts out and tried to go to sleep. Of course, Charles must have known that we had been partying so he dropped 4 or 5 large rockets, probably 122 mm, in the 101st Abn area which was to our west about 200 meters. A 122mm rocket makes a really big hole and blast the shit out of everything near it. It appeared that the enemy had calculated their altitude incorrectly and instead of hitting Bien Hoa Airbase, the rockets fell short and hit the 101st area. No one knew for sure if this was a pre-emptive strike that was to be followed by a ground assault so we all got dressed and readied our gear. After an hour or so, it was decided that it was just short rounds so we were allowed to go back to bed but remained fully clothed with our weapons and ammo close by. Not a problem for a Lurp, because we slept with our rifles every night we were on a mission.

It's a good thing they didn't attack, because all of us that had been drinking felt like shit and we were pissed off at Charlie waking us up. We were ready to kick some ass and a shot of adrenalin would have probably fixed our hangovers; however, Charlie rarely did what you would expect, so we all woke up with hangovers and a bad attitude.

Chapter 21

Intelligence Missions for the Alphabet Agency

After the Tet Offensive it was very obvious to anyone involved in actual war fighting in Vietnam, that all of the US Government intelligence agencies had missed or failed to recognize the intelligence that was provided to them by units like Company F, Long Range Patrol. They probably had better intel on what was occurring in Cambodia and Laos because they had numerous methods of monitoring that activity. They had specialized aircraft, actual boots on the ground like MACV SOG and other technical methods of monitoring the activity, especially along the Ho Chi Minh Trail. One of those devices used was the Box (restricted ID). It was basically a portable, self-contained, seismograph that had a VHF transmitter built into the device. The Box was about 24″ high x 8″ deep x 12″ wide. The problem with it was that it weighed about 30 pounds (long before digital electronics) and had to be planted in the earth by hand. The method it used to detect the enemy was that it had to be planted alongside a well used trail (not more than 2-5 feet) and it would record any vibrations occurring on the trail, like numerous enemy soldiers walking down the trail. It would then transmit those signals via a VHF radio signal to specialized aircraft monitoring the specific signals. It all looked good on paper, but what it really involved was some troopers carrying the device to a specific location/trail, digging a hole to hide the device in, activating the electronics, covering and camouflaging it except for a small antenna and then exit the area, undetected. Of course all of this had to be carried out without being observed by the enemy or being attacked by enemy soldiers walking down the same trail. It was not an easy mission and had a lot of dangerous activity involved in the entire operation. Of course Lurps were the perfect choice to carry out this type of mission. We had the reputation and the ability to move through the jungle without being detected by the enemy and to complete very dangerous missions in complete secrecy.

Team 1-5 was the first team to draw a mission for emplacement of the devices on trails coming across the border from Cambodia into Vietnam. I believe it was because of SSG Lavender's skill and reputation as a team leader. Of course if you were a member of Lavender's team, you made damn sure that you had your shit wrapped tight, because you didn't want to be the weak link for the team.

We were to be inserted near a high speed trail (very active) and very close to the Cambodian/Vietnam Border. I was lucky and didn't draw the short stick on who was assigned to carry that 40 pound box. Walking point did have some advantages.

The mission started out as typical Long Range Recon Patrol (LRRP) operation. The difference between it and a Long Range Patrol (LRP) was that it was imperative that the team was never compromised or never made contact with the enemy. If that occurred the mission would be aborted, at least for that day and location.

This was a true "sneak and peek" operation and it required a lot of skill to complete the mission.

It also required the team to adopt a different mentality, which was to be a ghost in the jungle and just disappear for the entire mission. We had to adjust our aggressive attitude so as not to attack any enemy patrols that may cross our path. It also required us to adjust our gear, because we would be traveling light and quiet as possible, which meant no M-60 machine gun, less explosives like extra grenades and Claymores, but with still enough ammo and firepower to execute an escape and evade operation if things hit the fan. It is a delicate balance because everything has weight. The more weight, the more you have to work to carry it quietly and the more energy you expend! Of course all of those weight/load factors get exponentially increased by the terrain, the distance and the temperature! No one said that being a Lurp would be easy and it wasn't. Fortunately all of the team members of 1-5 were the original 6 members. We had been running Lurp Missions for at least 6 months and we were all in great condition, both physically and mentally!

The insertion for a LRRP Mission was similar but different from the LRP Mission, especially with this high priority mission and the federal agency watching our every move. The skill to pull off a very quiet and uncompromised insertion involved coordination between the Lurps, the helicopter pilots and even the C&C ship, who would supervise the insertion. Whenever you got near the Cambodian border the danger factors for a Lurp team and the helicopter crews substantially increased. Essentially, you had thousands of NVA and substantial equipment setting just inside the border of Cambodia. The enemy soldiers included special NVA Hunter/Killer Teams searching for Recon Teams and excellent equipment to back them up, including substantial anti-aircraft artillery and SAMs. It would be similar to accidentally kicking an active hornets nest if you mistakenly crossed over the border or caused them to come across the border to take care of business in a most deadly manner! Of course you still had to get inserted within a reasonable distance of your mission target so that you had less exposure time on the ground. You had to have reasonably good cover and concealment to move toward your objective and you needed options depending on what the terrain presented to you.

Our insertion was probably around 5 klicks east of the border and 2 + klicks from the target area. It was a small LZ and an area with good overhead cover and good ground concealment vegetation. Most of it was double canopy so we had a lot of vegetation growing on the floor of the jungle. It made it harder to move through, but did give us a lot better concealment to hide in. The reason this particular LZ was chosen by TL Lavender was that it was sufficient distance from the border and from our target area; however, the target area could still be reached in one day of careful movement. The plan was to get inserted and once the insertion was confirmed as being uncompromised, we would move out in a northwesterly direction. We would slowly and quietly patrol our way close to the border and locate the active trail.

We had originally planned to make the move to the target area in one day of movement, but the heavy vegetation on the floor of the jungle coupled with an absolute requirement of quiet movement caused the team to take a lot longer to move toward our approximate destination. We had an approximate location of a particular trail that was identified by the US Intelligence Agency, where we intended to plant the Box. You may see a partial trail from the air and it appears to be moving in a fairly specific direction, but when you get on the ground that same trail becomes more like the path of a snake. The path of a trail is determined by the enemy soldiers making it and the terrain through which it passes. It is normally not a haphazard design, but is specifically built by experts to use overhead cover to hide movement down it from American and Allied aircraft and to confuse the observers who think they know where the trail is actually going.

I have seen trails that were literally cut out of the jungle. They looked like a subway tunnel coming out of a solid wall of trees and low bushes. The trails that didn't have a lot of overhead cover would be additionally camouflaged by bending and securing small trees and bushes over the trails. Other Lurp teams actually found locations where vegetation had been planted along the trail to prevent observation of its existence from our aircraft. The NVA and the VC excelled in camouflage because their lives, their movements and their supply lines literally depended on not being detected by American and Allied aircraft! Even when you're on the ground actively searching for a trail, they still jump out at you as if they just appeared like magic. It is a testament to the skills of the VC and NVA to adapt the environment for their use and to confuse us, their enemy.

We were approximately half way to the location of the trail when TL Lavender called for a halt to our quiet march. We were all physically tired and soaked with sweat from the efforts to move with the hot temps on the ground in the brush and small trees under double canopy jungle. Also, we were all more mentally alert for this mission, because we didn't want to fail. This was a test for Company F Lurps and we didn't want to let down the Company. It was more then a matter of pride, because we understood that if these Boxes worked like they were predicted to, then it could be a significant addition to the war fighters' tool box of weapons.

We found a good RON location in a clump of small trees that gave us additional cover and concealment. We sat up in a tight wagon wheel configuration and then settled in for the night. Once it was dark and we didn't have any questionable movement we could be reasonably assured that the enemy was not aware that we were in the area. There is normally more movement of animals in this double overhead canopy environment and more sounds from insects on the floor, most likely because they also have better concealment with all of the brush, vines and small trees that can grow in that particular environment. It is actually a great help to especially have the insects around your position at night. They become your instant alarm system, because they are familiar with the area and they are also on a "self preservation" alert status! Normally it starts with the small insects buzzing, chirping on making small noises as they move through the vegetation. It can be followed by larger insects, lizards and some night birds. It can be a complete symphony of insect sounds and they are quite soothing for a Lurp team on a mission. The movement of small mammals and rodents does occur, but most of the time they are specific to a certain area. Many a sleepless night was spent by a Lurp team on alert, because of movement through the brush near their position. At first light instead of enemy troops, the movement normally turned out to be jungle pigs, some being feral domestic pigs and some being natural for that particular area. Either way it can play with your mind when you can't see a thing, you can only hear the movement and you're a long way from any LZ in case things go to crap and you have to E&E out of the area.

There were large mammals in the jungle like elephants and tigers and some alligators, but it was rare to run into them. They normally detected and avoided you.

The most dangerous reptiles were the snakes, especially the cobras. They were both day-time and nocturnal hunters. They moved along the floor of the jungle and in the trees searching for prey. The most dangerous time for Lurp/snake confrontation was during the dry season, because the cobras/Kraits/Pit Vipers are cold blooded. When the temperature drops to the low 70s at night after being in the high 90s to 100 degrees during the day, they get cold just like humans do. Some also have the ability to detect prey with infrared sensors (Malayan Pit Viper/Kraits use infrared sensors in pits on the front of their heads for hunting prey at night so a warm human body lying on the floor of the jungle would look like a lit room to certain species of snakes. If they come to investigate they try to get right up next to a human to gain some of that heat. If the human moves or does anything to make the snake (Malayan Krait: one of the most dangerous snakes in the world; nocturnal; painless bite with neurotoxin venom like the cobras) think it's in danger or being attacked they will strike at the large target, like an arm or leg and they don't normally miss their target. They were like Lurps in a way; Strike first and ask questions later! Xin Loi GI!

Its rather peculiar that as a Lurp we just accepted snakes as another risk that the jungle presented to you. It was not high on your priority list because snakes usually avoided Lurps and the Lurps avoided the snakes! I only know of two events that involved cobras/Kraits in the 19 months I was actually in Vietnam. The score was one for the Lurps and one for the cobras. It would appear to be a tie except if you were the Lurp that got bit by a cobra/Krait.

Private Don Carnahan was with another team and they had gone into a RON position. In the middle of the night when he was off his guard duty position, he was lying on the ground with his poncho liner wrapped around him. He was asleep but woke up when he felt something fairly heavy crawling on his jungle boots that he was wearing, but were sticking out the bottom of his poncho liner. He was half asleep and said that he just kicked it away. Whatever it was it came back a second time so he kicked it away again and felt that it was pretty heavy, but he didn't think it was a snake. This animal was very determined and it came back a third time. Don said he kicked it again hard and this time it didn't come back. He didn't feel anything but within a minute of the third kick he had difficulty breathing and then went into convulsions. He doesn't remember anything else until he woke up in the hospital over 24 hours later. He had to have a full blood transfusion within the hour of being bitten because there weren't any antidotes for the snake bite and they didn't know what kind of snake it had been. The facts that saved him was that the team was close to an LZ where they were able to get extracted and get him to evacuation hospital within the GOLDEN HOUR. I talked with him several days after he returned from the hospital. He said all he remembered was that it was cold and he was wrapped up in his poncho liner trying to stay warm. He felt something brush against his leg and just kind of kicked at it. The last thing he remembered he was going into convulsions and doesn't remember anything else until he regained consciousness in the evac hospital. Based on his comments and the fact that he didn't feel any bite, the evidence would point toward a Krait. He said that when they examined his jungle boot, they observed that one fang had struck the reinforced webbing along the tongue on the boot, but the other fang had partially penetrated through the tongue of his jungle boot. That slight penetration had allowed enough venom to be injected into his body to cause the convulsions and what would have eventually been death.

The night was uneventful with only our natural concert performed by the locals for our team. We moved out after our normal hundred percent alert at sunrise. We all knew that today was our "make it or break it day" to complete the planting of the Box near a high speed trail.

It was early afternoon when we finally located the trail. Upon spotting the trail, we just circled the team for a while to watch the trail and see what type of activity it would have. The timing was perfect though, because it was the hottest part of the day, so the likelihood of enemy troops walking down the trail was at its lowest probable point! Of course if Murphy had joined the team on this mission, anything could happen!

The location where we discovered the trail was not ideal, because it was along a semi clear area, but it did allow the team to be able to watch both ends of the trail that came from the west and followed an easterly route. The plan as dictated by TL Lavender was that he and I would crawl out in the low brush next to the trail. We would find a dense bush and dig a hole in the middle of that bush deep enough to bury the Box and then cover and conceal it. The only thing above ground would be the semi-rigid OD green antenna. We set up a linear type ambush with two claymores pointing at the opposite ends of the trail where it came out of the jungle (west side of trail) and then re-entered the jungle (east side of trail). The semi-open area along the trail was probably 50 meters long so we had a great view. The problem was that to get to the location next to the trail we had to crawl through the low brush for probably 15 meters to reach the trail. That meant that if we were in the process of planting the Box and the enemy walked out on the trail, we would not have time to crawl back to the perimeter of the team. We would have to just hunker down and hope the enemy passed by without seeing us. The entire idea of planting the Box next to an active trail was counter intuitive to all of our training as a Lurp. The closer you got to a trail the chances of being compromised were exponentially higher then if you were back 10 to 15 feet from the trail. We had to just suck it up and do the job without thinking of what could happen if we had bad luck.

TL Lavender had already confirmed that the box was active and working. After turning on the device, he had completed a radio check on a specific frequency with an aircraft flying in area and they had confirmed that the Box was operational. We had been told that if the Box was dropped or mishandled during our march to the implant location, there was a chance that it would not work. Hell, that's all we needed was to drag this big ass 30 pound Box to a location to find out that it didn't work! We had handled the Box along the way like it was a sleeping baby. We didn't want to have to redo the whole damn mission on another day.

TL Lavender and I stripped off our packs and began to low crawl out to the trail with only our M-16s, our load bearing equipment, an entrenching tool and that damn heavy Box. It probably took us 15 minutes to actually make it to the area we had observed from the team's perimeter. We would crawl a short distance, lay still, listen and then move on. We were already soaked in sweat partially because of the exertion we used to get to that point and because of the added stress of knowing we were hanging our Lurp asses way out on the end of the limb. Once we got near the trail, TL Lavender spotted a particular thick bush about 3 feet tall and approximately 4 feet from the trail. It was obvious to us that if the enemy came down the trail and unless they were blind, they would spot us lying in the bushes. Our only hope was that the team would have initiated contact on the enemy before they got to our location. Once again this was one Lurp trusting another Lurp to cover their backs in case our luck ran out. We crawled to the location of the thick bush and we started to immediately dig the hole to house the Box. One of us would dig while the other kept an eye on the trail. We had some luck because the ground was soft and it was relatively easy to dig the hole; however, we were digging on our stomachs using only our arms as the force. We also had to be careful about not letting the soil we were digging up, fall out toward the trail where it could be observed by passing enemy troops. To dig a hole wide and deep enough to house that large box took some time. I would guess it took us at least 20+ minutes to actually get the hole dug, but it seemed like hours. Once we had a large enough hole we slid the Box into it, screwed on the commo antenna and carefully started to cover it. The antenna was approximately 14 inches long so we had to place the box in an upright position, but with the antenna in the middle of the branches of the bush so that it was completely concealed. If the enemy observed the antenna and then discovered the Box, it would be game over for that big Box. I would surmise that there was a Plan B if the enemy discovered the Box, but it was above our pay grade and we weren't told what would happen.

Once the Box was in the hole and completely covered we still had a lot of soil left over so we had to slowly disperse it in such a manner that it wouldn't look like a hill of soil lying along the trail for some suspicious reason. We had become very good at camouflaging ourselves, our gear and our locations, so it was not difficult for us to complete that part of the mission. Of course it took more time to disperse the extra soil and the clock was still ticking.

Once we completed the dispersal of the extra soil, TL Lavender and I slowly crawled back to the team's perimeter. As we low crawled I tried to put all of the bushes back to their normal position so that our track couldn't be observed from the trail. Once we were back in the team's perimeter, we had a long drink of warm water and took a well-deserved break. However, we didn't want to hang around the trail and get compromised so it was a short break. TL Lavender called in the code name on that specific frequency for the Box being planted, we saddled up and carefully backtracked out of the team's perimeter. The plan had been to plant the Box and then head out to an LZ for extraction, but because of our over-cautiousness of leaving the area without being compromised we actually spent another night in the jungle and extracted the next morning from a different LZ and probably several clicks from the trail and that damn Box! The cold beer that evening was especially delicious and it flowed abundantly for the team.

Chapter 22

A Week as a LURP/Standdown and Bellyman, February 10, 1968

All the teams were brought in for a stand down because Major Maus, our CO, had been promoted to Lt. Colonel and was being transferred to a new assignment. A loss for Company F! He was the best CO we had because we respected him for his experience and knowledge and how he commanded F Company LRP. Little did we know that the next two would be the worst COs we could possibly have as a Lurp Company Commander. They caused death and destruction of Lurp teams because of bad decisions. I was the receiver of one of those bad decisions and it nearly cost me my life along with most of my team.

Basically, a Stand Down is a time when all operations are ceased and all of the teams have a chance to rest up, prep their gear and of course party. We had really great stand downs because we would fill several jeep trailers full of ice and beer and the cooks BBQ'd whatever was available, usually chicken or steaks along with baked potatoes and some kind of salad. It usually got pretty rowdy once the beer was flowing and sometimes we did things like throw our officers in the trailers full of ice, water and beer. It was great fun and showed that we respected our officers and all that they did for us. We also threw the chopper pilots in, because everyone knew that they had all saved more than one Lurp Team's asses by coming in and getting us when the area was full of enemy troops firing everything they had.

Even though it was a Stand Down, someone had to pull guard duty and I was selected for some of that duty. It may seem like it was unnecessary to have guards posted inside the secure perimeter of the Bien Hoa Army Base. The problem was that the VC/NVA didn't give

131

a shit about what we thought and they were constantly trying to enter the base's perimeter and blow up strategic targets, like ammo dumps and aircraft hangers. Of course those were difficult targets to reach, so if they breached the perimeter they considered just about anything as a target. We had two important targets in our company area. The first was our TOC, an underground bunker, where all operations for the company were controlled. The second was the helipad where there were normally three Huey lift helicopters and two Cobra gunships sitting, ready for an immediate response if a team was in trouble. There was normally only one person on guard for each of those positions, but they were less than 100 meters from the berm which had manned bunkers every night. If some shooting started on the berm or in our company area, you can bet your ass there would have been a bunch of armed Lurps running toward the shots.

Of course, it was still boring as shit compared to sitting on a trail, locked and loaded, waiting for an unsuspecting enemy to walk into our kill zone. To counter this boredom all of the Lurps tried to be belly man during insertion or extraction of a team. The purpose of a Belly Man on an insertion or extraction helicopter, *per Recondo School SOP,* was to assist the team in either getting off the helicopter or more importantly climbing on a helicopter during an extraction. Because Murphy was always present during the war, it sometimes was not possible for the helicopter to actually touch down on an LZ, simply because of natural terrain features such as trees or ant hills. Of course, it was also complicated by facts like the enemy was pushing the team or had them surrounded and it was the only location where a Huey might get close enough to the ground for the team members to crawl up on the struts and then into the helicopter. The crew, especially the door gunners were usually up to their asses in alligators and were firing madly into the jungle to prevent the enemy from knocking the helicopter out of the sky. That situation left no one to help the Lurp team members on board, especially if they had wounded team members. Thus the belly man was expected to reach down or literally stand on the struts and help pull each team member up into the helicopter. It could be a crazy ass job with lots of risks on Hot LZs, so of course all of the Lurps wanted to do it.

There was a secondary reason for pulling a belly man position and that was for flight time and a possible air medal. Since none of us had a MOS as a helicopter door gunner or crew chief, we could only receive the basic Air Medal, but none of us were looking for medals in the first place. It was more about the adrenalin rush of being in the middle of a serious shoot out with the helicopter crew, the team on the ground and probably some Cobra gunships versus a bunch of pissed off enemy troops who had probably already lost some men in the initial contact with the Lurp team. Nothing like being in the middle of the shit and then getting everyone out with maybe a minor injury or two! It was back to base camp for cold beer and some really good war stories, fresh off the Huey!

Chapter 23

A Short Mission; February 11, 1968

We got our warning order in the morning and were inserted at 1700 hours and Lt. Clark, one of the Platoon Lts came along to get some combat experience. As soon as we got on the LZ, SSG Lavender spotted two VC and called in the gunships, who made a couple of gun passes. We faked an extraction and moved into a RON for the night. We had a lot of movement around us but they never found us and we never fired on them. Of course none of us slept so we moved out early hoping for some action. We moved several hundred meters through a swampy area with thick vegetation. We crossed over at least eight elephant trails, none of which were fresh. We continued on through this swampy area and finally took a break where three more elephant trails converged. We didn't know if the elephants were in the wild or were being used by the enemy essentially as a heavy lift truck. Based on the randomness of the trails, they were probably wild elephants on the move to water and feeding grounds. After a half an hour break we again moved out and found a good RON site in some bamboo clumps of trees, which provides good overhead cover and some cover to the front. As we were moving into the RON we discovered a well-used trail so we were essentially setting up an ambush in our RON site. Most of the time you were doing one or the other, because normally a RON site is for the purpose of resting up, so you find a really good location that gives you as much protection as possible. Plus, you are essentially hidden in the bush and it is nearly impossible for the enemy to find you unless you were followed and they saw you go into that site.

One of the big misconceptions of the jungles of Vietnam is that they are always hot and humid. During certain times of the year, especially the rainy/monsoon season that is very true; however, during the dry season it can get really cold at night. When I say cold I'm talking down in the low 70 degrees. That may seem like a pretty reasonable temperature, but during the daytime it is at least 100 degrees or more with probably close to 100 percent humidity. That causes you to sweat profusely and your uniform is basically soaked with your own sweat and maybe some water on your legs from walking in a swampy area. Then you go into your RON or ambush site, usually no later than 1500-1600 hours, so that you have time to set up before the anticipated probable movement of the enemy in the evening hours, *Per Recondo School SOP*. So now you're not moving, you're soaked to the bone and the sun goes down. Once the sun goes down, so does the temperature and since we were in a swampy area that also caused more of a fluctuation in the temperature. So by the time it's half way through the night you're freezing your ass off, even though you are wrapped up in a poncho liner with your head and arms out to look and listen and to react if the enemy is coming into your site. The problem is that your uniform is acting like an air conditioner and when the water evaporates off of your uniform and your body it naturally cools everything down, thus you're freezing and its 70 plus degrees. The only good thing about getting down to those temperatures is that the mosquitoes didn't like it either so they are not out flying around and trying to suck you dry of blood. The leeches didn't seem to mind it that much so you're still on the jungle menu, but it's from a ground attack by leeches instead of an air attack by mosquitoes. You have to condition your mind to not let those minor things like mosquitoes or leeches distract you from keeping your senses working and always looking for the enemy. We were notified on our evening sit rep that we were being extracted in the morning. Apparently the company was moving its missions to a different AO. We extracted at 0630 hours, but because we were not near a good LZ the helicopter had to hover and we all climbed on board with the help of that belly man. After debriefing and cleaning our gear, I actually slept for a few hours after not getting any sleep for the last 48 hours. Primed with a few hours of sleep, we all headed for the PX and then to the EM Club where we all got blasted. The main reason we would go to the EM Club is because we are all 18-19 or 20 years old so we're not allowed to buy hard liquor at the PX and it is marked out on our ration card. Xin Loi GI! Of course you can go to the EM Club and buy hard liquor over the bar, thus we drank a lot of hard liquor and got really drunk. We made it back at nearly dark and I finally went to bed for some needed rest.

Chapter 24

February 29, 1968, a Routine Lurp Mission

After 17 days of continuous guard duty, filling sand bags, shit burning detail, training and other bullshit that our Platoon Sgt came up with, we finally drew a mission. We had moved into a new AO and it was an extremely dead area for activity, thus most of the teams were doing a full mission of 4 nights and 5 days in the field.

Eric Johnson was transferred off our team to give another team more experienced Lurps. We now have Tony Thieu, a Chu Hoi, as our sixth man on the team. We all missed Eric, because he was an expert radioman and a damn good medic. Tony, of course was excellent in the jungle, but I would rather we kept Eric because he was a known entity and when the lead was flying hot and heavy, Eric was always there where you needed him.

We inserted at 0800 hours and moved about a 150 meters from the LZ and set up on a crossroads of trails. The 11th Armored Cav had driven APCS up and down the trails so the chance of the enemy using them was nil.

We were advised on our evening sit rep that we had to move out early in the morning because the 199th Light Infantry Brigade was going to be sweeping through our AO. That's just what we needed – a bunch of trigger-happy straight leg GIs (non paratroopers) moving through our area in force, probably company or larger formations.

We moved out of that AO on foot and crossed a plain of palm trees which was partially burned out. We went off the plain and down into some more palm trees where we set up our RON. It was unusually dark in the RON that night, because the palm leaves literally blocked any starlight from shining through. You could move your hand in front of your face and never see any movement. We hunkered down not wanting to get into firefight at night without being able to see a thing. Kind of like shooting by feel!

It was very quiet except for some medium size animal, the size of a small dog, that ran through our perimeter. We didn't know what it was, but it was spooked and made too much noise to be the enemy. It might have been a pig, but we never found out. It was good for a short adrenalin rush, but then everything went back to being boring as shit!

We moved out again in the morning for approximately 150 meters and found four bundles of reeds, approximately 6 feet tall and 12 inches in diameter. There were a lot of fresh signs of human activity, so our alertness was up on the scale and we were hoping for some contact. After another 50 meters we ran into a medium size river that was deep and moving fast. Aloft said he spotted a river crossing. We moved out approximately 300 meters but did not find the crossing, so we went into a RON back from the river, but still close enough to monitor any activity on it. *Per Recondo SOP, you never sat up an ambush directly adjacent to a fast moving river, because the noise of the flowing water could prevent you from detecting the enemy moving up on your position.* Also, common sense told you that one of your directions you might have to move out through if you were attacked was now a killing zone for the enemy. You always wanted to leave yourself room to maneuver if shit hit the fan in the middle of the night and you had to blow your claymores and commit to an E&E (Escape and Evasion) plan.

Tony, our Chiu Hoi had been walking point now for two days. All 4 foot 8 inches of him, but he had large balls! He was damn good on point, but I stayed close to him all the time, and just gave him directions by pointing where I wanted him to go. He was so smooth, quick and silent moving through the bush that I had to slow him down. He also saw a lot of sign that I might have missed in the bush and explained what it meant by basic sign language and some broken

English. He did know "Beaucoup VC" in English and when he says that I'm damn sure he knows what he is talking about.

Later on through an interpreter we learned how he became a VC. About 5 years prior to this, Tony was a young boy of about 15 years old and his family was rice farmers. The VC came into the village and told him, being the oldest of three sons that he was joining the VC. He said that he did not want to join them so they lined up his family and said they would start shooting each of his family members, starting with his youngest brother, if he did not volunteer to join them. Tony grasped the situation and became a VC from that day, until he was captured by the Americans, repatriated and then became a scout for us.

Tony was hell on wheels in a firefight, because he knew if he was ever recaptured by the VC or NVA they would slowly torture him to death. I had to take away his grenades, though, because he would try to throw one in a firefight, and it usually did not go far or would hit a tree and bounce back into our perimeter. We ended up dodging shrapnel from his grenades on more then one occasion. I also had to teach him to slow down and shoot his M-16 in a deliberate, aimed short burst. At first he just held the trigger down and about three seconds later he was reloading after probably putting just a few rounds down range and then the rest flying up into the air as an M-16 had a tendency to do if you fired a 20 round magazine on full automatic. He was, however, damn good at deploying his Claymore and camouflaging its location. I'm quite certain that was from prior training and experience as a VC!

We had a lot of monkeys in the trees around our RON site and once they got use to us being there they settled down. They were the best damn burglar alarm in the forest, but they're a two-edged sword. The bad side of the sword is that when you move into their area they raise all kinds of hell with a lot of screaming and jumping around in the branches way above where you are walking. Of course this alerted the enemy along with all of the other local animals that something was moving through their area, the only question is what.

Once the monkeys realize you're not there to harm them they usually settle in for the day or night. They're quite entertaining to watch if you're in a secure location and not on guard duty.

In the morning our C&C ship flew over and they got a good fix on our location. We were 300 meters out of our AO so we picked up and moved back paralleling the river but in good cover. We found the river crossing and it looked like it was made for an ox cart to approach the river. The brush was cut out right to the riverbank and it looked like there was also a boat ramp. Probably supplies came down the river and were placed in the ox cart, kind of a multiple-vehicle supply chain operation. We backed off and set up an ambush on the ox cart trail/boat ramp, hoping to score a hit on an ox, a boat and a bunch of enemy troops! Not a damn thing happened that night, just like so many other times when we had the perfect ambush set up and the only thing that happens is we got bit by mosquitoes and leeches and then cooked during the day time!

Today, March 4, 1968, is my 20th birthday and I am celebrating by lying in an ambush site waiting for the enemy to walk to the river launch point and for us to light them up. Nothing happen on our sunrise 100 percent stand-to and at 0900 hours Aloft flew by and told us to move out to a LZ for extraction. As we were leaving we threw a couple of trip flares into the very dry bushes along the river crossing area. It started a nice fire and there wouldn't be a problem again for Aloft to located that river crossing/resupply location. It also let the enemy know that we were aware of its location, so they would now have to change to Plan B if they wanted to off load supplies in the area. We moved about 500 meters and were extracted without incident.

Chapter 25

Deadly Shit Happens in a War Zone

The only thing better then executing a good ambush on the enemy was to get extracted back to our company area for hot food, cold beer and some actual sleep without one eye open! It was my birthday so I was also thinking of celebrating with my fellow Lurps. Platoon Sgt Sahms jumped on mine and Gross asses as soon as we walked off the helipad. He told us we had until 1100 hours to move out the extra wall lockers we had procured, WTF over? After we debriefed, we cleaned all of our gear and ourselves before we decided to work on moving the wall lockers. We had a lot of extra shit in those wall lockers so we first had to sort through that and then find a place to stash them until the Plt Sgt had other things on his mind. Then we would bring them back for our personal use! Of course we screwed off and didn't get the wall lockers moved by the time limit imposed on us! The platoon sergeant was on us first thing the next morning and told us that we had work detail all day. We protested and went to Lt. Cresi our Plt. Lt and pleaded our case. Not sure what the hell we were thinking, but it seemed like a fairly good idea at the time! It was the only time I ever tried to get around an order from a senior NCO and I never did it again! The Lt. got us off the detail and we thought we had beat the Plt. Sgt. at his own game; however, when the Lt. left the area, Dickie and I were assigned to dig a pit in the sand bag area. It was to be large enough to bury a ¾ ton truck, so we spent most of the afternoon digging that pit which we never completely finished. The moral of this story is: Don't fuck with the Senior NCOs or you will get bent over with extreme prejudices when the officers aren't around! Xin Loi GI!

Toward evening 1st Platoon got a volley ball game going in our home made volley ball court. We played with basically jungle rules, which meant there weren't any rules other than the ball had to be hit over the net by one person and on one shot. Of course there was an abundance of cold beer being consumed so the game could get pretty funny, crazy and sometimes just stupid!

The game finally ended because everyone was either tired, drunk or a combination of the two. As we were walking back toward 1st Platoon Barracks we heard two quick shots from an M-16 and it came from the first barracks in the line of barracks and was occupied by some of the Commo Platoon personnel. A lot of us ran to the barracks and found Private Alford lying on a bunk with two bullet holes in his chest and another Lurp standing next to the bunk with a M-16 in his hands and a very scared and confused look on his face. Four of us grabbed Alford and as we picked him up he did one last breath and stopped breathing. We carried him to one of our helicopters where the crew, who had been told of the problem, was in the process of spinning up the engine. We placed him on the floor of the helicopter and several of our medics were working on him trying to get him breathing on the flight to the 43rd Evac hospital. The last thing we saw was the ship lifting off and Spec 4 Johnson along with two other Lurps trying to keep Private Alford alive.

The ship and the Lurps returned an hour or so later to tell us that Private Alford was pronounced dead on arrival at the Evac hospital. Apparently one of the two M-16 rounds struck him in the heart and short of being on an operating table there wasn't anyway for the doctors to save him. Later on the medics became exceptionally experienced and trained. They saved a lot of lives. The dust off helicopter crews (the emergency rescue helicopters) were highly respected and renown for their skills in keeping wounded GIs alive while they flew them to the closest Medical Evac hospital in their AO. They were also known for their bravery in flying into very dangerous LZs during fire fights to pickup wounded GIs in an attempt to get them to an Army Surgeon within that Golden Hour. The pilots and their crews were at the top of the highly respected list by the war fighters. Those crews risked their lives on a daily basis just to try to save some wounded GIs and a lot of them paid for that dedication with their own lives!

That experience and training later became known as paramedic training. It was eventually adopted by most of the first responders in the USA and in the civilized world, because it saved lives!

Later we learned that his good friend and fellow commo platoon member had accidentally fired two rounds from his M-16 while unloading it. They had just came in from their assignment as a radio relay team from a fire support base and were in the process of breaking down their equipment when the accident occurred. The first round hit the floor and ricocheted up into Alford's chest and as the Lurp who had fired his weapon, fell back in complete shock he fired another round but by this time the barrel had been accidentally raised and the second round hit the Lurp directly in the chest.

The Lurp who did the shooting disappeared from the company and it was reported that he was taken to Long Bien Jail (LBJ) where he was held while an investigation was conducted. We never learned what his fate was, but some of the commo personnel told us that the two commo buddies had been smoking pot at the fire support base, prior to them being flown back to our company area. This would be the first of two incidents in which drugs played a role in the death of a Lurp. Drugs, like alcohol, don't mix with guns, especially in a war zone!

Chapter 26

Another Day in the Artillery War Zone

Artillery was a two-bladed sword for a Lurp team on a mission. The positive side was that we used them semi-autonomously as a very large hammer to pound enemy troops and their fortifications. My favorite artillery piece was the self-propelled 8″ Howitzer. They were very accurate and packed a big punch! You could call them in on a target and adjust them down to 25 meters + or -. We had a team that observed an underwater concrete bridge the enemy had built over a large stream (approximately 10 meters wide). During the dry season they had apparently formed up the bridge and poured it above the water line. When the rainy season came the water level increased because of the additional water and the bridge just disappeared under the flowing water. The bridge was about a meter wide and several inches below the running water. Once the team figured out what they had found, they backed off 200 meters plus and still had eyes on the bridge. They called for an arty mission. Luck was with them and they got a battery of 8″ Howitzers. The TL got the rounds adjusted to within meters of the underwater bridge but the guns couldn't get that last few meters adjustment cranked up because the rounds were either long or short. The TL explained to the Arty Liaison what was happening and he talked with the gun crew sergeant. The Sgt told them to hold for 5 minutes and then he called them back and said to give them the coordinates again. This time the rounds impacted directly on the bridge and blew it to hell. When the liaison officer asked the crew Sgt what he had done, he explained that they just backed the gun up a few meters and that gave them that extra adjustment for the gun. Obviously that gun had a very experienced crew who had probably fired thousands of rounds from that particular artillery piece and knew its idiosyncrasies.

The other side of the arty sword causes things to happen like what happened to our team, Team 1-5. We were on a typical recon mission in War Zone D and it was during the dry season. It was very hot and dry. Worst of all we were patrolling in an area with single and double canopy with some open areas that only had elephant grass and or small trees and bushes. It had been a long hot day with absolutely no signs of enemy activity, which made for a very boring and arduous hump through the jungle. The TL Lavender finally decided to halt for the day because we were all hot, tired and irritated with the jungle, which could be dangerous for a six man Lurp team deep in enemy territory. The TL found a large stand of bamboo that was in the tree line, but from inside the stand you could see a fairly large open area to the front. It also had some large termite mounds in the stand and toward the front. The bamboo trees were pretty old and some of the trunks of the bamboo trees (actually a grass) were larger then 4″ in diameter. It was a near perfect site for a RON. It provided good over head cover, concealment and actual protection from a frontal attack because of the termite mounds. There were four termite mounds and they were probably 3 feet high and 18-28 inches at their base, shaped like an inverted ice cream cone. They were constructed side by side, so essentially we had a 3′ x 5′ x 1.5′ wall that was as hard as concrete to our front.

There were two disadvantages to hiding in a grove of bamboo trees: first and foremost they were the favorite home for this certain kind of leech that was about an inch long and moved like an inch worm. Once you settled into your individual defensive positions and cleaned out most of the leaves, you could sit, watch and hear them slowly crawling toward your warm-blooded body. They made a very slight rustling noise as they crawled through the dry and dead bamboo leaves. You can become very attuned to your jungle surroundings once you learn to get into the "jungle mode"! Essentially the first hour or so if things are quiet as far an enemy activity is concerned, every team member committed genocide of the leeches, primarily by squirting them with the little bottle, about the size of an eye drop container, of "bug juice" we carried for that purpose. That is if we weren't sitting on an ambush position, because the juice did have an odor and if you used too much it could definitely be smelled a short distance from your position. If you were in an ambush position you would normally just squirt a little on your jungle fatigue pant legs where they were bloused in and duct taped to your jungle-boots. You also squirted some around the cuffs of both sleeves of your jungle fatigue shirt. Some guys also squirted it on the crotch area of their fatigues as added protection against a sneak attack during the night. At night and unless it got really cold the leeches were still active and they would find ways to get inside your fatigues especially in your arm pits and attach for a meal of warm blood. In the morning you could find them full of blood and almost an inch long and maybe an eighth to a quarter inch in diameter. Of course the only way to get them off was to spray some of that high octane bug juice on them which burned like hell and was such a pleasant way to wake up in the morning in your exclusive jungle hotel room!

The second problem with using a grove of bamboo trees for your RON location was that the active growth area, usually the outer perimeter of the grove had small green branches that had hooks on them. It was essentially like the claws on a cat that were extended when in the attack mode, only hundreds and hundreds of those claws. You had to carefully push them aside or they would just tear your skin and your jungle fatigues to pieces. This was another required/ acquired skill of a Lurp in the jungle environment.

I have seen team members that had to fight their way through bamboo to an LZ for extraction with the enemy in pursuit. Their jungle fatigues were literally in strips of cloth clinging to their bodies and a lot of nasty scratches and cuts from the same claws that tore the fatigues. Of course there was a flip side and that was that the enemy couldn't crawl into your position without being cut up and making a lot of noise in the process. So bamboo was a non-prejudicial jungle plant that would attack anyone or anything that rubbed against it!

After we actually got set up for the night and just before darkness came, we heard an artillery round coming in and it sounded like it was going to be fairly close. It landed and exploded probably two hundred meters to our front. It exploded in the jungle on the opposite side of the opening. Depending on the size of the gun, it could sound like a slight whistle to just a big explosion when a 175 MM round crashed and exploded close to your position. This sounded like a 155 mm or and 8″ mobile howitzer because it made a whistling sound. This was surprising because we hadn't called for an artillery strike and there weren't supposed to be any H & I rounds fired in our AO. The next round came in about one minute later and it was approximately 150 meters from our position just on the edge of the opening. We knew we were in trouble because it appeared that these were H & I rounds and they were "walking the rounds" toward us at approximately 50 meters a shot. TL Lavender got on the radio and was advising our command about the artillery rounds when another one hit and exploded about half way across the opening and it was too damn close. As it came in and exploded we heard this whirring sound and then a big clunk, which caused one of the larger bamboo trunks to the right side of our perimeter to partially fall forward because it had been cut off approximately four feet above the ground. That was followed by a thumping sound and large piece of smoking steel landed next to my feet. It was probably 10 inches long and curved along its vertical axis to make it approximately 6 inches in diameter. It was irregular shaped and had all of these irregular tiny steel fingers sticking out from its edges. It had cut the 4″ bamboo trunk in two like a hot knife through butter and would have removed a human head, limb or body part if it had struck one of us! We had all been kissing the earth when that round landed and exploded. We also thanked our lucky jungle stars for the termite mounds to our front, because it sounded like some other smaller pieces of shrapnel had actually struck the opposite sides of the termite mounds. By now it was painfully obvious that the next round was going to be right on our position! What are the odds that a H & I round randomly fired into a random patch of jungle was going to take out a Lurp team, who had randomly picked this location for a RON? Probably 10 zillion to one, great odds unless you're the team and its happening to you! By this time, TL Lavender pulled out all the caution and just yelled into the mike, "Stop the fucking artillery!" We all hunkered down expecting the next round to be right on top of us, but nothing happened. It seems that our artillery liaison had finally made contact with the artillery command for that area and they had stopped firing their big guns in our AO. A short time later, TL Lavender got a return message on the PRC-25 that said the artillery commander had apologized for firing the H & I rounds in the wrong AO. They were confused and thought they were supposed to be firing H & I rounds in the North AO where the Lurp teams were conducting recon missions, when in fact they were suppose to be only firing H & I rounds in the south AO! No shit, Sherlock! We definitely had Murphy trailing along on that mission!

After we had settled back down and our hearts had returned to near normal beats, I reached over and picked up the large shard of metal shrapnel. I was thinking about taking it as a souvenir but when I picked it up, and while it was still warm to the touch, I estimated that it weighed more then 10 pounds and I changed my mind about carrying an extra 10 pounds of weight around for the remainder of the mission. Based on its size and weight I think it was probably an 8″ self propelled howitzer that had been mistakenly firing in our AO. Arty was truly a two edged sword for a Lurp team on a recon mission!

Chapter 27

Supervision 101 in the Combat Zone

Our original First Sgt. was at his DEROS Date and was returning to the US. His replacement was picked from one of the platoon sgts and we thought things would be good. We were wrong, the new first sergeant tried to run the company like an airborne company in a US garrison. We had reveille every morning and on going inspections, which we didn't mind that much, they were just a pain in the ass. The one thing that we did mind was that he made a new rule that said your bunk had to be properly made (quarter bounces on the top blanket) and you couldn't lie on it until after 10:00 hours. That meant that if you came in late at night from a firefight and extraction or early in the morning you couldn't try and catch some sleep from all you had missed while on a mission. What you found was that most of the Lurps who needed that sleep would go down by the ammo bunkers and lay on their poncho liners to catch a few Zzzzzzs to try to get back in sync with their body clocks. It pissed all of us off, because there wasn't any good reason for the first sgt. to be doing it other than fucking with the troops to show them who was in-charge. He seriously miscalculated the deadly abilities of the Lurps he was supervising.

One late night and less then one month after the new first sgt took control of the company, there was an incident that changed everything for Company F.

We were all woke up around 02:30 hours and each platoon had to stand in formation and an individual head count of each man in each platoon was conducted. After about an hour we were allowed to go back to bed and no one knew for sure what had occurred. Most of us thought that some Lurps had missed the return time from a pass in Bien Hoa and were now AWOL. The next morning we got the straight scoop from a Lurp of 1st platoon that was pulling guard duty for the TOC.

The Tactical Operation Center was to the north end of the compound, buried under ground to prevent it being hit by mortar, artillery or rocket rounds. It probably had four feet of sand bags stacked on top of a roof built from 6 x 6 beams and plywood. The roof projected high enough above the ground that you couldn't see the opposite side of the perimeter wire. It was isolated from the barracks and had a tent next to it where all of the debriefings occurred when we returned from a mission. It had concertina wiring staked down around its perimeter and the only way in was through the gate directly in front of the steps leading down into the bunker. This is where the guard was positioned. Also at the gate and just outside the wire was a generator that was used to charge all of the batteries for the radios in the TOC. It was part of the TOC guard's duty to start the generator around 01:00 hours on the AM shift and let it run for about 30 minutes to recharge the multiple batteries used for the numerous radios operating in the TOC Bunker.

On this particular guard duty assignment that night was one of our men from 1st Platoon. As was normal for that guard duty position, you could walk around the outside perimeter of the TOC Bunker, to check that the enemy hadn't made it over the berm and was positioning an explosive charge to blow a hole in the roof of the TOC or was a rally point for the enemy prior to making an assault on the bunker through the gate and of course over the TOC Guard.

The Lurp had just done his walk around the perimeter and wasn't in any hurry to complete it since he would do the same thing in about another hour and so on until relieved at 07:00 hours by the day shift guard. He had also gone down into the bunker to get some coffee which was always there in the TOC for the radio operators and of course the guard who was protecting their asses!

150

When he came back out of the TOC it took him a minute or two to adjust his eyes to total darkness compared to light inside the bunker. The generator was the small standard issue Army generator which meant you had to wrap the pull chord around the engine pulley to get it started. There weren't any electric start generators that were that small in probably the entire Army's TOE.

He said he had just wrapped the chord around the engine cranking pulley and was about to give it a long hard pull to spin the engine and get it started, when his night vision came back and he noticed something peculiar on the engine. These were single cylinder gas engines and the spark plug protruded out the top of the engine. He noticed that the spark plug had an extra wire wrapped around the top where the current is sent through the spark plug from the coil and into the cylinder to ignite the gasoline, which causes the engine to start.

It wasn't his first time being on guard duty for the TOC and he had never seen that wire there before. He immediately thought that some enemy sapper had crawled in and placed an explosive charge with an electric blasting cap to blow a large hole in the TOC. He was already locked and loaded so he put the weapon to his shoulder and did a 360 degree sweep of the area looking for any movement or odd shapes like the enemy lying prone in the darkness. He didn't see any thing and so he found the wire and followed it while gently holding it in one hand and his M-16 on full auto in his other hand. He expected the wire to make a left or right turn and slowly track around the perimeter wire of the bunker to the back side of the bunker where it would be attached to a large explosive mine/bomb. The problem was that the wire tracked due south toward the barracks. He thought the enemy had set up a large claymore mine pointing at multiple barracks with Lurps sleeping inside them. Once he saw where the wiring was tracking, he informed the TOC personnel about what he had found and they came out to standby at the gate while he followed the wire toward the barracks. It continued due south but was headed toward the Senior NCO hooches which were four small tin hooches about the size of the chicken coup we had on our ranch in South Dakota. It had two bunks inside for two of the Senior Company NCOs. The wire ran directly to and about 10 feet away from the front of the first hooch which is where the 1st sgt and the 1st platoon sgt. slept. At the end of the wire was one of our claymore mines, with the blasting cap in the well and positioned to blow directly through the front wall of that NCOs' hooch. The two bunks with the two senior sleeping NCOs in them were positioned one on each side of the front door and on the floor. If the mine had blown, it would have ripped out the front of the their barracks and probably outright killed both of the sleeping sgts or mangled them so badly that they would not have seen the sun rise in the morning.

By now the runner for the TOC/Company F had contacted the CO, Major Maus and he was at the TOC. The Lurp told Major Maus what he had discovered. The wire was immediately removed from the spark plug of the generator and then Major Maus walked with him to the location of the claymore mine. The Lurp had not touched it, thinking that it could be booby-trapped and explode if he disturbed it. Major Maus woke up the 1st sgt and the 1st platoon sgt and had them evacuate the hooch. Everything was locked down at that point and that is when the company formation was called. Of course everyone was accounted for so it was a mystery as to who had placed the claymore to kill or maim the 1st sgt and the 1st platoon sgt. The one thing that was certain was that even though the claymore never blew it had the same affect as if it had, save for a couple of NCOs' lives. By early the next morning the 1st sgt was unceremoniously transferred out of Company F to never be seen or heard from again. I don't think CID was ever called in and so the whole incident disappeared from the records of Company F; however, I'm quite certain that every senior NCO of Company F learned a valuable lesson about not screwing with "spun up for combat Lurps" while in the combat zone.

To this day, I don't know who set the claymore, and quite frankly I don't want to know. I'm not in favor of fragging or other forms of murdering officers and NCOs. I'm quite certain, however, that if the 1st Sgt had continued his "leadership by harassment" of the troops, eventually someone would have been killed or wounded because of lack of sleep or unnecessary stress caused by his actions. The simple fact is, "Thou should never unnecessarily screw with combat troops in a combat zone!" Xin Loi GI!

Chapter 28

R&R in Australia

Every military person, regardless of rank or MOS was supposed to get one week of leave at a designated R&R Center somewhere in the Pacific. Most married men chose Hawaii because their wives/girlfriends could fly there and meet them. Young, unmarried men – pumped full of adrenalin and testosterone from being in a war zone – chose other less sedate locations such as Bangkok, Thailand, Singapore, and a few other locations where the booze and drugs flowed freely and the women enjoyed being with young horny GIs!

Sidney, Australia, was kind of in the middle of the "entertainment rating" being not too crazy but a great place to party and meet women. It did have one thing that boosted its rating in my mind, "Round Eyed Women!" All of the other R&R locations had mainly Asian women, most of whom were young and beautiful, but I was looking for a change of pace. The other reason I chose Australia was because, as a farm boy from South Dakota, I knew I would probably never have another chance to visit such a far away place.

Now, a lot of people will read this book (hopefully) and think that it was a very prejudicial and perverted system that basically flew young soldiers, sailors, airmen, marines and coasties to some location in the western Pacific to party and have sex with the local women. I guess if you refined it to its purest level that would be a correct analogy; however, it was different because all of these young men and a few young women (primarily Army, Air Force & Navy nurses) were coming from a war zone. Most had seen and/or been through some horrendous events in their young lives and they all had the potential to be killed as soon as they re-entered the war zone. As in any war, they needed a break from the death and destruction of the war.

Most war historians would probably disagree with me, but I believe that "sex" is an essential part of any war and it is as much a part of the whole system as the "Beans and Bullets"! Having lived through almost two years of being in the war zone gave me a unique perspective of what really happens in a war zone, regardless of the geographic location of the war. In spite of what your moral or religious beliefs are, being in a war zone had a certain feel of danger about it and that was further enhanced by adrenalin that was a constant factor in combat. The saying, "Eat, sleep, drink and be merry for tomorrow we may die" is dead on.

Chapter 29

Murphy and the Grim Reaper Pay Team 1-5 a Visit; April 12, 1968

I very much enjoyed my R&R in Sydney (April 3-10, 1968) and yes, I met young women, drank outstanding Australian beer and did a few tourist things. Of course all good things must come to an end and they did for me. I was back in the company area by the night of April 10 at 1800 hours. I was tired and somewhat in a funk from just having left a modern city/country and now I was back in this shit hole they called South Vietnam.

The following morning, April 11, my team had an assigned mission scheduled for that afternoon. Originally it was only supposed to be three hours in duration. It was just supposed to be a sneak and peak mission to confirm some other intel. That decision was quickly changed to a 3 day mission, which really made more sense. We were inserted at 1415 hours and I didn't like the look of the LZ. It took us a long time to get into the LZ and we had to cross over a well used trail that paralleled the LZ. This was of course a basic violation of *Recondo School SOP,* but again you played the hand you're dealt. We only moved about 50 meters from the LZ and set up for the night. As soon as we were in our ambush site on another trail we had discovered, we heard voices and saw some chickens roaming around on the trail. The combo of those two things told us that we were near a VC base camp, since this was a free fire zone and there weren't supposed to be any friendly villages in the area. To compound problems, we could not establish communications with the radio relay team at a fire support base and so it was decided to extract us. The extraction was executed without any contact with the enemy and we were back in the company area by 1700 hours. I was in my bunk by 1800 hours having just returned from R&R 24 hours before with very little sleep for the 7 days I had been in Sydney and completing a short combat mission in that same time frame.

In the morning after reveille, some of us, including SSG Lavender, decided to go to the Air Force PX, which was on Bien Hoa Airbase. The reason we liked going to the AF PX was because it was a serious upgrade from the Army PX. The difference being like going from a small mom and pop market in South Dakota to shopping at a mall in Los Angeles. Most of us returned back to the company area after about three hours, but SSG Lavender stayed on the airbase at one of their NCO Clubs, which were air conditioned.

I decided to completely strip my rifle down and clean it, even though it was fairly clean having only been in the field for about four hours total time on the ground. I had made myself a desk and stool from parts of a wooden pallet I had scrounged from the dump/ burn pile. I was sitting at the desk with my rifle completely stripped down and lying on an old towel so I didn't loose any parts as I cleaned the M-16. Spec 4 Rennolet, aka Dickie Gross and Sgt Vargo, aka Sgt. Rock, our assistant team leader had just walked in the back door of our hooch. They had been drinking or smoking pot and were obviously under the influence of something, but no one gave a shit because we were at the bottom of the rotation list to be re-inserted for a mission, so everyone was relaxing in their own manner. Gross and Rock were standing near the front of Gross's bunk and talking about something that was humorous. I heard this loud crack and then there was fire shooting out in all directions from Gross's bunk. If you're not familiar with having a high speed rifle round pass very close to you it makes a very sharp crack noise and this is what I keyed in on. I jumped up from my table and turned to run towards the front of our barracks, which was further away, but in the opposite direction of the fire. This was done automatically and was one of those fight or flight survival skills that all humans possess and was honed to perfection from being in firefights. I made it probably two or three steps when I felt this extreme pain in my lower right back area. By now I knew the fire was from a willie peter (white phosphorus) grenade that had exploded under Gross's bunk! I guess I knew this from the smell and the type of flames that were flying out from under Gross's bunk. As I continued to run toward the front of the barracks, I reached back with my right arm and tried to remove the piece of burning phosphorous that was stuck to and burning a hole in my skin after it had burned through my OD Green T-shirt. When a willie peter grenade explodes it causes small chunks about the size of a quarter of burning phosphorus to be expelled out from the grenade in full circle out to approximately 10 meters. Explode is probably the wrong term, because the small detonator inside the grenade simply fires and the pressure from that small explosion ruptures the thin corrugated metal skin of the grenade allowing the burning white phosphorous to be ejected out in a circle.

I was successful in removing that chunk of burning phosphorus from my skin by flicking it several times with the thumb on my right hand. This occurred as I exited the front door and the burning piece of phosphorus fell harmlessly to the ground; however, that little double flick caused a second degree burn on my right thumb and it hurt like hell. About at that time a Lurp came running by shouting "Someone is burned really bad at the rear of the barracks!" I turned and ran to the rear of our barracks and I saw Dickie Gross lying on the ground. The only reason I recognized him was because of his build and what he was wearing. The willie peter had hit him square in the face and his face looked like someone had taken a torch and melted it! Where his eyes, nose and mouth should have been were nothing but holes partially covered by burned and melted skin. He had been wearing a white t-shirt and all of the skin from the top of his arms below the t-shirt was rolled up in a neat roll in the palm of each hand. He also had chunks of burning phosphorous in his chest and some of the Lurps were trying to remove them with their knives.

I was in shock and just stared for a few seconds and then I noticed that Dickie was trying to talk. I kneeled next to him and ask him how he felt. He replied, "Well at least I'm going home!" I stated "Yes, Dickie, you're going home!" it was the last time I ever spoke to him.

Sgt Rock was also there and had some willie peter burns on his upper torso, but Gross had taken the blunt of the blast since he had been closest to where the grenade was.

By this time the company officers had been alerted and one of the chopper crews was spinning up a Huey to transport us to the Field Hospital at Long Bien. We carried Dickie to the helicopter. I and Rock also got on along with one of our company medics. We immediately lifted off and flew at high speed to the field hospital about five plus minutes flight time, where the doctors and staff were waiting for us on the landing pad. On the flight over Dickie was trying to talk and as he breathed out he was exhaling white smoke from the grenade. Dickie was placed on a wheeled gurney and we all went running into the emergency room. The doctor in charge took one look at Dickie and yelled for some carbon tetrachloride, which they didn't have in the emergency room and someone had to run to the medical supply room to get it. In the meantime the white phosphorus chunks in Dickie's chest were still burning deeper into his body. White phosphorus is a very insidious chemical and it will burn underwater because it burns so hot (5,000 degrees fahrenheit) that it coverts the water into oxygen and hydrogen. I did not know at the time, but apparently carbon tetrachloride is one of the chemicals that will extinguish the burning phosphorus through a chemical reaction instead of a thermal reaction.

As they started to work on Dickie, we were all removed from that room and placed in another room where we were treated by additional doctors and nurses. The only thing they could do for me and Rock was to clean the wounds, put antibiotics on them and then bandage them. I don't remember if they even gave us anything for pain but I was so deep in shock that I don't remember any pain after leaving the field hospital.

We rode back on the Huey and walked back into the company area. The smell of the willie peter and burnt flesh was very prominent in and around our barracks and to this day I can still smell that smell and it makes me feel ill.

Everything had been left as it was because willie peter smoke is poisonous and can be deadly if inhaled. Also, there was going to be an investigation by our officers into how the accident had occurred and so nothing was disturbed. All of us from that barracks were moved to another barracks for one night to let the barracks air out.

I was still in shock, because just a little over 24 hours before I had been in Sydney, Australia, having a great time with not a care in the world and now I had a willie peter burn on my back and on my right thumb. One of my best friends and the only other Lurp from South Dakota was critically burned, was blind at the very least and would be horribly scarred for the rest of his life. Sgt Rock was also injured, so it was a complete shit day for our company in general and team 1-5 in particular. SSG Lavender never returned until later in the afternoon and that is when he learned about the death of Spec 4 Rennolet!

The following day I caught a ride over to the evac hospital and tried to visit Dickie. I actually saw him, but he was unconscious. His head and arms were completely swathed in bandages along with some on his chest. I did notice that his head had significantly swollen apparently from the burns. The nurses told me that he was very critical because of the massive third degree burns on his upper body.

The following day I went back to see if Dickie was conscious, but he was not in his assigned bunk, so I found a male orderly and asked him where they had moved Gross. He looked at me and matter of factly stated, "Oh, he died last night." I wanted to just grab the orderly and rip his face off because I was very angry at what had happened and shocked by the orderly's blasé attitude. I guess in retrospect, he had seen so many deaths in that hospital that they all just seemed to be part of a routine day for him.

I caught a ride in an Army deuce and half, back to the company area and walked over to where most of the platoon was filling sand bags. Someone asked how Gross was and the only thing I got out was, "He died last night!" I had been holding it together, but I lost it at that point and I walked away crying. I found a private location up near the berm and I cried my eyes out for some time. I finally got my emotions back in control. Needless to say, it was a very dark day in the company area.

An investigation was conducted and it revealed that Dickie Gross had not followed company policy and removed his hand grenades including the M-26s and the willie peter he liked to carry. He should have done that as soon as we were debriefed after returning from the mission last night. We were in fact supposed to remove all explosives from our gear and place it in the ammo bunker, but the fact was that most of us only removed our grenades and put them in the ammo bunker, to prevent accidents like the one that had just occurred. The main reason for not returning the claymore mines, det cord and C-4 to the ammo bunker was that they were very safe and almost inert if they didn't have a blasting cap attached to them. Also, each claymore was made up by the person who was carrying it and at the time we didn't have individual platoon ammo bunkers. Each Lurp made up their claymore to their own specifications, so the 75 foot cord on the mine was wrapped in 10 ft lengths and secured with a rubber band, as taught by Recondo School. The purpose of wrapping the wire, which looked like a two-wire brown lamp cord, was to only expose the amount of wire you needed to set up your claymore and to prevent the excess wire from being seen or found by the enemy. We also placed the excess wire to the front of the claymore but still in the claymore bag, which added to the shrapnel that was blasted out at the enemy.

Because the investigation was revealed to be an accident that could probably have been prevented if Spec 4 Rennolet had followed policy, someone had to be held responsible for the death. It was decided that SSG Lavender would be held responsible for the death, because he was the team leader of team 1-5 and he was also the highest-ranking NCO responsible for the team members. It was *Recondo School SOP* that the assistant team leader was responsible for making sure the team members removed all of the explosives, especially the grenades, upon returning to the company area after completing a combat mission. Sgt Rock had failed to follow that procedure and was also at fault for the death of Dickie Gross and the injuries of myself and his own injuries.

It was never established why Dickie did not remove his grenades from his gear, but as I had previously noted Dickie ran pretty loose and ignored a lot of the orders he was given. I suspect that that was partly because of his age, having just turned 18 years old when he got shipped to Vietnam. Either way, it was all put on SSG Lavender's head, which I thought was wrong, but I was just a team member and my opinion apparently didn't count.

Shortly after the determination was made to hold SSG Lavender responsible for the accident, he was med-evaced to Japan because he had a serious case of Hepatitis B. I suspect he was probably going to be disciplined using the USMCJ (US Military Code of Justice) but apparently that was dropped and it was decided to not award him the Silver Star that he had been written up for involving the ambush of the VC Company on January 3, 1968. Ironically, Spec 4 Rennolet eventually received a Bronze Star with a V for Valor for that ambush and 46 years later, Sgt Eric Johnson, our medic at the time also received a Bronze Star with a V for his actions that day. Eventually it was decided that it was an error not to award SSG Lavender his Silver Star for Valor and which he so rightly deserved. I believe he actually received the Silver Star after he had been medically retired from the Army.

Of course no one was left unscarred for the accidental death of Spec 4 Rennolet, aka Dickie Gross. Myself, Rock and Lavender all will carry that with us for the rest of our lives. It also hammered home to me, while still in country and now a Team Leader, how important it was to follow the SOPs and to always be checking on my men to make sure they were doing what they were supposed to be doing 24/7!

I was out of the field for about two weeks, because the burn injury on my lower right back area was right where my pack made contact with my back. It would rub the sore and cause a lot of pain. Of course that didn't mean that I was free to just lie around and recuperate. Hell no, it was a "no slack do" kind of operation so I was pulling a lot of guard duty at the TOC, the helipad and CQ runner. Basically they used me where they needed a warm body, which was good for me because it gave me time to get back in the groove and not think about Gross and his shitty luck!

Chapter 30

Our New AO; Cu Chi; April 23, 1968

We were given a new AO by Two Field Force, because they needed intel about the area around Cu Chi, which happens to border Cambodia on the extreme west side of Vietnam. Cu Chi, which is approximately 30 miles northwest of Saigon, is the base camp for the 25th Infantry Division. It is also known as Rocket City, because of its daily dose of rockets and mortars that it receives from the enemy.

We were lifted one platoon at a time by the CH-47 Chinooks, aka Shit Hooks and it took all day to get the entire company operation into the Cu Chi base camp.

The Shit Hook is known as one of the heavy lift helicopters, since it can sling-load large amounts of ammo for the artillery guns or also carry up to 30 fully loaded troopers. It is noisy and dirty getting onto the rear ramp of the Shit Hook with the engines running and the twin rotor blades turning, but once you get inside it is fairly quiet, with the standard aluminum and cloth seats along the exterior walls to sit in and all of your combat gear and shit stacked on the floor of the helicopter.

I did not like riding in them though because they had a bad habit of falling out of the skies in Vietnam from mechanical failures. They had large, twin, four-bladed rotors turning in opposite directions and if something failed in either transmission then everything became out of sync and they usually fell the earth and burned. They had the same aerodynamics as a Grand Piano when the rotors stopped turning and I don't believe they could even auto-rotate like a Huey if it lost it's engines.

Once we were dropped of by the Shit Hook we had Deuce and Halves transport us to our temporary company area. The so-called barracks we were given were basically of metal construction and cement floors and that was about it. They had been abandoned for some time and structurally they were in bad condition. On a four star rating for accommodation they were about a -1. The big problem was that they didn't have any doors on them or the ones that did didn't have any screens on them so the mosquitoes and other flying or for that matter crawling insects, etc. had free access and had so for a long time. The accommodation didn't surprise us because we had been sent to other areas at temporary base camps and we always got the shittest barracks accommodation they had. I don't know if it was because the commanding generals of the regular Army didn't like us working in their AOs or it was all they had to offer. Either way we usually got the shitty end of the stick! We were used to this and we had adapted to the situation. Most of us carried a hammock in our personal gear, since we usually didn't get enough bunks for everyone and no one wanted to sleep on the concrete floor even if you had brought along an air mattress for the your accommodation in the rear. The added benefit to the hammock was that you could put a mosquito net over it and were somewhat free of bites while you slept. The other benefit was that it took you about two minutes to break it down and be ready to move out back to our home base!

Chapter 31

Loches; Hunter Killer Teams

I became a Team Leader as Spec 4 even though it was suppose to be a Staff Sergeant position. My selection as a TL was partly because of attrition and partly because I had proven that I could handle a team since I had worked every position on the team except for TL. My team number was 1-3.

We were on a mission and on the move from an RON to try to find another ambush/overview site to set up on. It was midday, clear and hot. We had been in double canopy and then we came upon this area of single canopy with a lot of elephant grass and small trees that were probably no higher than six feet. We could have gone around this area, but it would have been out of the way. There was plenty of cover for us on the ground but we would be exposed from the air. I had a gut feeling that we should take the long route, but it was hot and I wanted to get the team back under some cover to keep from over-heating and using a lot of our water. We headed across the single canopy and we were about half way across when I heard this loud buzzing sound. I was just thinking, what the hell is that noise, when up popped a Hughes 500 Loche, with a mini-gun mounted on the port side and a door gunner in the right rear door. They were probably 50 meters from us and about 15 feet off the ground. I could clearly see the pilot and he could clearly see all of the team in camouflaged uniforms, especially my point man who was one of the Chou Hois. We just stared at each other for what seemed like minutes, but was probably seconds, when I held up the radio hand set, which was attached to the PRC 25 I was carrying. The pilot did nothing and the Loche just sat there with that "Menacing Mini-Gun" pointed directly

166

at us. I told one of the team members to show him a ID Panel which he did, but again the pilot just looked at us, the Loche was buzzing away and the mini-gun ready to fire. If he would have given us a two second burst we would have all been KIA on the spot, because he couldn't have missed at that distance. What I didn't know was that there were also two Cobra gunships circling just out of our sight and even if the Loche didn't get us all, the Cobras would have finished the job. Later on they were called hunter/killer teams, with the Loche right down on the deck looking for the enemy and when he saw them or was fired on the door gunner dropped smoke and they immediately pulled pitch and left the area. The Cobras would be rolling in on gun and rocket runs with the smoke as their initial target area and would saturate the area with death and destruction. The 1st Air Cav were infamous for their hunter/killer teams called Pink Teams!

By now it had been well over a minute and I was getting pissed, because I felt the Loche was compromising our position. I finally, out of frustration, just gave the pilot the middle finger and said "FUCK YOU!" He gave me a short hand salute back, pulled up from our position and disappeared over the jungle canopy. I was very relieved by his actions and we quickly moved on and got out of the single canopy. After that experience, I very rarely ever took my team across single canopy terrain, knowing that we had been damn lucky, but the chances of being that lucky again were nil! To this day I don't know why the pilot didn't just light us up as soon as he saw us, since we would have looked like a VC or NVA Squad, but wearing camo. I think he might have estimated our heights and had a feeling we were GIs, but I will never know for sure.

Chapter 32

24 Hours in the Life of a LURP at Basecamp

Depending on the AO we were operating in, your team after a successful 4 nights and 5 days mission would be placed at the bottom of the list of available teams (15 to 25 teams) and you might be at your base camp for less than 24 hours or you could be there for up to 5+ days. The time in the rear was directly proportional to how hot the area was we were operating in. If it was really hot/high enemy activity, like along the Cambodian border, some teams never made it off the LZ or were in a firefight and compromised before they were able to move far off the LZ. In those cases where a team was in a serious firefight and had expended a lot of ammo and or had personnel wounded they would be extracted and returned to base camp to be placed at the bottom of the list. If they had only been compromised or exchanged a few rounds with the enemy they would be extracted from that LZ and re-inserted at their secondary LZ to Charlie Mike/ continue mission.

As a team leader I would typically get a warning order 24 to 48 hours prior to the actual insertion date and time. The warning order would give me the basic info such as: approximate date and time of insertion; AO with general coordinates of where I was expected to patrol; size of my team, 6 man recon or 12 man ambush/hatchet team; type of patrol; area recon for enemy troops or fortifications, find targets of opportunity, locate trails and monitor or set up ambushes on known trails.

Typically 2-4 team leaders would get their warning orders at the same time. This was to facilitate coordination between the team leaders and team members, especially if it was going to be a heavy team ambush mission (two six men teams combined for the 12 man team). This entailed assigning members from each team certain extra equipment, like an M-60 machinegun, M60 ammo; M-79s and ammo, claymore mines; LAWS Rockets; along with their standard weapons, ammunition, hand grenades, smoke grenades, Lurp rations, water, cammo gear, first aid kit, signal devices such as mirrors or panels and whatever else they were assigned to carry. It should be noted that the M-60 gunner only carried the gun and between 500-800 rounds; a few carried 1,000 rounds of belted 7.62 mm ammo. Everyone else including the team leader and assistant team leader shared in the carrying of M-60 ammo, M-79 ammo and claymore mines.

After the briefback the team leaders and some time the assistant team leaders would do an over-flight of the AO to pick a primary and secondary LZ for their insertion points. The aircraft lead pilot would mark those locations on his map after giving it his approval, so that he could go back and brief the other pilots of the LZs we had picked. Any significant problems they observed were also noted as to being able to get into the LZ because of obstructions like termite mounds or tree stumps or even swampy/semi-open water. The trick to picking your LZs was that you wanted them fairly close to your patrol area/specific trails but not too close. You wanted an LZ that was just big enough for one ship to land or for two ships to land if it was a heavy team. You never wanted to use the really big open areas because the VC usually had LZ Watchers to give the alarm if something like a company of infantry was landing, something like 25 helicopters at a time setting down in this large LZ and disgorging maybe a company(100-125) troops. Of course if they only saw one helicopter land and drop off 6 troops they would still give the alarm and the Lurp Team's problems started as soon as they were on the LZ.

Once the LZs were picked we returned to base and then I would inspect my team's load and gear to make sure they had what was required and not things I didn't allow on my Lurp patrols, like C-Rats, cigarettes, ponchos and various other pieces of crap some of them wanted to bring along. The primary reasons being those items created noise and or odors that could compromise the team and get someone wounded or killed. The good thing was that all of the team members knew that everything had a weight and the more weight meant the harder it was to hump that load. Also you never wanted to run out of ammo so everyone loaded up on M-16 mags, grenades and ammo for the M-60. Initially we probably took more ammo then we needed but refined our loads with experience. Most team members carried 12 to 16 magazines of 18 rounds of 223 ammo, a couple of M-26 hand grenades and normally one six pack of M-79 ammo and always at least one claymore mine! I personally carried 21 magazines, 2-4 M-26 hand grenades, 4 smoke grenades, usually one willy peter grenade, one claymore mine in addition to the PRC 25 Radio, an extra battery, an extra mouth piece, a home made triangular radio antenna that we built at Recondo School and a pen flare gun. Of course I had to also carry my food, usually 5 Lurp rations and 2 to 4 canteens of water. If it was the dry season I also carried one fat rat, which was a plastic container like a zip lock bag with a spout with one gallon of water in it. The total weight of my pack was probably around 50 plus pounds and then my load bearing gear, aka pistol belt and pouches was an addition 30+ pounds. I believe our average weight was probably around 86 pounds but that could be + or – 10 lbs.

After everything was checked and OK the individual team members were released to relax but they had to stay in the company area unless we were more than 24 hours out for an insertion. Of course that could change in a moment's notice so you basically stayed in the company area and tried to relax. You obviously didn't do a lot of drinking or dope smoking because you knew that the clock was ticking and you didn't want to be the weak link on the team and let your team members down.

It should be noted that when we were in the rear and not on the list for probable insertion with 24 hours, I didn't care if my team members drank or smoked MJ. Everyone had their own way of relaxing and winding down. I did care if we were going to be inserted later in the day or the first thing in the morning and my team members knew this. One of the first things you learned at Recondo School was that you had to be flexible like a trunk of bamboo and not like a steel beam.

Even for a LURP, life can go from a complete adrenalin rush to up to your ass in boredom in the form of work details; shit details; TOC guard; gate guard; berm guard duty; etc.

Years after being honorably discharged from the Army, I recreated in my mind a typical 24 hour time period for a Lurp in Company F. It would be similar with other LURP Companies, but the rear time would depend a lot on where the LURP Company was stationed. Company F happened to be stationed at Bien Hoa Army Base, because that was also the initial base camp for the 173rd Airborne Brigade. When the Brigade moved further north Company F took over the company area of one of the 173rd's infantry companies. The barracks and the general area were in need of a lot of work, thus a lot of work details were necessary to bring it up to our Officers and Senior NCO Standards. Of course they were all "Lifers" and had been at numerous state side and foreign bases through the course of their Army careers, so they had an excellent idea of how a squared away company should appear and function.

The barracks were approximately 60 feet long by 15 feet wide and each platoon had four barracks. This translated into a lot of physical labor by the privates, spec 4s and the buck sergeants! Since we were definitely in a war zone, we needed to increase the protection standards of the barracks and the bunkers so that if a rocket or mortar hit in the area of the barracks, personnel inside the barracks would be afforded some protection from the blast and the flying shrapnel. If it was a bad day and it hit on the roof or inside one of the barracks the only thing that would be left would be bodies and a real fucking mess. It would probably contain some of the explosive force and shrapnel, so indirectly the personnel in the barracks on either side of the explosion would be afforded some protection and it would save most of their lives. To make the barracks somewhat protected,

171

required sand bags to be stacked around 4½ feet high along the exterior walls of the barracks. To stack sand bags that high you had to establish a good base/foundation for all of those vertically stacked sand bags and the entire weight. To make it work and not have the sand bag wall collapse when you're at the top row, the base had to be at the minimum 4 bags wide. One row of 4 wide sandbags would not work so there would be a couple of 4-sand bags wide rows around the entire barracks except for the front and rear doors. The next probably three rows would be 3 wide sandbags followed by probably four 2 wide sandbag rows and finally a single sandbag row at the top. It was like building a rectangular pyramid with a flat top, except instead of stone we were using 25 pound sand bags, a lot of fricken 25 pound sandbags for each barracks. After the barracks were finished with sand bag protection, there was a rocket and/or mortar attack bunker between each of the barracks. They were approximately six feet wide with a five feet deep trench fifty feet long, covered with a half of a steel culvert. Each of those required at least six rows of three high sandbags. Again a lot of fricken 25 pound sandbags. By the time we finished with all the sand bagging details, we had a hole in the ground that you could drop a deuce and a half in and not see it.

You're probably wondering if we really needed that much protection inside the wire and behind a bunker line. The answer was a definite "YES" especially where our company area was located. F 51's company area was on the extreme north end of the Bien Hoa Army base and approximately half way between the east and west perimeters. That in itself was not especially problematic, but what was is that we aligned with the Bien Hoa Air Force Base that was on the extreme south end of the combined Army and Air Force bases. The VC and NVA would come out of the jungle to the north and approximately 5 miles from the perimeter where the rice paddies started and set up rocket and mortar firing positions in the middle of the night. They would simultaneously fire off several 122 mm or 107 mm rockets and some 82 mm mortar rounds, aiming for the Air Force Base/aircraft/runways, then quickly break down their firing positions and fade back into the jungle. The big problem was that their aiming devices for the rockets were for the most part rudimentary at best, so when they fired off their rockets they might have aimed too low which meant they landed short of the Air Force base and somewhere on the Army base. It was not uncommon to be on bunker duty at night and see the flashes to the north and you could see and hear the rockets passing overhead our company area. Of course we called it in but by the time they scrambled a helicopter gun crew or fast movers the enemy was long gone. I personally saw the hole made by a 122 mm rocket that fell short and landed in a roadway on the Army Base and it made a hole approximately 20 feet wide and probably 3 feet deep. If that were to hit on a runway or near aircraft it would definitely cause some serious damage. I also saw an 82 mm mortar that fell short of its target and failed to explode. It was approximately 300 yards from the company area and had landed on a blacktop road next to some barracks. It was buried about halfway in the blacktop and the MPs had just put a tape perimeter around it and split. I'm sure later on the EOD guys showed up and probably disarmed it and took it to their range to explode it. Yes, it could have exploded at any time, so we took a quick look and split because as I said before, Murphy was alive and well in the Vietnam War!

Chapter 33

24 Hours in the Life of a
LURP on a Mission

As indicated in Chapter 9, there was a lot of preparation before a Lurp team got on the helicopter for an insertion. It was extremely important that the prep was completed in a specific manner and then checked by the team leader and the assistant team leader. It was too damn late when you were on the LZ or worse, in the middle of a firefight and you find out that not all of the team had loaded the 100 rounds of M-60 ammo or the 6 pack of M-79 HE ammo.

The final event before entering the helicopter was to have each team member, including myself, jump up and down with all of their gear on. This was to check for any noise made by the gear, especially metal on metal. Sound was a great aid to a Lurp team in the jungle. It could also be a killer if an unwanted sound happened while lying on a trail with the enemy passing by at less then 15 feet. Sound was always a two-edged sword as was sight and smell. Each provided additional safety alarms for the Lurp team, but each could also be detrimental to the Lurp team's safety!

There was also one other task that all experienced Lurps did before or just after getting onto the Huey. Almost everyone on a Lurp team wore some kind of head cover, partially for the camouflage it provided for the head, partially for the shade and protection it could provide while humping through heavy brush or elephant grass. It could even act as a washcloth/wet rag to rub water on your face or neck, if you were lucky enough to have found a running stream and had time to safely do it. Most of us wore boonie hats, but some wore berets and some wore the old style Army garrison caps. Regardless of what you were wearing, you always tucked it in the front of your fatigue shirt because the down draft from the spinning main rotor had a lot of force and it would rip the cover off your head and usually throw it up into the spinning blade where it disappeared forever. It was a minor thing, but could be a major problem especially during the dry season when it was hot and you had a better chance of getting some sun exposure. During the rainy season/monsoon the cover protected your head from the direct contact with the rain, but of course it was soaked through as was everything thing else including your camo uniform and your boots. Fighting a war in the jungle is not for the weak minded or weak hearted. Of course, regardless where your particular war zone was located, the environment always provided challenges for the fighting men and women. You learned early on that you had to be flexible and adapt, adapt, adapt!

The loading onto the Huey of the 6 man recon team as well as the 12 man ambush team was choreographed by the team leader and the assistant team leader for specific seating positions. One Huey for a 6 man Lurp team and two Hueys for a 12 man ambush team. This was a critical situation because you never knew if there would be a problem on the LZ, like it was a hot LZ (enemy fire) with the team having off loaded and now in contact with the enemy. The second Huey could have landed in the wrong location on the LZ or it was a hot LZ and the pilot aborted the landing! A lot of bad ca ca can happen on a LZ and the insertion was probably the most dangerous part of the initial mission for a Lurp team.

As the team leader, I always rode in the right front position of the Huey for several reasons. First and foremost the rest of the team watched me and if I exited the helicopter they always followed, because if they didn't I or at least half the team (3 Lurps) would be on the LZ and the others would still be on the helicopter as it lifted off. I also wanted to be in that position so that I could assess the situation as we came into the LZ: if I saw something I didn't like or it was the wrong LZ, I would signal the crew chief, who sat in the right gun position on the helicopter, he would radio the crew and the left seat pilot (the officer in charge of the ship) would abort the insertion. I also had the M-60 machine gunner on my side of the ship so that if we encountered fire on the LZ we could immediately establish fire superiority and hopefully silence the enemy guns. I had the assistant team leader ride on the opposite side of the helicopter. There were two main reasons for this: first if we took fire during the insertion and I was hit or killed the ATL should still be OK and would take charge of the team. Secondly, the ATL carried the other radio (Air Force Downed Pilot; URC-10 Survival Radio) while I carried the PRC 25 Radio which was our primary means of communication. With an Air Force survival radio, you could talk directly to Air Force air crews whose radios were UHF while our radios were VHF radios. It also had an emergency beacon signal when you activated the radio and that signal would be picked up by all of the aircraft flying in your general area. If you left the signal on for 24 hours straight and didn't acknowledge anyone trying to contact you, then it was assumed that you were dead or captured and the Air Force would drop bombs on the beacon until it stopped transmitting.

Once safely and hopefully undetected on the LZ, the team moved a short distance off the LZ to do a listen, wait and see, for approximately 10 minutes. The insertion helicopter(s) left the immediate area so that it appeared that there weren't any US Troops on the LZ.

The aircrews also had an intricate air ballet that they completed. The C&C Ship (Command and Control) was normally high up (3,000 feet AGL) so that Chief Pilot could watch the insertions and give the pilots of the insertion ships any additional information that they observed from their vantage point. Some of the time the pilots, especially when doing a single 6 man Lurp light team insertion in a very active enemy AO, would be down on the deck a kilometer + from the LZ, at just above tree level or even flying around the higher trees as they flew at full speed toward the LZ. A second Huey, the chase ship, would be just behind them and to one side. The C&C ship would be talking to their pilots especially letting the insertion

176

ship know how far out they were and the correct heading. When they got to the critical distance from the LZ, the C&C ship commander would tell them to start to flare just before they came over the LZ and then the insertion ship would literally drop out of the sky onto the LZ for the insertion. The chase ship would overfly just to the right or left of the landing of the insertion ship, which would produce confusing sounds so that the enemy wouldn't know if a helicopter actually landed or was just flying low over the area. Added to this choreographed scene was two Cobra gun ships that were paralleling the flight of the insertion ship(s) and approximately 200 meters and 300 meters behind the insertion ships. They were in a staggered formation, one to the right and one to the left of the flight pattern of the insertion ship(s). This allowed both gun ships to have adequate time to acquire the target(s) and fire their 7.62 cal. mini-guns and 2.75 rockets if the insertion ship(s) encountered enemy fire on the LZ. One would overfly to the right or left of the landing insertion ship while the second Cobra was just far enough behind, opposite side to the other Cobra, the insertion ship(s) to provide additional cover fire as the insertion ship(s) lifted off with or without the Lurp team exiting the helicopter. The first Cobra would immediately make a hard right or left turn depending on which side they had over flown the LZ and would be covering the rear of the second Cobra as it made its gun runs on the enemy. The first Cobra was covering the insertion ship and the second Cobra by firing from the nose turret, which held a 7.62 cal. mini-gun and enhanced power automatic M-79 to provide additional fire on the enemy.

If everything went according to plan, the entire insertion should take less then 60 seconds to complete. The Lurp team should have exited the insertion ship, met at the front of the helicopter and quickly proceeded into the jungle next to the LZ. This should have occurred in the first 30 seconds of the insertion. Of course it depended on the how fast and close the Huey could get to the ground or hover, all of which depended on the actual conditions of the LZ and the skill of the pilots.

Now the cat and mouse game began and it was on the shoulders of the TL to make sure that his team carried out their mission; however, it was of primary importance that everyone made it back to base camp alive and hopefully uninjured.

From all of the loud noises produced by the Huey coming in fast and then landing, it was now deadly silent in the jungle, at least to man-made noises. The 10 minutes of waiting near the edge of the LZ was the critical first step for a Lurp team. During that time the team would be in an area that provided the best cover and concealment as directed by the team leader. All of the team members would be in rough wagon wheel perimeter facing out and on full alert. No one moved and they were all intently listening and observing what was happening in the jungle in front of their individual areas of responsibility. This maneuver could flush out LZ watchers or enemy troops that just happened to be moving through the area and observed the insertion of the Lurp team. The LZ watchers usually signaled with a gunshot, a whistle or sometimes banging on something metal to raise an alarm. If it were enemy troops that observed the insertion they normally would attempt to quickly follow the team so that they didn't loose them in the jungle. Most of the time they spotted the trail leading off the LZ and would walk right into the motionless Lurp team, which immediately erupted into a firefight that was up close and could be deadly. Of course as soon as a team member detected the enemy it was hand signaled to the team leader who would call it in to the C&C ship that was off in the distance. The radio call would go something like this in a whispered conversation: Team 1-3 to Silent Shadow 6 (army officer in charge of the Lurp team's insertion – 6 designated the company commander) over; This is Silent Shadow 6, go team 1-3; team 1-3 reporting movement at 270 degrees approximately 30 mikes from our location; Silent Shadow 6, roger that team 1-3, have you actually seen enemy troops over; team 1-3 negative, but we did hear equipment banging together so we are certain that it is not an animal over; Roger that team 1-3 what is your plan over; team 1-3 will wait an additional 10 minutes to see if anything develops or if the enemy went a different direction over; Roger team 1-3 keep us undated, Silent Shadow 6 out.

If nothing happened in the following 10 minutes the team would pick up and move out in a different direction from the possible enemy movement. Once they were away from the immediate area, the TL would give the point man the direction of the march and the team would slowly and cautiously make its way from the insertion point.

If the team didn't encounter any problems on the LZ they would move out after the 10 minutes, "listen, wait and see" period. I would give the point man an azimuth and hand signal how far to move. If the terrain allowed for it we would initially take a different azimuth to confuse the enemy about our true direction of travel. As an example: if we inserted on the east side of a LZ say at 90 degrees on the compass, but the direction we were actually going to go was south, 180 degrees on the compass. I would initially have the point man head out on an approximate 45 degrees heading and continue that for maybe 100 mikes, again depending on the terrain. This of course was to confuse any enemy that might be following our trail and also to gain some distance from the LZ so that we weren't paralleling the LZ/open area. If the enemy was tracking us, they may hear our movement or even observe us moving and with that information, they could move ahead of the team and set up an impromptu ambush. Once the team was out a 100 meters (+ or –) from the LZ, then we could turn and head back generally in a southerly direction. If I felt like something didn't seem right about what we saw or heard on the LZ, I may have the team move a short distance and then circle back to set up a linear ambush on our own trail. If nothing occurred after 15 + minutes then we would move out for the actual prescribed mission.

This may seem like a lot of effort with nothing to show for it, but the number one thing was to always stay flexible as the TL. It was important for the TL to never get into the same routine every time they came off the insertion LZ. You should also never lose sight of the fact that the enemy had good intel on the ground and you should never drop your guard or think you were better then they were. If Murphy was hanging out in your AO, things could quickly go to shit even if you were doing everything right. The high speed, top secret units that operated "across the fence" in Cambodia and Laos actually had NVA counter-recon teams with dogs searching for them as they left the LZ. These NVA teams were highly experienced and were there to specifically locate, and kill or capture all of the recon team members. They proved to be deadly efficient!

Once we were on our true course to recon a specific area of the assigned AO, then the entire team got into a cautious patrol movement through the jungle. I liked to call it "The Jungle Dance"! Some team members were very good at it and I prided myself as being one of those troopers. I had walked point for the 4th Battalion in the Central Highlands, not because I was good at it during that time, but because I was a FNG and I was considered expendable by my squad leader. Basically the point man was normally the trip wire that caused an ambush to be sprung on the line of troops following the point man. In Company F, I honed my skills and was normally the point man for Team 1-5 unless I was humping the M-60. I liked walking in that position because I could see everything that was happening to the front of the moving team. I used my previous point man experience in the Central Highlands along with my hunting experience from back in South Dakota to become an excellent point man. I can honestly say that, because I never walked the team into an ambush or caused us to walk directly into an enemy patrol or camp that was occupied.

The terrain normally dictated the movement of the team. The basis for the 6 man recon team was to move through the jungle, making the least amount of noise, leaving a minimal trail if not a completely undetectable trail and collecting Intel, like an old, narrow trail running 270 degrees to 10 degrees. We would move until I felt it necessary to stop and take a break, sometimes that may be a 100 plus meters or sometimes less. There were really two purposes for those breaks; first was to listen to see if we heard any suspicious noises and second to actually give each team member a chance to take a physical break. During this break all of your equipment was kept on and you simply sat down or knelt down facing out covering your assigned area. If I felt we needed to extend the break time because of excessively high temperatures, heavy vegetation or just a gut feeling, I would put the team in the wagon wheel configuration and indicate to them that they should take off their packs. In those extended breaks and with good cover and concealment, I may allow some of them to eat a meal, but normally that didn't occur while on the move. Usually a quick drink of warm water from your canteen; wipe the sweat off your neck and face with a drive-on rag (an OD green triangular bandage or part of an old OD Army towel that was wrapped around your neck); maybe apply some more camouflage stick on your face and stretch out your legs to give them a break. By then it was time to get up and start moving out.

Rarely did we have specific orders to reach a certain location in a specific time period, primarily because of unknown terrain features. It was also a very bad idea to try to speed through the jungle to get to a specific area and it defeated the actual purpose of the recon team – to move undetected through the enemy's territory and collect good intelligence.

The majority of communications between the team members were exchanged by hand signals and on very rare occasions, by whispering the info, primarily to the TL. It is important to note here that the TL controlled every aspect of the team and individual team members to include who did what; where they were placed on an ambush site; when and how they ate their meals; who was on guard; who was on stand-down; who slept and who stayed awake. This was not a superiority complex problem with the TL, it was an integrated part of the entire team's complex makeup and literally preserved the life blood of the team. Everyone needed to know exactly what was happening at any moment, regardless of day or night hours, especially the TL. Granted it was more about touch at night because we didn't have the night vision goggles that future war fighters would have in their kits. That was the reason for the wagon wheel formation if we weren't in an ambush position. If we were in an ambush position then it was more of a linear position; however, each team member should be able to touch at least one team member lying next to them.

Depending if we were in an ambush mode or just in a RON (Rest Over Night) for the night, the TL would set up the guard schedule. It could start with any team member including the TL, but there was always at least one Lurp on guard, 24/7. There were two rules that were always adhered to on my team; first when you were on guard duty you always sat up, never laid down, and you had to have your weapon ready to fire instantly. You had the rest of the team's safety sitting on your shoulders. The reason you were required to be sitting was so that you didn't nod off to sleep and the other team members could look and see who was actually on guard. Secondly, the person on guard always had the TL's watch. This provided the guard with additional stimulus to stay awake, since he had the evidence in his hand of who was on guard; secondly the watch told the guard when his one-hour of guard duty was over. He quietly tapped the next guy awake and handed him the watch, making sure that the new guard was actually awake before he laid down.

As the TL, I eventually trained myself to wake up every hour on the hour and check to see if the guard was sitting up and actually awake. It was just one of those extra things I did to ensure that the team was operating in the safest manner, because, like a Captain on a ship, the TL was responsible for whatever occurred with the team. A heavy responsibility, but you kind of grew into that role!

For me as a Lurp and for most of the team members, it took about 24 hours to get into the jungle mode; this included getting a feel for the jungle in our patrol area, including the rhythm of the vegetation, wild life and insects. They were "The Jungle" and if you could get in sync with these living organisms, then you could truly feel the jungle and in most instances you could survive for some days or maybe even for weeks; however, there were very few GIs that could survive indefinitely in the pure jungle. In fact the only Vietnamese people that could live in the jungle were some of the Vietnamese villagers in the flat lands and the Montyards, in the highlands, who lived and worked in the jungles and rice paddies, but they still had contact with the cities and some form of selling and buying basic supplies.

Secondly, within 24 hours you had absorbed enough of the jungle via dirt, vegetation and sweat that you didn't smell any different from the environment around you and that was what you wanted. Smell could be just as deadly as sound when you're lying in an ambush 10 feet off of an active enemy trail. Also the configuration of the trails in the really heavy jungle areas caused the trails to act like miniature wind tunnels, which carried the smell of enemy troops approaching and could also carry a member of the team's smell, such as smoke if someone on the team tried to smoke a cigarette in the jungle. Some of the old lifer dudes were so addicted to nicotine that they couldn't make it for 5 days without a cigarette. Fortunately none of my team members were smokers, so I didn't have that problem. Other smells such as c-rats could also cause problems and I didn't for the most part allow team members to carry c-rats. It was more about the noise caused by the metal c-rat cans then it was about the smell.

During the dry season you would sweat profusely and I would drop 10 plus pounds in the 5-day mission, primarily from loss of water/dehydration/sweat and also from only eating maybe one small meal a day or sometimes just a snack. Added to that, was the controlled stress of being always at 110 per cent of your mental and physical self. I also never slept sound while out on patrol, especially as a TL.

On one occasion after we extracted late in the evening, I just stripped off my camouflaged uniform and left it hanging on a nail in the wall of the barracks next to my bunk. In the morning when I picked it up to take it to be laundered it was stiff as a board. I could actually stand the pants in the corner like two camouflaged stovepipes. I examined it and I could see a lot of salt stains from the sweat, mixed with dirt, vegetation, some bug juice and whatever else got rubbed on it while lying on the ground of an ambush site. It basically smelled like the jungle floor and that was exactly what you wanted it to smell like! To this day my sense of smell is highly active and alert and it has caused me some problems because of what the smell reminds me of. Of course after a quick reality check, I would be back in the moment.

Chapter 34

Patience is a Required Virtue for a Lurp Team/Team Members

Patience was the supreme rule for a Lurp team and each individual team member. It manifested itself in a lot of different ways. Lying on a trail in an ambush mode on semi-high alert state was probably the greatest test of patience. All experienced team members knew that this quiet blissful state of boredom could go to shit in a milli-second if Charlie came down the trail and was in the kill zone before any team member saw, heard or smelled them. So even if you had an excellent ambush site with good cover and concealment, your mind and your body were still there for every second of every minute of every hour for what could be days. Of course the twin of patience is boredom and the juxtaposition of the two could be very dangerous for every member of a Lurp team on a mission. Most of us just relaxed when not on guard duty and tried to sleep with one eye open. A few brought a small paperback book to read, which I did not encourage the team members to do. It made noise and white paper in the green jungle was like an arrow pointing you out to the enemy. Some Lurps on other teams did stupid things like talking and a few smoked. Almost everyone of those teams got fired up by the enemy at some point and usually they ended up with some wounded Lurps. I don't know why the TL would allow that to occur, but I didn't and if you couldn't comply with the rules I had for the team members, including myself, while on a mission, they could join a different team. My main objective on every mission was to bring back the whole team alive and hopefully not wounded. Accomplishing the goals of the mission regardless if it was a recon or an ambush mission closely followed my first priority of team safety.

Chapter 35

Near Death First Mission after Returning from Leave in South Dakota

By the middle of July, 1968 I had completed my one year in Vietnam and was scheduled to rotate to CONUS; however, because of my particular enlistment situation I decided to extend for 6 months. I knew that if I rotated to the states I would probably be there a year and then would be rotated back to Vietnam. I was a Sgt with combat experience so I'm sure I would have been assigned back in a line unit of grunts and that would not be a good assignment. Thus I figured I would stay where I was and keep my team along with the fact that I was completely integrated into Company F and how we conducted Lurp missions. I was also aware that our company had probably one of the best combat support systems in Vietnam as to lift ships, gun ships, artillery and Air Force/FAC liaison. This was a very significant reason why Company F had such an outstanding combat record and low ratio of KIA or WIA Lurps to the number of enemy killed, wounded or captured. Of course it was a war zone, and things could change in a heartbeat.

When I picked up my rifle from the armory, it wasn't my rifle. I asked the Armory Sgt where my rifle was. He told me that he had issued it out to a FNG and that he was issuing me a brand new M-16. He thought he was doing me a favor, but in actuality he had screwed me. I started to protest, but figured it was too late to do anything about it. The problem was that it had taken me some time to get my original M-16 dialed in for up close and personal combat. I had spent numerous hours just switching the selector switch from Safe, to Semi-Auto, to Full Auto. The reason being that on a new rifle there was an obvious click from one position to the next of the selector switch, similar to the problem with the A-47. That single or double click sound could be fatal for any Lurp at the beginning of an ambush. Secondly, I shoot long guns left-handed and the original M-16s didn't have ambidextrous selector switches. I had moved the selector switch with my left thumb without it being around the pistol grip and I didn't want any resistance in that movement because half a second delay could be a death sentence for me.

Third, there was always the superstition about not making changes to anything if everything was working fine and so far my luck had held. I'm not saying that the new rifle changed my luck, but I did become a bullet and shrapnel magnet during the next six months.

My team was on a mission and wouldn't be in for several more days, so the TL from another team asked me if I would be their M-60 gunner for his heavy team. They were going to be doing a stay behind ambush after a reaction platoon and a Navy Seal team completed a sweep of this particular area. The idea was for the Reaction Platoon to provide security while the Seal team did a dive trying to locate an underwater cache of weapons. This information had been obtained by another team in documents they had seized and by additional information obtained by one of the intel agencies operating in Vietnam. The idea was that we would all insert at the same time into this particular location and then when the mission was completed by the Seal team, they would all be extracted and the heavy team would stay behind to ambush whoever came into the area to check out what this particular US Army unit had been doing. Of course it was believed that with that many GIs on the ground the enemy wouldn't notice that not all of the GIs had left the area. The second problem with this assumption was that the enemy observers wouldn't notice that some of the GIs were wearing camo uniforms while the majority were wearing the standard GI OD green combat uniform. The third problem with the same assumption was that the enemy wouldn't count the number of helicopters that were used to insert all of the GIs and that that same number of helicopters didn't land to extract all of the GIs.

I had to completely change my web gear because I wouldn't be carrying an M-16 or any mags for it. I didn't remove the ammo pouches but took out all of my mags. I could put some hand grenades and other small gear in the pouches. I also emptied out my pack except for my poncho liner and some Lurp rations. The majority of the pack was reserved for M-60 ammo in the 100 round cardboard boxes since no one in their right mind would carry the ammo in the metal can which added a lot of weight. I was going to carry 500 rounds in the pack, 200 rounds in the assault pack each gunner made after being at *Recondo School* and an approximate 30 round assault belt to be on the gun. It was a load for someone my size but in reference to machine gun ammo, it was better to have more then less. Most of the other team members would also carry one 100 round box of M-60 ammo, I should have a total of around 1,500 rounds to fire from the M-60 if we got into deep shit. We never carried an extra barrel for the gun, again because of the weight. Also if you were burning out your barrel that meant that you were firing too many rounds in each burst and that was just a waste of ammo. I liked to fire between 8-12 rounds for each burst, because you had good control of the weapon and would be dead on target.

I can think of only one time where the barrel of an M-60 got burned out. A heavy team ran into probably a NVA Battalion and had a real shit fight, which included smoking the barrels on the M-60s. After an initial firefight, the NVA regrouped and would go on line to charge the heavy team's position. There would be the haunting sound from their calvary trumpet at which time the NVA would charge across an open area, start up the high ground toward the heavy team that had two M-60 guns and two of the craziest gunners in the company. Those two gunners usually carried 1,000 rounds each for their M-60 machine guns and the rest of the team members also carried M-60 ammo. Each gun probably had nearly 2,000 rounds and they burned through well over 1,000 rounds for each gun. They did heat up their barrels; however, it was one of those necessary actions based on the combat situation they were involved in.

The gunners told me they would just mow down the line of NVA troops with the two M-60 guns and then the NVA would retreat and try it again. Of course the rest of the heavy team was picking off the NVA with their M-16s. The reason the team even stayed around is that in the initial firefight, the PRC-24 Radio was hit and knocked out of action so the team didn't have any communications with HQ to let them know they were in trouble. The TL decided it was better to stay and fight in a good defensive position instead of making a run for it and have a lot of pissed off NVA troops chasing them.

The NVA finally retreated and took a lot of dead and wounded troops with them. Apparently the CO of that NVA unit finally realized that a frontal assault was not going to work and who ever they were attacking had two M-60 machine guns and lots of ammo! Plus the fact that they ran into two of the craziest and best M-60 gunners in all of Company F. Xin Loi NVA!

Once our heavy team was loaded out we walked to the helipads and boarded two Hueys for the ride out to the insertion LZ. The lift ships had already inserted several squads from the reaction platoon along with the Seal team, which I believe was 6 Seals. Everything was going great until we got within a few clicks of the LZ and the crew chief advised us that the LZ was hot. "Shit," I thought, "my first mission after 30 days of leave back in the states, and I just drew a Hot LZ Card from the deck of Lurp Playing Cards!" I was kneeling down in the middle of the deck of the first insertion ship and in that position I could actually see through the front wind-screen of the Huey between the two pilots. We started to drop down for the landing on the LZ in a straight shot off the nose of the bird pointed at the LZ. We were probably 500 yards from the actual LZ and several hundred feet in altitude, but we were hauling ass with a lot of speed because of the LZ being hot. I heard the pilot say something and felt the helicopter take a sudden drop of probably 30 + feet. I just caught movement in front and just above our ship and I realized it was an RPG round passing overhead. "Well great," I thought, "not only did we draw a Hot LZ Card, the bastards are firing RPG 70s at us." We were still probably 200 meters out and 100 plus feet in the air when a second RPG came flying at us. This one was lower and passed under our ship by probably 20 feet, but it was still a real pucker factor.

The LZ was a flooded rice paddy with probably 6-8 inches of water on top of the ground. Because the pilot brought the chopper in fast with just a little flare, the skids of the helicopter went into the water and when they touched the submerged ground we continued forward in a sliding motion for a few meters before it was time to bail out. As soon as we had cleared the deck of the helicopter it lifted off because it didn't want to be sitting on the ground waiting for another RPG round to come in. That was fine with the Lurps because we had no cover and we needed to get to the berm of the rice paddy to our front, which was at least 50 meters away. We all started to run and at the same time heard a hell of a firefight going on to our front. I took maybe two steps when I hit a shell hole that was submerged and hidden from view. It was probably an old mortar shell impact point, because the hole was only about 24 inches deep and maybe 5-8 feet wide. The problem was that first of all I didn't know it was there, and secondly, I had the M-60 on a sling around my neck and to my front, plus the 200 round assault pack hanging on my left side and the 500 rounds in my pack. As I stumbled into the shell hole, I fell forward and was carried forward and down by all of the weight. The machine gun and the 200 round assault pack acted like two giant pendulums and swung forward. I expected to just fall to my knees and then regain my balance; however, all of that shifted weight just drove me face first into the rice paddy water and then I just kept going down. I realized as I bottomed out that my head was probably 12 inches or more underwater and I had drank a lot of the nasty rice paddy water on the way down. I let loose of the M-60 but it was still attached to my upper body by the strap around my neck, plus the assault pack and all of the rounds in my pack were all holding me down and underwater. I hadn't expected to do a face plant and then a face dive in the water so I was out of breath and sucking in paddy water. I did a quick push up type action and my face just about cleared the water before the weight submerged me again. I quickly realized that I wouldn't be able to just push myself up out of the water and by then things were starting to get a little fuzzy. I had probably been under water for around 20 seconds which wasn't that long if you were prepared for it, had taken an extra breath and closed your mouth before you hit the water, but of course I hadn't done any of that. I realized that if I didn't do something quickly, I was going to drown in this damn shell hole in shitty rice paddy water. I knew, because of the configuration of the machine gun strap and the strap to the assault pack around my neck, that I wouldn't have the time needed to take them off my body before I passed out, so I had to come up with Plan B. The M-60 was acting like a log attached to me on my right side, so I could only move one direction and that was to my left away from the gun. I had enough sense to try to dig the tip of my boots into the side of the tapered shell hole to use my leg muscles to help me move. I remember thinking well its "all or nothing" and with that I shoved forward with both legs and simultaneously rolled in the opposite direction of the gun. Somehow, I made it far enough in the roll over that my head cleared the water and I got my first breath of air. I got a couple more breaths and had enough strength to remove the strap holding the M-60 machine gun around my neck. My entire body was still underwater except for my head and a short length of the left side of my neck. I managed to roll all the way on my back with my pack still on, which cleared my head, neck and part of my shoulders. I then basically wiggled and skidded on my back using the heels of my boots and my arms to propel me upwards out of that damn shell hole. It probably took me a minute to get up out of the hole and be sitting on the flat ground of the submerged rice paddy. I managed to get to my knees and then pulled the M-60 out of its submerged location. Of course the war was still going on and now the enemy were dropping mortar rounds in the rice paddy to my front and right side. I decided it was better to make a run for it than sit there and get hit by a mortar round. I managed to get to my feet and made a quick bent-over walk toward the west dike of my rice paddy, swimming hole! I made it there without falling down again and lay up against the paddy dike, which was probably 4 feet high and had small trees and bushes growing on top of it. It was sloped so I would guess it was probably more then 4 feet thick/wide at the bottom, which meant nothing short of a tank or artillery round was going to pierce it, at least on the bottom where it was sitting on the rice paddy ground. One of the Lurps was hunched down to my right on the dike and to my left was a Sgt from the Reaction platoon and he was doing the same thing. There were a shit load of rounds striking the top of the dike or passing overhead. There was a machine gun fairly close to our left front that was working out, firing in probably 30-50 round bursts. I yelled at the Sgt, "Hey Sarge who in the hell is firing that machine gun?" He yelled back, "It isn't ours!" I thought oh shit this is turning into a real bad scene because we are taking heavy fire to our front and now the left flank. I realized then that a stay behind ambush was out of the question, because we had stirred up a real hornets' nest and they were keeping more than a platoon of GIs pinned down behind a rice paddy dike.

Right after I spoke to the sgt, I heard the distant whoosh of what I thought was another RPG round being fired. Within several seconds I caught some movement to my upper left as I was lying on my back facing out toward the open rice paddy. I saw a RPG round hit the small tree that was growing out of the top of the rice paddy berm. This particular tree was about 4 feet high and had branched out into a Y formation about a foot above the ground. The RPG 70 round had hit the tree right in the middle and as it passed through the small branches the round and its tail fins had passed directly between the upper part of the Y branch. The four stabilizing tail fins, which extend out about 8 inches from the body of the RPG had snagged on the two branches. I knew I was dead, because I could reach up and touch the warhead of the RPG 70. It had sagged down after coming to a sudden and complete stop. If it had exploded both I and the other Lurp would have been hamburger meat and probably the Platoon Sgt also. I just kept looking at it and wondering when it was going to explode. The original RPG rounds were point detonated and I could clearly see the silver fuse on the end of the green RPG round, so I knew it wasn't a dud. During that time the little voice in my head kept saying, "You dumb ass, you just volunteered for 6 more months of this shit and you might die on your first mission!" Xin Loi GI

After maybe half a minute I realized that the RPG round was not going to explode unless something struck the fuse on the front of the round. There wasn't anywhere to move to and with the warhead of the RPG round sagging down in the tree it was below the top of berm, so unless another RPG round or a mortar round landed close by, the RPG wasn't going to explode! Of course if they landed that close, we were dead anyway so it really didn't matter if the RPG round exploded or we got hit by an additional enemy round and it caused the RPG round to explode as a secondary. Dead is dead, regardless how you die.

I was thinking, "What the hell else could go wrong on this mission!"

I had been lying against the berm with the other Lurp for about 10 minutes and the fire from the enemy hadn't decreased, which told me they had a lot of ammo and they were protecting something of value.

It was at that time that I started to feel a tingling in my finger tips and toes. Kind of like when your hand or foot has gone to sleep and was now coming back. I thought it was rather strange, but with all of the shooting going on, I had other things to worry about. Within a minute after the tingling started my legs started to go numb along with my arms. In probably another minute, my entire body was numb, but the reason it was numb was that my entire body was paralyzed. I tried to move my arms but nothing happened. I could move my eyes and I could actually speak but had no control over the rest of my body. I yelled at the Lurp on my left and told him to come over. He did and I told him about my problem. He checked me out to see if I had been hit somewhere that was causing the paralysis. He didn't find anything so I told him to let the TL know that I had a problem. I'm not sure if the TL got the info then or later upon extraction. This was terrifying because if I somehow I got left behind I would be captured by the enemy and probably tortured if not killed straight out. We stayed in our positions for probably another 5 minutes when word passed down that we were going to be extracted. The seals would go on the first ship and the first half of the Lurp heavy team would go on the next ship. After that the rest of the heavy team and then two ships for the two squads of the Reaction platoon.

By now several other Lurps had arrived at my location and after talking to them it was determined that they would basically drag me out by my arms or uniform shirt to the landed helicopter, like a wounded GI and would unceremoniously throw my ass on the helicopter. By now I was beyond scared and was transcending into a very pissed off Lurp. Not only was I in danger, but now I was putting my fellow Lurps in danger, because they had to drag me out to the helicopter and some of the other Lurps had to carry all my equipment including the M-60. It was also embarrassing as hell because I wasn't wounded but I was still paralyzed. It could be extrapolated out that I was so scared that I froze up and that was a very bad rep for a Lurp to have!

The first two ships came in and landed amid more mortar fire and machine gun fire from the enemy. The area to our front near the tree line and approximately 150 meters from our position had been worked over by a pair of gunships, but it hardly deterred the enemy. In fact the mortar team was getting more accurate and was dropping rounds closer to the berm we were lying against. That was bad because if they got close enough we would have to crawl over the berm to the other side and that would expose us to their machine guns and rifle fire. Kind of like rats on a burning ship!

The first half of our Heavy team ran to the second ship and the Seals ran to the first lift ship. Per our training at *Recondo School*, the heavy team leader and the other five Lurps would be on the next lift ship. That way the TL knew what was happening with his team and he would be the last one on the ship. I would be part of that second team with the TL and that meant that I would be dragged out through that damn submerged rice paddy again. It also meant that if they dropped me or they got hit I would submerge into the rice paddy water and simply drown, since I was still completely paralyzed.

The Seal team was about three quarters of the way to the first helicopter when a mortar round land very close to them and one of the Seal team members dropped his scuba tank, but continued to run to the helicopter. I could see all of this occurring in front of me because I was propped up against the berm like an unused puppet and had a front row seat.

The scuba tank was just floating in the rice paddy all by itself as the two ships lifted off. It was really weird, like some portrait on a very non-classic piece of art! Maybe an Andy Warhol!

It took about 15 minutes for the two lift ships to return and then it was our turn. Another set of Cobra gunships had arrived and they were making gun and rocket runs on the tree line to our front where the main concentration of enemy were. So off we went with two Lurps dragging me like a rubber doll across the damn submerged rice paddy to the first helicopter. The two Lurps had to lift me up and then throw me into the middle of the helicopter and of course with no muscle control I just slumped down like a wet noodle. Fortunately they had dumped me on my back so I didn't do a face plant on the deck the Huey. There was a lot of firing going on as we lifted off, primarily from the two door gunners of the helicopter. It seemed to be an eternity before they stopped firing and I knew we had cleared the LZ without taking hits or being shot down. The TL checked on me and I told him I was good except for the fact that I couldn't move. It took approximately 10 minutes for us to land at a fire support base and be unloaded because the lift ships had to go back and pickup whoever was remaining from the Reaction Platoon. Probably a squad plus around 10 to 14 GIs.

When we landed the team had to drag me off the helicopter and sit me upright against some stacked sand bags at a helicopter revetment. About 15 minutes after we landed I started to feel tingling in my finger tips and my toes. After about 5 more minutes I had feeling back in my entire body. I tried standing and was able to without any noticeable weakness. Once I was up I walked around and then spotted the TL. I approached him and said that I felt OK. He asked me what happened and I told him I didn't have a clue. I said the only thing different from all the other combat assaults I had been on, including Hot LZs was that I fell in a shell crater and drank a bunch of rice paddy water.

Shortly thereafter the two slicks returned with the remainder of the Reaction Platoon, miraculously no one got hit during the entire time the group was on the ground. The Reaction Platoon leader also had recovered the set of scuba tanks dropped by the Seal and gave it to them. Within 30 minutes the Captain of Company F decided that we had had enough fun in the sun and getting our asses fired up. We would just return to our company and call it a day. He was still airborne in the general area of our little stay-behind exercise, because the artillery liaison on-board the C&C ship was dropping artillery on the enemy location. Later our FAC flew into the orbit and had some Phantoms out of Bien Hoa Air Base drop some bombs on the location. I'm not sure if II Field Force(II FF) ever sent a company or two to check out the area, because the enemy definitely was protecting something . Maybe they had a base camp there. Company F had done their part in locating a large force of the enemy in kind of an ass-backward way. Now it was up to the General of II FF and his S-2 (Intelligence Unit) to decide how they were going to react to the contact with the substantial enemy force.

About a month later, I was reading the *Stars & Stripes* newspaper and saw this article about GIs being paralyzed by drinking untreated rice paddy water. I thought, "NO Shit, I must have drank a couple of gallons while trying to drown myself in that rice paddy swimming pool!" The article went on to say that doctors and research personnel from an Army Medical Unit had identified a microscopic parasite that lived in the rice paddy water. If a GI drank the untreated water, the parasite would move into the lining of the stomach and then into the blood stream. It would stay in the blood stream until it was transported to the brain. It would attach itself to brain cells in the area that controlled the large muscles movement and feelings of the human body. This caused temporary paralysis in a human until the parasite died which could be from 30 minutes to one hour plus. After which time, the body regained its feeling and mobility. Up to that point, I was thinking it was probably more like poppa-san and his water buffalo both crapped and peed in the water and I just drank some of it, after which I became paralyzed! The article didn't say if they had a solution for the problem other than don't drink untreated rice paddy water. At first I was thinking what happens to that dead parasite, does it just stay there or is it absorbed into the body? More importantly, does the paralysis ever return to the affected body? No answer on that, so I had to "keep on truckin' in the land of the Lurp".

I took the article and told everyone in 1st Platoon about it, including the TL with who I had been on the stay-behind ambush in his heavy team. I did it for two purposes: the main one being that I wanted to clear my name of any doubts that I could function under extreme stress like in a firefight. Fortunately, I already had a good reputation as a TL and had tons of experience as a Lurp. Secondly, I wanted all of my fellow Lurps to know not to drink the untreated water from a rice paddy! Like they didn't already know that! It appeared that I was the only one concerned about what had happened to me, since most of those team members had been on other missions and some had already been in other firefights. As Lurps it is best to store the useful information in your brain but not to dwell on it. You needed to be on your A Game every time you inserted for a new mission. I did that and forgot all about it until I started to write this book.

Chapter 36

An Ambush Initiated By Smell

On November 19, 1968, I was the team leader for a heavy team. We had inserted in the early afternoon into an area of War Zone D near the Cambodian border. We had traveled a few 100 meters (mikes) from our insertion LZ when we came upon a well used trail. It wasn't the best location for an ambush, but because it was late in the afternoon and this was a high speed trail (very active trail), I didn't want to be screwing around next to the trail looking for a better location with the enemy "active hours" approaching. The active times for most trails were the time periods when Charlie liked to move down the trails in larger groups; primarily first light in the morning and late afternoon. The reason Charlie chose those times was because of the rising day time temperatures especially during the dry season, their logistics which included humping heavy loads long distances and to avoid US Line Troops, who tended to move out later in the morning. They also believed that there wouldn't be as many US aircraft, especially helicopters, up early in the morning or toward evening after the previous day's long flight times. They were partially correct on their assumptions, but the Lurp heavy teams that ambushed them changed the rules and they got caught a lot of times in deadly ambushes. This was of course another method of inflicting casualties on the enemy, but it was equally important in the fact that you got inside their heads. They were very uncomfortable traveling down their trails if the word was out that there were US soldiers conducting ambushes in the area. Some of the time they knew it was Lurps and some of the time they believed it was Special Forces conducting the ambushes. They were correct in both assumptions because the majority of the Lurps were trained by Special Forces, so whether SF conducted the ambush or some of their trained Lurps did, the results were the same! Death, destruction and Psych Ops Warfare!

With 12 men in a heavy team it takes some time to get the ambush set up. During that time, the team is very vulnerable because they are all moving to position/interlock their claymores if they have been assigned to the area designated as the kill zone of the ambush. The rest of the team is placing their claymores to protect the team's other significant danger areas. All Lurps at some point are also clearing out leaves, sticks and rocks to make a quiet position for the ambush zone or while protecting the flanks and the rear area of the position. There were always a couple of Lurps watching the trail while their fellow Lurps placed and then camouflaged their claymore mines in a specific area of the kill zone so that all of the claymores' direction of blast were interlocked in a crisscross pattern. It was equally important to place the claymore mine at an oblique angle to the location of the team, because the 1.5 pounds of C-4 in each claymore created a deadly back-blast, especially since most of the time the claymores were set out at approximately 10-15 feet from the team and they were designed to be deployed at 75 feet. The reason why they weren't deployed that far out was because the Lurp team member, who deployed the claymore would have no idea what was happening with his claymore at night when his night time vision was down to almost zero. If the VC or the NVA knew where your position was, they would try to crawl near or into the perimeter and turn the claymores around causing them to be pointing into the Lurps' perimeter. To counter this, some team members would take anti-personnel mines (M-14), called "Toe Poppers" and place them in front of their claymore so that the enemy would step or kneel on them while trying to find the claymore and reverse its lethal ball bearing flight path. I never actually used that technique because my claymores were always deployed at what they would now determine to be "danger close!" I know of one Lurp who had deployed the toe popper and after a successful ambush in which his claymore was not detonated, went out to recover his claymore. He forgot about the mine and stepped on it, which detonated and caused some serious damage to his foot and evacuation back to the US via a hospital stop in Japan. The obvious question would be, What the hell were you doing in front of your own claymore? You had to keep your head screwed on tight, because Murphy was always there looking over your shoulder to capitalize on your mistakes!

Also consider the fact that most heavy teams usually deployed 4-8 claymores in the kill zone. If everything went as planned, all 4-8 claymores were detonated almost simultaneously. That's 6-12 pounds of C-4 exploding at a very close distance. The back-blast of flying jungle vegetation/dirt/rocks and sometimes parts of the claymore mine itself made for a very dangerous situation at detonation time. As an example of how much shit is blown into the air, the ambush that we executed under S/Sgt Lavender's control on the VC company was during a sunny, early afternoon time period. The sky actually turned dark and blocked out the sun like it was almost dark. In that particular ambush, team member PFC Schmidt actually got hit in the chest by one of the claymore's metal legs that was blown back into our perimeter. It actually penetrated his chest by about an inch, but since it came in at an oblique angle it didn't cause any major damage. Our medic, Eric Johnson, pulled it out and slapped a bandage on it. PFC Schmidt was told he could carry on and he did by firing his M-16 into his designated area of the ambush zone.

Secondly the shock wave/sound wave would be tremendous and it normally resulted in the loss of your ability to hear anything except for gunshots and explosions, which sounded like they were in a cotton tunnel and far away. It could affect every Lurp in the immediate area of the kill zone and sometimes the entire team. Long-term affects/ years later were that most of the Lurps developed tinnitus and loss of hearing! Welcome to the Combat Tested Lurp Club!

With the ambush/kill zone in place, we settled into our normal routine, which was several Lurps on guard duty while the rest tried to relax. Depending on the configuration of the ambush site, again normally dictated by the specific terrain, I usually liked to be in the

200

middle or near one end of the ambush site so that I had a reasonable view of the trail and the kill zone. On this ambush I ended up on the extreme right flank of the ambush site and then 5 more Lurps were distributed along the linear ambush to my left with the other 4 Lurps in a horseshoe shape to the flanks and the rear. We had only been in place for approximately one hour when I caught a very strong smell of sweet smoke. I immediately recognized it as the smell that was associated with enemy troops cooking rice over a wood fire. I had not heard anything nor seen any movement down the trail to my right. Regardless, I half turned to my left and gave a snap of my fingers on my right hand to alert the team. As I turned back, to my surprise there was an enemy soldier standing just to my left and approximately 15 feet away on the trail. He had either heard me or detected my movement and he was turning to his left and coming up on target (me) with a submachine gun. I had also started to bring up my M-16 on the enemy soldier but he was ahead of me by probably a second. Instinctively I just pointed and fired my M-16 at his center mass without aiming because there wasn't time. I shoot left handed with long guns because my master eye is my right eye instead of my left eye. As I fired a short burst at the enemy soldier, he simultaneously fired on me. Because of shooting with the left hand, arm and shoulder I had turned my body to the left to assist in firing my M-16. That movement had put my body perpendicular to the trail and the firing enemy soldier. His aim was partially on target and I got a grazing hit under the right forearm. It caused a burning sensation but hardly any pain at that point. My rounds however were dead-on center mass and he was hit with 3-4 rounds in the chest. The impact of those rounds knocked him backwards, but as a true soldier and as he fell down, he continued to fire his weapon, which turned out to be a Chinese 9 mm submachine gun known as a PPSK with a 30-round magazine. The rounds he fired snaked through our perimeter and shot the belt off the M-60 with the gunner and gun lying next to me on my left. The rounds continued through the perimeter shooting off the heel of the jungle boot of the Lurp lying on the left flank and finally culminated with four rounds into the pack of Spec 4 Moyer, who was in charge of the rear security. All of the shooting took maybe three seconds max. We had some return fire from the right flank before the remaining enemy troops fled the location. With no more enemy firing I had the team secure both ends of the trail and I stepped out onto the trail to check the enemy soldier to see if he was dead, recover his weapon and any intelligence items, which included his pack and any other gear he was carrying. In this particular instance, the soldier was dead and had probably died while still standing, since it appeared that several rounds from my M-16 had struck him in the heart and exited out his back. That would account for why he simply fell down instead of trying to seek cover. Most likely his last conscious move was the finger pull on the trigger of his submachine gun. I collected everything of value including the submachine gun and left his body on the trail. The other enemy troops knew how he had died so it wouldn't be necessary to hide his body. This was of course another way of getting inside the head of the enemy. It would be like you walking down a specific street in your neighborhood and having an aggressive dog come out of a yard and attempt to bite you. The next time you walked down that same street, you would probably walk on the opposite side of the street or choose a different route for your daily walk. That would be getting inside your head not only for your own safety, but also causing you to alter your plans to prevent more problems or worse from getting bit! Welcome to psych warfare on the home front!

Based on how the contact occurred, the soldier that I killed was probably walking point for a squad of VC, since they didn't try to flank the team and attack us. I immediately called in a CONTACT on our radio to get the helicopters spinning up and heading our direction. As it was, it would take approximately 25 minutes for the extraction helicopters and the Cobra gunships to be "on station", so that initial radio call was very critical. Twenty-five minutes is a life time if you're in heavy contact with the enemy, and even a heavy team would have to conserve its ammo to be able to sustain a firefight of that duration.

It might even require the team leader to decide to simultaneously blow all the claymores in the kill zone, quickly followed by blowing the flank and rear security claymores before evacuating the area. This technique was used to clear out an area close to the team's location. It would act as shock treatment to keep the enemy soldiers either down or moving out of the way, hopefully with some of them wounded or dead. That type of movement was called an E&E Tactic with stood for an Escape and Evasion movement. What it translated into for the team in contact was that shit has hit the fan and its time to "Shoot and Scoot" the hell out of the area, because Charlie is pissed and he wants a piece of the team! Sometimes, literally running and shooting movements were over relatively long distances. Without the assistance of the helicopter gunships, the team could be in big trouble and getting chopped up along the way. This was especially true if it were NVA soldiers you had ambushed. They were excellent fighters and would press the attack on your position. This also illustrated the importance of the Lurp Team working together to keep their fire controlled, while still maintaining a secure movement away from the enemy troops. It also illustrated how important it was to have an excellent point man, because other then giving him an initial direction, he was on his own to negotiate the best and fastest route away from the ambush site.

Once the gunships were overhead the assistant team leader or designated Lurp would drop smoke at the rear of the team and using the PRC-25 radio would give the direction of movement of the team in reference to the smoke, along with the direction and approximate distance of the enemy troops. In certain areas, especially triple canopy, the smoke would drift and would not be a true representation of where the team actually was. If the smoke drifted away from the team it wouldn't be a problem, but if it drifted toward the team and the gunships were shooting just to the left or right of the smoke, they might actually be putting fire into the team's perimeter, which occurred more then anyone wanted to think about it. On one occasion a team was running and being chased by NVA they had ambushed.

The ATL, last Lurp in the line of Lurps, had dropped smoke behind the running team and then a gunship made a run with their mini-guns, with one bullet actually hitting the smoke grenade on the ground. That would be a very exact definition of "Close air support"!

Once the gunships had a general idea of where the team was, they would then start strafing runs with their 7.62 cal mini-guns, 2.75 rockets and the enhanced M-79 rounds from their nose turrets. Normally that would cause the enemy to disengage their assault and move away from the area. Sometimes, however, it would take a lot more firepower, like fast movers dropping 250 lb bombs or making 20 mm gun runs to break up the enemy attack. Because of numerous friendly fire incidents in which the bombs or 20 mm fell into the perimeter of the friendly troops, FAC would usually send the fast movers in at a right angle to where the friendly troops were, so that nothing landed in the troops' perimeter. In that type of situation none of the Lurp teams ever got away clean and they usually had wounded or dead Lurps!

We landed at the slick pads just outside the company area and made our way to the debriefing tent that was next to the underground TOC bunker. The debriefing was short and we handed over the soldier's pack and the rest of his gear but I kept the PPSK after it was examined by the intel officer. I took it back to the barracks to check it out. We then broke down our gear, removed the grenades and placed them in the ammo bunker to prevent any further accidents in the barracks. As I was removing the M-16 magazines from the right front ammo pouched to check and clean them, I observed that the first mag in the pouch looked somewhat deformed. I examined it closer and observed that it had a bullet hole in the right front side. I unloaded the rounds out of the magazine and found that a bullet about half way down in the line of bullets was bent inward and upon looking inside the magazine I found an expended 9 mm full metal jacket round that was slightly deformed on the nose. I then examined the ammo pouch and found a neat 9mm sized hole in the face of the pouch. Apparently the enemy soldier had fired more accurate shots at me then I first thought. Based on how the enemy soldier had fallen when I hit him in the chest, it would appear that the first round he fired actually hit my ammo pouch and probably the second or third round had grazed my lower right arm before the rounds continued on through the team's perimeter. I reconstructed the ambush in my mind and believed that I must have come up on my right leg to a kneeling position and that had placed my two right ammo pouches/stomach directly in the line of fire.

Lady Luck had been with me on the ambush, because that first round would have torn into the mid line of my intestines and would have caused a lot of destruction and a nasty wound. Gut wounds were known to be a particular dangerous wound because they not only allowed the contents of your intestines to be spread through the stomach cavity, but they also deposited a lot of probable infectious material into the wound because of the bullet traveling through your uniform and your skin which had to have a lot of dirt and other undesirable material sitting on the exterior of your body. Would I have died immediately, probably not unless that round had penetrated deep enough to hit a major artery; however, I certainly would have been in a lot pain and would probably have made the one-way trip to Japan for medical treatment, before being shipped home.

I tossed the round after holding on to it for a short time to provide a great prop for a definite crazy war story! In combat everyone has their superstitions and I believed that I had been lucky, but there was no sense in tempting fate. That bullet might be a bad omen and I had already used up some of my 9 lives!

Chapter 37

Selecting a Primary and Secondary LZ

The ability to pick an excellent LZ while flying in a Huey at 2,000 feet and over 100 miles an hour took some time to develop. I managed to grasp it with some experience and having a good mentor like TL Lavender; however, it was an art that was not natural for humans while flying through the air. You knew the approximate area where you would be conducting your patrol, based on your topo map spread out on your legs and your briefing. You could see some LZs based on the map, but most of those were too large to use for an insertion. What you wanted was the LZ located close enough to your mission patrol area to prevent extra humping time and distance to get into your AO, but not too close. There was a specific sound that occurred from the helicopter(s) main rotor as the pilots slowed the Huey to touch down at a relatively slow speed. You did not want the enemy to hear that sound as you inserted, thus a small LZ that was surrounded by dense jungle as a sound barrier was ideal. The LZ also had to be small enough to get one Huey or two at the most into the LZ for a quick insertion. It should not be too big because of LZ Watchers. The main problem was that you were looking down on the LZ so you saw it as a two dimensional picture rather then a three dimensional objective. Once you picked your primary LZ, the chief pilot, who was also looking at the LZ but with very experienced eyes having safely completed hundreds of insertions, would make the final decision for a yay or nay. Some of the reasons that LZs were not approved was that the pilot(s) would see objects like trees too close that the main rotor could strike them, or tree stumps, termite mounds, and/or an irregular surface that could cause the helicopter to strike the object or the ground with the tail rotor. The tail rotor on a Huey was its Achilles' heel! To understand the process, you had to have landed in a Huey from a forward speed of a 100 + mph to almost a dead stop as the Huey settled down into the LZ. The process of slowing the Huey required the pitch of the main blade to be angled upwards at the front of the rotation of the main rotor, which then caused the tail of the Huey to be moved down. Basically the Huey in flight was like a giant spinning gyroscope that if you applied force on one side the other side would react in the opposite direction with equal force. There's a physics formula for it, but it was not important for a Lurp to understand, just the pilots. If you looked at a Huey sitting on the pad you would see an extended, curved rod approximately 1.5 inches in diameter approximately 3 feet long, that was attached to the tail of Huey, just below the tail rotor, and extending down toward the ground, but terminated about 4 inches from the pad/ground. It was called the STINGER by the Huey crew and it was there to prevent the tail/tail rotor from striking the ground as the pilot pulled a lot of pitch on the main rotor, to rapidly slow the Huey for an insertion. In our mode of work, if the pilot flying the helicopter struck the stinger on the ground during a fast and hard landing, that pilot bought a case of beer for the Huey crew! The tail strike was dangerous for the helicopter's crew and could be damaging to the airframe of the Huey. For a non-helicopter pilot, it would be like parking a car a little too fast and striking the parking curb with the front wheels. Embarrassing and it could also cause damage to the front wheels/alignment. The near perfect landing was for the Huey to come in fast at tree top level, pull pitch and have the Huey settle down on the LZ using the cushion of air caused by the main rotor as a buffer. It was a beautiful ballet of a skilled pilot and his Huey in perfect form and synchronization. Of course war was not a ballet theater and Murphy was always there to throw a wrench into the insertion. The primary problems were caused by the terrain and what looked good at 2,000 feet was not what was actually there on that particular LZ, so the Huey pilots had to adjust literally "on the fly", and it had to be right the first time!

For the six Lurps sitting untethered in the left and right doors of the Huey, they were along for the ride and what a hell of a ride it was. Flying at 100 + miles an hour at tree top level or sometimes below tree top level, just flying around the taller trees, it was the most exciting and dangerous roller coaster ride you could ever take. You were 100 percent committed to the skills and experience of your pilot and the crew and if they made a mistake everyone suffered the consequences. Once the helicopter flared and begin to slow down for the rapid descent into the LZ, it was game time for the Lurps and the serious shit began, while your heart spun up for the unknown events that were about to occur! There was also a dramatic change in the sounds that were around you. When flying in a Huey at fairly fast forward speed, all you hear is the whine of the main rotor and the air rushing by, but as you descend into the LZ all hell breaks loose because of the sounds that are generated. First that 48 foot main rotor is striking the air at a steep angle, creating a very fast and loud whopping sound as the main rotor blades are biting into the air at an increased pitch. When Huey settles down near the ground you get the additional sounds of the rapidly disturbed cushion of air moving downward, striking the surface you're about to land on and causing a lot of additional sounds including the roar of the turbine. Additionally there might be large amounts of debris flying into the air depending on the terrain and the season (dry or monsoons). It was organized chaos created by sounds and shit flying around you and the Huey, but it was game time and you had to make the decision as a "go" or a "no go!"

One of many "OH SHIT" moments for the Lurps as the Huey settled down onto the LZ was that you would hear the snap snap snap of what sounded like automatic rifle rounds passing close by your head and you were frantically looking for the enemy who was firing at you. The problem was that the door gunner on your side of the Huey was not firing back at the enemy and even with his helmet on he would certainly have heard or seen a weapon being fired at the Huey. The Huey gunners were known for having a very light touch on the trigger of their aircraft-modified and mounted M-60 machine gun they were sitting or crouching behind. They were truly "The Quick or the Dead!" So in a millisecond you had to decide what the hell was that snapping noise and then you remembered that it was the dry season and those snapping sounds were caused by debris, primarily dried leaves, being struck by the high speed leading edge of the two main rotor blades. Of course in that millisecond the bird had landed and it was time for the TL to make a decision to un-ass the Huey or call for the pilot, by signaling to the door gunner, to abort the landing. Normally you just went for it and quickly exited the Huey by stepping off the skid onto the ground and followed by the rest of the team.

Another type of insertion that really increased your pucker factor was jumping off the Huey struts into a swampy or visible water on the surface, although the jump was actually just stepping off the strut like exiting the door of an aircraft on a parachute jump. Normally the helicopter was hovering around 5 +feet, depending on the terrain and obstacles. Again this was choreographed because three heavily loaded Lurps standing on the right or left strut and three similar heavily loaded Lurps standing on the opposite strut created a balance issue for the pilot/Huey. If you remember the gyroscope analogy and it being perfectly balanced in the air, then approximately 700 pounds (three Lurps and their gear) all stepping off the right strut at the same time, leaves 700 pounds still on the left strut and the gyroscope/ helicopter naturally dips to the left because of that extra weight on the left side. The pilot has to anticipate this and must be prepared for this, because he has milliseconds to respond and the controls on the Huey have about a one second response delay. That is why it was so important for all six Lurps to step off the struts at the same time. I'm not sure we ever got it perfect, but no Hueys every crashed during our insertions.

What caused the main pucker factor in a waterborne insertion was that it was known that the enemy would place vertically, long (3-5 feet), fire hardened, sharpened, bamboo stakes in those swampy areas primarily to prevent helicopters from landing. They especially liked to place them where there were tall grasses/reeds so that the helicopter crew would not see them until it was too late and they would pierce the bottom of the Huey/fuel tanks or strike that vulnerable tail rotor. A cheap but effective anti-helicopter landing prevention method and sometimes a silent anti-aircraft weapon that could bring down or at least wound a helicopter and maybe some of its crew. This was a typical technique/or mentality for guerilla warfare and it was effectively employed by the enemy.

My team and I had at least two waterborne insertions, not because we purposely chose them, but because they were the only LZs within range of our patrol area. This was very typical for the areas along the Cambodian border and some parts of War Zone D.

On the first waterborne insertion the helicopter got us as close to the tree line as possible, but had to hover approximately 5 feet above the reeds and tall grass because of possible unknown obstructions hidden in the reeds and tall grasses, such as long sharpened bamboo stakes in our thoughts or tree stumps in the thoughts of the Huey crew! As I stepped off the strut and the rest of the team followed, I half waited for the pain of a long bamboo stake driving through my crotch and up into my gut, assisted by gravity and around 250 pounds of human flesh and gear falling to the earth. Nothing happened to me or the rest of the team, but we were now approximately up to our waists in water, thick reeds and grass with all of that weight on our backs and shoulders. It took a few minutes for all of us to waddle our way to the solid ground during which time we were very vulnerable for an attack. Why an attack probably never happened was that the enemy thought that no sane, regular infantry grunts would try to use it as an LZ, because of all the issues/terrain features they would have had to overcome. Obviously they initially didn't know about Lurp teams and that we normally did a lot of unusual things to keep the enemy off guard while they tried to ascertain if we were in their area and where we were! Xin Loi Charlie.

On the second waterborne insertion, which occurred near the Cambodian border, it was a similar situation but enhanced by the

Pacific Ocean tides that influenced the height of the water along the large rivers even though the ocean was nearly 100 miles away. The tides actually caused the rivers to flow slower into the ocean and thus rise in height. You learned never to underestimate the power of nature, especially the ocean.

As the Huey hovered and we prepared to to step off the struts, we/I thought the water was approximately 3 feet deep based on the area I was observing as we came in for the insertion. I stepped off the strut as did the rest of the team and we all literally hit the water with a splash, feet first as the beginning of a good PLF (parachute landing fall). It was not as I had anticipated, so when I sank past my knees and kept on sinking, I was beginning to wonder how deep the water actually was? Past my waist and still sinking I begin to worry about all of my equipment getting wet and then the light went on and I begin to worry about going in over my head and still sinking. It was very apparent by this time that I could be in trouble and trying to jettison all of my gear, especially my pack would be very difficult and time consuming. Our packs were partially sealed so there was captured air in them but not enough to float it, so in essence it became dead weight once it submerged. I kept sinking and at the upper chest area, my feet finally struck something solid on the bottom of the jungle pool. At this time most of my gear was under water except for the top of my pack/the radio and my M-16 that I had instinctively raised above my head when I hit the water. I had time to look around and noticed that most of the team was only in waist deep water and they were headed for the solid ground and safety of the jungle vegetation. Just my damn luck and affinity for finding submerged artillery shell holes on an insertion! I was the last to make it to the solid ground and as I exited the water, I must have looked like a wet, camouflaged dog coming out of the water. Unfortunately, I didn't have the ability to shake off the water and besides it would have made too much noise for such a small action and of short duration. I entered the wait and listen perimeter that the ATL had already established. Several of my team members had a slight smile on their camouflaged faces which I understood as a "no slack due" moment even for the TL. We waited and drained off the water for approximately 10 minutes, after which it was Charlie Mike (continue mission) and we moved out on our recon mission.

That particular mission had us in water for three days including one night where we all slept in water about 2 inches deep near our heads having our upper bodies propped up on our packs, but much deeper water for our lower bodies and our feet. During that mission some kind of microscopic bug got in my left ear drum, probably assisted by the multitude of ear damage and at least one ruptured ear drum caused by large explosions, such as claymore mines exploding 10 feet away.

When I returned after the mission was completed I went to the hospital and told the medic/nurse of my problem. His solution was to rinse my ear out with cold water (like sticking an ice pick in my ear drum) and sending me on my way with some SPCs, essentially aspirin. A couple of hours later I returned in extreme pain with the ear drum being so sensitive that I could not talk because the vibrations felt like the ice pick had returned to finish off my ear drum. This time I asked for a doctor, and as soon as he examined my left ear he realized I had an acute infection on the ear drum. He first dripped liquid morphine into and over my ear drum to kill most of the pain (I could have kissed him for that pain relief) and then he prescribed some heavy duty antibiotics to kill the (probable) bacteria that was causing the infection. It took at least three days to completely kill the bacteria and for the pain to completely subside. Charlie Bacteria one point; Ed the Lurp no points, but still in the game! Xin Loi GI.

Chapter 38

Top Secret Intelligence/Need to Know

Before and after the Tet Offensive we were given a lot of Bomb Damage Assessment (BDA) missions. Essentially HQ at II Field Force requested a recon of a certain aerial bombing mission. Company F would send a Lurp team to see what type of damage had been inflicted on the enemy and their positions. Primarily it was to check on BDA caused by B-52 bombers who were dropping 1,000 pound bombs with delayed fuses onto suspect enemy concentrations or enemy complexes. A 1,000 pound bomb with a one second delayed fuse would penetrate the jungle floor probably 8-10 feet before it exploded. This penetration and subsequent underground explosion was supposed to cause any underground bunkers or tunnels to collapse from the pressure wave generated by the bomb.

The first thing you noticed on a BDA from a B-52 bombing mission was mass destruction at ground level. At approximately 100 m from the actual impact zone you would start to find large chunks of red clay with the stumps of trees and damaged bushes sticking out of them. When I say large, I mean about the size of a VW bug, sometimes smaller and sometimes a little larger. It depended on the terrain and the type of tree cover that the bombs fell in. As you got closer to the epicenter of where this particular bomb impacted, you would see that there weren't any trees standing. It was essentially an open area devoid of anything standing probably above 4-6 feet. This was caused by the tremendous blast force/high pressure wall of super heated air that emanated from the 800+ pounds of liquid explosive contained inside the bomb. If that wasn't enough, the casing of the bomb was made from steel and when the explosion occurred that produced hundreds of pieces of high-speed steel, flying through the air. It would have been like a spinning saw blade flying through the air and cutting through anything in its path.

When we got to the actual impact location, we had to crawl on our hands and knees to the edge of the crater. When I say crater I mean a hole in the ground approximately 12 feet deep by 75 feet wide with the next bomb impact maybe 30 meters from the previous bomb strike. There would be this continuation of bomb craters in pretty much a straight line for approximately a quarter of a mile. It was one hell of a long strip of destroyed jungle with nothing much of anything alive near these craters. And since it was normally a three-aircraft bombing mission, you had three of these parallel strips of destruction running through the jungle.

In theory it probably looked like a great idea, but in fact it didn't quite work that way. First and foremost was the fact that these were dumb bombs with no guidance system. Once they dropped from the belly of the B-52 only the laws of physics guided them in. Secondly the B-52s were dropping those bombs from an altitude of more then 20,000 feet. They normally flew in a three-aircraft flight with the bombers arranged in an echelon position so as not to get in the way of the other aircrafts' bombs and to produce a wide area of destruction. Essentially it was carpet bombing like they used in the Second World War. This type of bombing was very destructive to a city, but not so much in an open jungle environment.

The bombing runs by the B-52s were called Arc Lights in Vietnam ground pounder slang, because at night you would see this bluish white light in the sky followed by a tremendous rumble of the sound of large multiple bombs exploding in a long chain. If you were close enough, you could also feel the ground shake and vibrate under you. Initially when they started using Arc Lights in Vietnam the SOP was that they could not be dropped within 10,000 m of friendly troops, then it got reduced to 5,000 m. During and after Khe Sahn it was 1,000 meters. The primary reason being that the shock waves caused by the massive explosions could kill or injure any human (friendly or enemy) near the target area.

All of these B-52 bombing sorties were Top Secret Missions and known only to a few Generals in the US Command Structure in South Vietnam. I believe the B-52s were flying from Thailand or Guam, but since it was a secret no one knew for sure. It also was a 24 hour delay to order a B-52 strike by troops on the ground, including Lurp teams with eyes on the enemy. Which meant if you observed a large enemy troop concentration, but they were on the move, a B-52 strike wasn't going to work, because of the fact that the enemy could move a long distance in 24 hours. Static troops or troops in a bunker complex would be a different story and a prime target for a B-52 Arc Light!

My team along with other teams were given warning orders for DBAs in the dry season of 1968. These Arc Lights were after the Tet Offensive and were being used to clean out any troop concentrations that stayed after the offensive was over. They were in the area of War Zone D, C and the Iron Triangle.

As our protocol required, the team leaders had to complete an aerial overfly of their recon area to pick primary and secondary LZs. We lifted off from our company area helicopter pads in one of the UH1D insertion ships to conduct the selection of LZs. It was around 0900 hours on a clear sunny morning with unlimited visibility and a perfect day for an over flight. We normally conducted the over flights from an altitude of around 2,000 AGL. This was high enough to make the enemy think that it was just one of the thousands of Hueys flying around in the skies of Vietnam on any given day. It was also low enough that we had a good view of the terrain and could easily pick out medium and even some small LZs from that altitude. We were in the area where previous Arc Lights had already occurred, because you see the ugly parallel scars on the jungle surface from those previous strikes. The area we were to conduct the BDAs in was to the west of the previous strikes and closer to the Cambodian border. At the time we didn't pick up on the fact that there weren't any new bomb strikes in that area. Also, our Warning Order was not very specific about the date we would actually be inserted.

We were about halfway done with our over flights and I was looking out and down the port side of the Huey searching for one particular opening that was showing on our topo maps. We were flying in a north to south direction. All of a sudden the jungle under the Huey just exploded and turned into a mass of boiling dust and flying debris. A short second later we got hit with the shock waves and the helicopter started bouncing up and down while twisting right and left, like we had just hit a real bad area of head winds and up drafts, but this was worse than the norm! I started to tell the pilot that we had a problem when I heard him say through the speakers in the flight helmets we were wearing, "Oh Fuck!" This was an indication to me and everyone else that we had a problem and it was something unexpected for the flight crew. The chief pilot did a hard left banking turn and put the nose down on the Huey to pick up speed. We could feel the helicopter picking up a lot of speed by the vibrations in the frame of the bird. By that time, I had a lot of hours of flight time in Hueys because of insertions, extractions, and doing over flights. This was probably the fastest I had ever flown in a Huey and the pilot was not backing off. After probably a minute to two minutes of flight time we leveled out and slowed our speed back to the normal flight speed. The pilot turned the Huey back to the right so that we were flying parallel and probably 5 + klicks from where we had been minutes before. We could see the approximate area that had exploded under us but it was still covered in clouds of dust and with some of it rising above our flight altitude. We also caught the glint and then saw three B-52s flying at a high altitude to the south and directly in line from the bombing run.

It was apparent to everyone that we had just flown through a B-52 Arc Light bombing run and had somehow managed not to get hit by a 1,000 pound bomb(s) which even if it hadn't exploded, would have shattered the Huey into match stick size pieces of aluminum along with its passengers. I believe each B-52 dropped 50 x 1,000 pound bombs, multiplied by 3 comes to a grand total of 150 x 1,000 pounders dropping down to the ground at terminal velocity! Based on the fact that the bombs exploded behind, under and to the front of the flight path of our Huey, suggests that by a very slim margin the bombs fell just behind the Huey but at a steep angle because of the altitude they were dropped from. I would think that if we had been looking to the rear of the Huey, we would have probably seen the mass of falling bombs pass just behind our flight path! It had to have been by the smallest of margins that the bombs missed us and pure luck that the Huey was at that specific location at that specific time. We had made several north and south parallel passes over the area as other team leaders picked their insertion LZs and had probably been flying in the general area for approximately 20 minutes.

As we flew back to our base, the pilots were using a lot of MF profanity in regards to the Air Force and those B-52 bombers. All of the Lurps on board were in agreement with their comments. It was also obvious to all of the Lurp team leaders that the pilots had not received any info as to a restricted air space on a given day at these coordinates! I guess it was a "need to know" basis and we didn't qualify for that US Government Security Rating! It was only later that I started to think about the totality of the incident. I was wondering if I, along with everyone else on board would have been listed as, "MIA, KIA or just we don't fricken know what happened to the Huey. At this time it is late for its scheduled return, NFD!"

It was also obvious to me that after being hit by a 1,000 pound bomb at 2,000 feet altitude and even it didn't explode, our body parts along with parts from the helicopter would have been spread over a large area directly where the bombs exploded. The chance of recovering any human body parts or helicopter parts would have been almost nil! Besides any body/body parts, friendly or enemy were just another meal for the creatures and insects on the jungle floor. Xin Loi GI!

This Arc Light incident was just another example of how things can go wrong in a very active War Zone. As I have previously mentioned, a Lurp's chances of getting killed by "friendly fire" instead of "enemy fire" were very high!

Several weeks later we were doing recon missions to the south and many clicks from where the original BDAs had been conducted. After the BDA was completed we usually continued on with a recon mission. You could usually do a BDA in a day or less, because the bombs either hit something or just made big holes in the jungle. The latter was generally what we saw. I don't know how many millions it cost for those B-52 bombers to fly in, drop their bombs and return to their base, but I would guess that it was a multi-million dollar operation if you included all of the support units such as mid-air refueling etc. It was the most expensive form of farming I ever knew of, because they normally just destroyed a large area of jungle that could now be cultivated for rice etc.

We were inserted into an LZ near a river junction of the Son Be and another smaller river. There was a village at that junction on the northeast side of the river junction.

This was one of those free fire zones/no fire zone areas depending on what time of the day it was if you could shoot someone or let them pass. Usually from 1800 hours to 0600 hours it would be a free fire zone where anything/anyone moving through the jungle or on a river would be fair game. That is of course that they had to look like an enemy soldier wearing combat gear. You wouldn't fire up a sampan that had women and children in it, but you would probably fire up a sampan loaded with men wearing military type clothing and obvious military gear, like rucksacks, web gear and of course weapons like a AK-47. Of course some of the Vietnamese ranger units would use this technique to do an insertion, but they normally would have American advisers with them. Either way you had to have your head screwed on properly to make the right decisions about initiating contact or letting them pass.

These areas were a pain in the butt for Lurp teams, because you didn't want to get spotted and compromised by some Vietnamese farmer out in his fields. The problem was that you didn't know if he was a friendly farmer by day and a VC at night. It was assumed that if you were compromised by a Vietnamese civilian, your location would eventually be given to the VC and NVA in the area. It meant that you had to pack up and move out quickly and quietly so that if the enemy were warned, you wouldn't be where you had last been seen. The enemy also liked to use mortars in those open areas around the fields, because they didn't have to get close to attack you and they were damn good with their mortars.

We had a clean insertion and moved off the LZ in an easterly direction far away from the river so as not to be spotted by anyone using the river as their transportation route. We had only moved several hundred meters when we ran into a pineapple growing area that also had sugar cane growing around its perimeter. We circled south around the small growing area that was fairly clear of brush and small trees and then northeast back to our original azimuth. It was a testament to the abilities of the Vietnamese farmers who planted the pineapple and sugar cane. I didn't even know that they could grow pineapple in Vietnam. We had over flown that area and never saw anything from the air, because if we had I would have avoided that area and picked a different area for our insertion LZ.

After circling around the growing area and near the east edge we spotted a small hooch (8' x 10') made from bamboo trees and palm frawns. It was typical for this area and it appeared to be abandoned. We did a quick recon and confirmed our suspicions that it was a temporary shelter, probably for the farmer when he was working in the growing area. It did, however, appear to have been recently used and it made me think that the farmer might have been here working, but when he heard the helicopter land near by he knew American soldiers were in the area. He had moved because he didn't want to meet up with them.

We continued on for another 50 meters and then moved north toward the river to see if we could find a location where we could have excellent cover and concealment and still have a good observation of the area. We had moved only about 30 meters when we found a near perfect area that was slightly raised and gave us a view of the river junction and a partial view of the south end of the village near the junction. It had excellent overhead cover and ground concealment for the team. It also allowed us to partially see the growing area, especially the hooch. On any other recon mission in a free fire zone, I would not have set up our observation point that close to a hooch, because it could be an indication that there was a lot of enemy activity in the area; however, our primary mission was to observe the river traffic to see if the B-52 bombings pushed any enemy troops and equipment to this area to prevent being hit by the bombs. Thus you had to compromise on your position so that you could complete the mission. It just meant that we had to keep some eyes on the hooch and growing area 24/7. There weren't any trails leading to it so apparently who ever was growing the pineapples and sugar cane must have come in via a sampan to work their fields.

We thought this also had excellent potential for us to eat some of the local fruit/pineapple and sugar cane, to supplement our lurp rations. It started out that way, but by the end of the second day we all had gastric problems because we had liberated several of the green pineapples from different locations in the growing area and had all eaten pieces of them. They weren't exactly sweet but they weren't sour either. We also had taken some sugar cane from various locations and it was definitely sweet to chew on once we pealed off the bark. My suspicions were that the green pineapple worked like a laxative, because by the end of the second day on the recon site all had made multiple dashes to the bushes behind our observation area. We had to dig a hole and deposit copious amounts of liquid crap into the holes, wipe, cover the hole to prevent any odor from indicating there were humans/GIs in the area and return to our recon position. There was still grumbling in your stomach as a warning that you might have to make a return trip to complete another bombing mission. I bet that Uncle Ho would have laughed his ass off at the idea of dumb GIs eating green pineapples and receiving the wrath of Vietnamese revenge for taking the fruit and not paying for it!

The routine for activity on the river worked like clockwork. From 1800 hours to 0600 hours the river was empty, not a thing moved over it. At exactly 0600 hours it was rush hour traffic and a large number of sampans, big and small were on the Song Be and some coming from the smaller river to the north. The majority were farmers moving vegetables and rice down the river toward the bigger towns and ultimately to Saigon if they were going that far. Most were man-power operated but a few of the larger ones had some type of motor on them to power the sampan.

On the morning of the third day at 0600 hours something radically changed. There wasn't a sampan on the river, nor at 0615, 0630 or 0645. It didn't take a genius or a Lurp to figure out that something was up. My initial thought was that we had been compromised and that all sampans were avoiding this area, I immediately knew that couldn't be the case. These were farmers and all they cared about was getting their crops to the market!

I radioed in to our HQ-TOC, and advised them of the above information. At that time the C&C ship came on the air and told me to move out to a secondary LZ to be extracted. I was surprised to hear the C&C ship on the air, because I didn't have any indication that teams were being inserted or extracted. I advised the LT on the C&C that I had an excellent observation point and requested to stay at least one more night. I was advised that this was an order and to be on the LZ in 15 minutes. I acknowledged the order and advised the team to roll up their claymores and prepare for an extraction.

It actually took us about 30 minutes to clear the recon site and march to the secondary LZ which was several 100 meters to the south. We extracted without incident and flew back to our company area. In the debriefing we were advised that the area we were in was going to be hit with a B-52 Arc Light bombing strike later that day. Well it was obvious to us that everyone knew about this strike, especially all of the locals and they had left the area. So our question to the officer at the debriefing was how in the hell did the Vietnamese farmers and their neighbors know about a B-52 strike coming in since this was all rated as TOP SECRET by the Army. They advised us that the district chief was notified 24 hours prior about bombing to occur in the area. It was then passed on to the village chiefs and eventually to all of the Vietnamese living in the general area. So basically everyone in the general area, including the enemy knew when and where a B-52 strike was going to occur. Anything of value, including a lot of their most cherished equipment and supplies would be moved out of the area of the strike. If you ever saw the VC and NVA on the move they would be loaded down with their gear and equipment. You would liken it to an ant hill where they could move a whole damn insect 5 times their size very quickly and efficiently because of team work.

I was thinking, What the Fuck, I along with other TLs and a helicopter crew almost got blown out of the air by a B-52 strike that we weren't advised of because of it being a Top Secret Mission; however, every Vietnamese farmer (VC relatives) and their families knew about a Top Secret B-52 strike 24 hours in advance! That was one hell of a way to fight a war, especially a guerilla war! Fricken politics in a war zone is a back breaker for the GIs on the ground! Xin Loi GI!

Chapter 39

An Arc Light that Hit a Target

Several weeks later my team was assigned a mission about 5 klicks to the east of the Cambodian border to catch any NVA trying to cross over the border. We had been inserted around 1630 hours. We had a canal several hundred meters to the north of our LZ and that was what we were going to set up on as both an observation point and as a possible ambush site. That depended on the timing and whether the number of enemy soldiers was small enough for our 6 man recon team to initiate contact. We found a great site with some heavy brush around us for concealment but with double canopy overhead to protect us from the sun and rain. The canal ran basically west to east and we were situated about 10 meters from the south bank of the canal. The canal, approximately 10 meters wide, had water in it and would have allowed a small sampan to use it to ferry enemy supplies east from the border. It also had a well-used trail on top of the north bank of the canal, so we actually had two excellent locations to observe for enemy movement.

The first night was uneventful but we did see and hear activity to the northwest of our position. It was mainly an Arc Light strike probably 20 klicks or more away and it had to be right on the border between Cambodia and South Vietnam. After a 100 percent stand too at sunrise we got back into our regular routine of one Lurp on guard duty and the other five members relaxing, sleeping or eating. Around 1000 hours I had to pee so I took my M-16 which had two 20-round magazines attached. One in the magazine well and one taped upside down so that I could remove the magazine that was empty and quickly insert the other magazine with a total of 36 rounds in the two magazines. Again this was pounded into our heads, *per our Recondo School Training, that you never were further away from your weapon than you could reach!*

I crawled to the rear of our position and indicated to the team that I was going to take a leak. I then crawled out of the immediate perimeter may be 3 meters, but still behind the claymores that had been deployed for rear security. I wanted to make sure that the team members could see me and that I could see them in case things went to shit. There was a small tree where I had crawled to so I used it to pull myself up to a standing position so that I could pee on the trunk of the tree to prevent any noise of the actual urine hitting the dead leaves. The tree also provided additional cover for me and I could do the deed while still watching the team and the trail to my right. It is also easier to stand and pee when you're holding a rifle and you don't pee on yourself like you could if you were just kneeling. I shot the M-16 left handed but I'm actually right handed so I could do both actions fairly easy. I was about half way through taking care of business when I detected some movement on the trail to my right front area of vision. I immediately brought up my M-16 and came up on target, while still peeing. The movement was actually an NVA soldier in uniform carrying a backpack and with a walking stick in his right hand on the trail of the north bank of the canal. He was probably 30 meters from my location and he was walking east at a very fast pace. He was just coming out of a bamboo thicket that was alongside the trail when I locked on his chest. I don't know if he heard something but he slowed down and started to turn towards our position. I had a semi-clear shot at his chest and I squeezed off one round. The NVA immediately fell down like he had been hit with a hammer, but then he sprung right back, put both arms in the air and started yelling, "Chu Hoi, Chu Hoi!" He dropped his pack and came running toward our position. He had to cross the canal, which he splashed across with his hands in the air. The water in the canal was probably around 3 feet deep so he made it across without a problem. After firing at the NVA I moved directly back through the team area and was standing on our north perimeter where the NVA could see me. I was yelling "Dien Day, Dien Day", which means 'come here' in Vietnamese. He apparently understood me, because he came up the canal bank directly to me. I had him kneel down and another Lurp check him out to make sure he wasn't carrying any weapons on his person. I advised the rest of the team to keep an eye on the trail in case he was the point man for a larger group following him. His uniform was the North Vietnamese tan shirt, but instead of trousers he had on shorts and of course his Ho Chi Minh sandals. I guess that was their dry season uniform? He was probably in his early 20s, lean and in great physical condition. After the Lurp checked him out, we brought him into our perimeter. He was babbling in Vietnamese but none of us could understand what he was saying. He eventually produced several Chu Hoi pamphlets from his shorts pocket and showed them to us. I motioned to him that it was OK and that is when I noticed that he had blood running down his right upper arm and some blood in the palm of his right hand. I had another Lurp cover him and I checked out his wounds.

He had a clean .223 caliber bullet hole in the lower middle of the palm of his right hand. I then checked his upper right arm and found a small exit wound just above the elbow on the lower triceps area of the his right arm. I was confused how the bullet had moved from a dead center chest shot to a palm, arm and upper arm wound. I believed what happened was when I fired the round at his chest, he was just turning toward us and he was still on the edge of the bamboo thicket. Apparently, my round hit a bamboo branch and changed direction just enough to initially hit him in his right hand/palm, then it traveled up his arm and exiting above the elbow of his right arm. I remembered his right hand holding the walking stick, which was about even with the area of his chest that I had fired. He was very lucky because if my bullet had struck him in the chest he would have been dead. Or if it had hit any bone it would have probably tumbled and exited his upper arm leaving a very big exit wound. I guess the NVA also have the same Murphy Luck, about when you do or don't get your ticket punched!

He appeared to be in some pain as I examined his wound so I gave him a couple of pain pills we carried in our medical kits and he gulped them down without hesitation. I had given the enemy meds before, because once they are no longer a threat to us they are just humans playing for the other team.

We recovered his pack and it had two RPG rounds in it and a few miscellaneous clothing items. Not much for a hardcore NVA soldier.

I radioed in that we had taken a prisoner and he was wounded. I was advised to prepare for extraction. One of the other good things about this recon site was that there was an LZ about 50 mikes to the southwest of our position. We couldn't use it for an insertion because it was too close to the canal and trail, but it was perfect for an extraction. It took the team about 10 minutes to roll up their claymore mines and get loaded up. I handed off the PoW to another team member so that I could concentrate on getting us to the LZ in a safe manner. We reached the LZ in about 15 minutes of careful movement and waited near the edge of the LZ for the lift ship to come in and extract us. Right after we arrived the C&C ship was in rotation near our position and directed in the extraction ship. It was an easy extraction and we had the PoW sitting on the floor in the middle of the chopper with a Lurp watching him. He appeared to be rather excited and not scared, as I was sure that this was his first ride in a helicopter.

It was during the ride back that I noticed that my camo trousers were still unbuttoned from my peeing episode that had changed to an ambush episode in the blink of an eye. I casually buttoned up when no one was looking. You can't be a hard core TL if you're walking around with your dong hanging out!

We landed at our pad and were met by our Intel Sgt who took charge of the prisoner along with several soldiers including a Vietnamese interpreter. I advised them of his wounds and they immediately took him to the PoW camp where they had a Doctor to treat his wounds.

We did a quick debrief and then headed to our hooch to drop our gear and take a cold shower before getting something to eat and of course a cold beer or two! We were all in a great mood because we were out of the field early, we had captured a PoW and since he was alive, the team would get a 3 day in-country R&R at Vung Tau on the South China Sea.

Later that day our Intel Sgt told us what they had learned from NVA PoW. The PoW had been in a battalion (400 plus soldiers) of NVA soldiers that had marched all the way down on the Ho Chi Minh Trail from North Vietnam over several months of time. They had just crossed over the border from Cambodia into South Vietnam and had stopped at a hidden base camp to rest up before moving deeper into South Vietnam. During the first night, the base camp got hit by a very large air strike, probably the Arc Light we had observed our first night in our ambush site. The NVA was knocked unconscious and when he woke up it was daylight. He only saw three other NVA that were alive and the rest of the camp, his battalion and the camp workers were all gone/blown to hell. He believed that they had all died from the bombs because the base camp was completely destroyed and the other three NVA acted like they had concussion and could hardly walk. He decided to surrender and saw a lot of artillery flares far to the east of his position. He picked up what he could find of his own equipment and headed out toward the flares. Along the way he found some Chu Hoi pamphlets and picked them up to use as a way to make contact with the Americans. Fortunately for him he got shot/snatched by our team (1-3). He was lucky that he didn't have to walk all the way to a US Base and try to surrender without getting killed along the way by US troops, artillery or gunships as he walked along the trail.

Chapter 40

Viva Los Cambodia

To keep spun up and of course to keep the adrenalin flowing, some of the Lurps in Company F also flew in the "back seat/observer position" with our FAC. We would be part of the radio relay system when the teams were on missions too far out for the PRC-24 radios to transmit to a ground-based radio relay team at a fire support base. It was a good assignment because you got to see how the Air Force operated especially when the FAC was directing fighter-bombers in on a target that a Lurp team had discovered. Of course it could be boring just flying around but it gave you a real perspective of how difficult it was to locate a team on the ground in the dense jungle.

I was selected to ride in the back seat in OV-1 and it was the rainy season, so the weather was always on the pilot's mind when flying over the jungle in this little two seater aircraft with a small engine and wings compared to other fixed wing piston driven aircraft like a Sky Raider. It was your choice what you took with you on the flight, beside some food and water. On the first and only flight I got to fly with the FAC, I elected to take my full combat gear just like on a mission; however, some Lurps just took their M-16 and a bandolier of probably six magazines. I didn't like the feel of being out miles from any base camp/fire support base/air-field with only a rifle and some mags. I had been around long enough to know that shit happens and you should be prepared for the worst!

We took off from Bien Hoa Air Base around noon and headed northwest toward where the teams were operating along the Cambodian border and north of Cu Chi. It was a tough area for recon missions because there were a lot of water hazards like swamps and

228

canals coming out of Cambodia. Of course it was the perfect location for the enemy to cross over into South Vietnam, because they used the canals as small highways to transport their personnel and equipment on small to medium size sampans. The enemy also knew that there weren't a lot of GIs in the area just because of its location and difficult terrain. Of course it was also one of the best locations for Lurp teams to operate in, because they could set up ambushes on the small canals, which created a very target rich environment! The problem was that the teams needed communications with our company command, because a team could get into trouble very quickly with large numbers of NVA coming across from Cambodia.

It took us probably 20 plus minutes to get on station and relieve the other FAC that had been flying since probably around midnight. The pilot had already explained to me on the flight up, how he flew the mission and what to expect, so I was prepared for the mission. We flew somewhat of a figure 8 pattern over probably 20 miles long by 10 miles area, so that we could stay in communication with the various teams, but not compromise their positions.

The weather was typical for the monsoon season with various rain and wind storms passing through the area. Most of the storms for this area came from the west and south west off of the southern tip of the Vietnam and from across Southern Cambodia. This particular day the weather was coming in from primarily the south and unusually from the east. We continued to do our radio relay flight and it was starting to get dark. It was at this time that the pilot notified me that the weather was closing in from the east and that Bien Hoa Air Base was socked in. We needed to try flying south to miss being enveloped by the heavy rain and wind that was showing in the storm to our east and South East. To do this we would have to fly along and parallel to the Cambodian border. As we started to fly south the weather came in very fast and we were now blocked from flying east or southeast. To fly around and not through the approaching storm we were still in South Vietnam but right on the border with Cambodia. By now it was just about dark and the storm was right on our left wing. We were

229

getting some rain and a little buffeting from the wind. The Bird Dog is not an all weather aircraft and certainly not made for high winds that could be generated by a monsoon storm. The pilot came over my helmet speakers and calmly said, "Well I didn't want to have to do this but were going to have to fly in Cambodian air space to get around this storm!" Of course I wasn't a seasoned pilot, but I understood that flying over Cambodia at around three thousand feet in a little tail dragger aircraft was not an ideal situation! He made a banking right turn and within just a few seconds we were in Cambodian airspace. He said he was going to try and circle to the right and up a few miles and then hopefully we would be past this regional storm and we could cross back over into South Vietnam airspace.

We had all heard about the numerous anti-aircraft guns in Cambodia which they called Triple A. I really didn't think it would be a problem now because we were on the edge of the storm and it was dark. About that time I observed this orange dot coming up from the dark jungle floor below and to the right front of the starboard wing. I started to tell the pilot about it as it passed by within 50+ meters to our right front. It now appeared to be about the size of a glowing orange soft ball. The pilot said, "Oh Shit, this is no place for a thin skinned aircraft to be", and did a hard bank to the left doing an 180 degree turn in a very short time period. I said, "What the hell was that?" He replied, "A 37 mm anti-aircraft gun!" Now I wasn't an experienced combat pilot, but I had seen pictures of 37 mm anti-aircraft guns and I knew from experience that it was a lot bigger round then a 20 mm, which was large in my mind. So one hit from a 37 mm round would probably have blown parts off this aircraft and we would have been heading for the ground in an unplanned landing, in Cambodia. Once we completed the turn and were on a due south compass heading. I started to see what were basically a long line of lights and I figured out that they were campfires, hundreds and probably thousands of them running parallel and probably not more than 5 miles inside Cambodia. I was amazed at the numbers I saw and knew that around each one of those campfires was a group of NVA soldiers. I jokingly told the pilot I would like to call in multiple B-52 bomber strikes on the campfire and he said, "Wouldn't we all!" We both knew that was forbidden according to the rules of this war, which really sucked. I think you could have wiped out several divisions of NVA and all of their equipment in a continuous bombing raid for about 24 hours. Sometimes the rules of war just flat out SUCK!

I'm quite certain that some of those troop formations were shooting large caliber weapons at us in our blacked out flying state, like 12.7 mm Russian and Chinese heavy machine guns, but I didn't see any tracers near our flight path. We continued south and the pilot said that we would have to continue to fly south in Cambodia until we were south and west of Saigon and then circled in behind the storm. If necessary land at Tan Sa Nout Airbase or back to Bien Hoa Airbase. I would estimate it took us nearly an hour to circle around the storm while flying in Cambodian Air Space but we finally passed the southern tip of the storm and turned back into South Vietnam Airspace. We both took a sigh of relief that we made it back without getting shot down in Cambodia. Even if we had survived a crash at night in this little tail dragger, the chances of us making it out of Cambodia were about one in a million and we both knew that. Of course some NVA soldier might have been very happy and rich because all Lurps that could be taken alive as a PoW's had a bounty on their head. I would guess the FAC pilots also had a nice bounty. You could think of it as a two-fir win by some lucky NVA. Of course I had along time ago made a pact with my other team members that we would not be taken alive by the NVA, so I'm not sure if the pilot ever knew that he was also included as a team member in that pact!

When I finally made it back to Company F after landing at Bien Hoa Airbase, I told all of the Lurps in 1st Platoon about my little adventure. I reiterated the fact that they should be taking a full combat load with them while flying as an observer on a OV-1 aircraft. They all agreed, passed me a cold beer as I was heating up water for a Lurp ration while at the rear of 1st Platoon's barracks, since I had missed supper in the mess hall!

Chapter 41

The Boom Boom Girls of Bien Hoa

If you read news reports about Vietnam you would occasionally find in-depth reports by allegedly experienced war correspondents about what the entire war experience was like on the ground. One of the subjects that the journalists would express surprise and concern over was the number of whore houses in any city of almost any size. Of course it was inherently and negatively directed at the thousands of GIs who visited those houses to obtain the service they were intended for. If the truth was known, a lot of those male journalists also got their wick dipped in one of the houses albeit a more expensive and refined establishment!

If you wanted to analyze the social reality this event presented, it was still pretty simple. You had a young man 18-22 years of age, horny as hell, who was pumped up with testosterone and bravado, who probably had just come in from the field and had been in numerous fire fights and had friends killed or wounded. He was there in the Boom Boom House to unwind and relax after having his internal psyche spring wound extremely tight from combat and the luxurious use of adrenaline. His attitude was probably somewhere between, scared as shit (not showing of course) and fuck it, tomorrow I may die! He was looking at a young, beautiful, exotic looking Vietnamese woman who had all the right attributes and was there for your pleasure. It didn't take a PhD recipient to figure out what was going to occur.

To me a whore house/Boom Boom House in Vietnam was just another part of the war environment for GIs. It was also part of the micro-economy for each city where the houses sprang up. The house could be anything from an old French villa converted to a whore house with a bar and bar maids, which were of course the most expensive establishments, but also had the most beautiful young Vietnamese women. Or it could be a falling down shack with built in wooden bunks, a mattress and a thin sexually-soiled curtain covering the front of the bunk and curtains on each end of the line of bunks. Kind of like a boy scout camp housing unit, but I assure you there weren't any boy scouts, at least active at that time, visiting those whore houses!

The typical Boom Boom/Whore House (middle to upper class) would be a medium sized building, normally an old French building of stone and stucco. The house had lot of rooms converted to bedrooms; however, no GI ever slept while he was in the room.

It had a fairly large open area off the entry way and that is where the girls would be on parade in their best DIU. I would say the average age was probably 20 years old, but some might be younger and some were definitely older. I never saw any coercion by the Madam/Mamasan of the girls and most appeared to be happy or at least OK with the business they were involved in. I don't know what the community they lived in thought of them, because I didn't speak Vietnamese; however, for most of the Boom Boom Girls, it was the economics that attracted them to this line of work. There was also that slim hope by the girls that some young GI would fall in love with them, marry them and take them back to the USA. It did happen on rare occasions, so I guess hope for them was a good thing.

A typical visit went like this. You would be escorted into the large room where all the girls were standing against a wall or moving around the room. Mamasan would tell you in broken English, "You pick girl." The price would be negotiated but most of the better houses had a fixed price, say 20,000 Vietnamese Pia ($20 in military pay certificate, MPC). That was for straight up sex that lasted somewhere between 2 minutes and 10 minutes, depending on the GI's sexual state (horny or not) and how well the girl performed. The proverbial "Short Time" which was usually around 10 minutes max, or the "Long Time" which could extend out to 20 to 30 minutes max! It was understood by most every GI that if you went past the allotted Short

Time Sex (unwritten time limit), you would be expected to pay more to Mamasan or at least give the girl a tip while not in the presence of Mamasan. Mamasan was operating a business that was all about making money and you damn well better not mess up her program.

The girl you picked came and took you to one of the rooms. She got undressed and laid down on the mattress on her back. The GI did the same and usually mounted up. There was very little conversation and that was more for breaking any tension between the Boom Boom Girl and the GI. From a fly on the wall perspective it was a very mechanical/almost rehearsed scene by the girls and depending on the experience of the GI it could be a short time or a long time. Normally a joyous Short Time Experience!

Most GIs had been schooled about various venereal diseases that some of the girls carried, most likely contracted from some stupid GI that was too damn lazy to put on a condom prior to having sex. I believed the stories and saw first hand (a Lurp who contracted the Black Dick/gonorrhea, I believe) what could happen if you were stupid and didn't wear your rain coat!

I personally used whore houses as a form of unwinding that psyche steel spring that was wrapped damn tight by the time I completed a Lurp Mission. Sex has a way of assisting in the unwinding of the spring, of course lubricated with alcohol and, for some, drugs.

I visited most types of whore houses from the near upper class to using a sandbag as a mattress and getting it on with a Bom Bom Girl while out on a sandbag detail. A Vietnamese guy just drove up on a small motorcycle and seeing that I was in charge of the detail they approached me. A quick conversation, mainly about the price, 10,000 Pia ($10), since I wouldn't be enjoying the obeisance of the House and the girl was somewhat used! Not to be a complete prima donna, we went behind some trees to complete the quick act. I have to say I found it to be one of the better uses of sandbags while in Vietnam and the sex was surprisingly good.

Of course, I don't want to promote the idea that these were exotic adventures by young men and women, because they weren't. They were usually dirty, funky smelling establishments that cared nothing about hygiene for the girls or the GIs. They were there to collect your money and it was up to you to find the pleasure past the stink and nasty environment.

A really funny sexual event occurred outside of a regular whore house. Most of Team 1-3 including me and some other Lurps from 1st Platoon all met at a bar in downtown Bien Hoa. We were all drinking beer and about half wasted. We had bar girls hovering around us or sitting with us, asking us to buy them a Saigon Tea (a very weak tea in a small glass). The entire purpose of the Saigon Tea was to get the GIs to spend money on the tea and thus increase the profit margin of the bar. Of course there was always some kind of nefarious sexual events occurring in the bar, even though it was not a whore house per se. Unbeknownst to all of the Lurps, one of our team members – his name removed to protect the guilty – had negotiated a hand job from one of the Saigon Tea Girls who had extended her business abilities. We were all drinking and laughing and having a great time when all of a sudden, the un-named male yelled out, "Bloody Hell, she shot it into my boonie hat!" The interpretation being that as he ejaculated into what he thought was her warm hands while we were all sitting around this long wooden table, what she had done was to calmly reach over and secure his boonie hat and, when the cannon fired, the round actually landed inside his inverted Lurp hat, AO! This was obviously not her first Rodeo! Funny shit and not unusual for a bar in Bien Hoa. Xin Loi GI.

Chapter 42

Sometimes, you're the HUNTER and sometimes, you're the HUNTED

Team 1-3 got a warning order on November 28, 1968 for a heavy team mission. I, along with my ATL, Sgt Bolt, and several other TLs did our over flights to pick our primary and secondary LZs. There was some intelligence that indicated that the NVA were moving into the area "In Force!" The AO we were to recon was near the Cambodian border. We expected to find NVA who would easily cross over from Cambodia to conduct assaults on US and Allied bases and troops. They would be rested, heavily armed and spoiling for a fight to crush the American troops in the area.

The 6 man Lurp teams that had been previously inserted into the area had found numerous high speed trails. Those recon teams had some minor contacts with primarily VC and a few NVA, but nothing significant; however, the teams believed that there were significant numbers of NVA in the area. This information was based as much on "gut feelings" as it was on hard intel like the hard packed high speed trails they had observed.

The specific area that team 1-3 was to recon/conduct ambushes in, was bordered on the west and north sides by a large natural open area. It looked like an inverted "L" from the air. It was probably over a klick (kilometer) long from north to south and approximately 300 meters wide. The east to west open area on the north end was approximately ½ klick long and probably 200 meters wide. There weren't any other LZs within the general area so I had to pick an LZ in that large open area. The actual LZ was just a little indentation in the east side of the open area and probably about three quarters of the way down toward the south end of that large open area. It did afford a limited view if an LZ watcher was on the east side of the open area, but on the west side of the open area they could look right up our asses as we offloaded with the insertion. I didn't like primary LZ, but I had to play the hand I was dealt. Xin Loi GI!

You would think that a large LZ would be an ideal location for a heavy team insertion, because there wouldn't be any problems of landing the two-ship configuration simultaneously. The problem was that because it was such a large potential LZ there would be LZ Watchers. You could have easily inserted an entire infantry company in probably one lift with 25 + Hueys. You would still have a lot of room left over for the large CH 46s to come in and drop a weapons platoon or artillery battery into the same LZ and in close proximity.

As a Lurp Team Leader this was one of the lessons you remembered from RecondoSchool and from your own experiences. You wanted to be inserted in an obscure LZ with little commotion and without being seen. If you got in without being seen and you made a clean getaway from the LZ into the jungle, you would be good to go. Similar to the way the Boomer Class nuclear subs disappear into the ocean depths for 90 days where only they know where they are. Of course we were a hell of a lot less costly and sophisticated in our operations, but we still had US GI boots on the ground and a mission to complete!

We inserted on November 30, 1968 at around 1000 hours because a lot of teams were being inserted in this AO. Since we were a heavy team and required two Hueys for insertion, we had to wait at the pad for the lift ships to return and pick us up. I didn't like the wait because I was mentally spun up for the mission and I had 11 other Lurps just sitting there also all spun up. We eventually got loaded on and headed toward the LZ which was approximately 60 + kilometers away. Of course the C&C Ship had stayed in orbit over the general AO so they were in position to talk the two insertion ships into the landing zone. Because the LZ was so large we wanted to be inserted without over flying the entire open area so we came in a northwesterly direction

237

at tree top level. With the C&C ship directing the landing the two insertion ships came in fast and flared at the last seconds which caused them both to drop out the sky at tree top level and immediately be in the landing configuration. It was a hell of ride and when it is done correctly it is a beautiful thing to see and feel from inside the Huey. I guess that's why I like to ride fast rollercoasters!

Both teams cleared the helicopters in seconds and we made our way into the jungle at the edge of the LZ. It appeared to be a clean insertion without being spotted and with no enemy signal shots during our 10 minute wait prior to permanently leaving the LZ and starting the mission. My internal, First 24 hours, clock automatically initiated itself as soon as my feet hit the ground on the LZ. Having picked a LZ at the south end of our designated recon area, it was necessary for the team to move in a northeasterly direction to get to the area assigned to us. The assigned areas were obviously very loosely described so that the TL had the option to move as necessary based on the environment and enemy activity. I had the point man head on a 90 degrees heading for about 50 mikes and then we turned to the north. We had probably moved several hundred meters when we came into an area that was different from the jungle we had just passed through. It had been primarily double canopy upon leaving the LZ, so there was a lot of brush and small trees on the ground, which is exactly the type of terrain we loved because it provided excellent cover and concealment. As we moved into this somewhat different area most of the small trees and bushes disappeared but there were clump of bushes and elephant grass at the base of a lot of the trees. This sparked my attention and set off that silent alarm in my Lurp brain. Something was not right and I knew I was looking right at it but not conceptualizing it in my brain. Like when you look at a mind puzzle and you have to change your way of looking at it, then the picture rises out of the maze. I was walking third in the line of march and I passed one of the medium sized trees with elephant grass growing around its base, I looked down and to my left, because from the angle I was looking I could see that inside the clump of elephant grass, there was very well concealed spider hole. I nearly had a heart attack because the point man and pace man had both missed it. I immediately signaled a halt. Once the team kneeled down in the linear configuration we had been marching in, I moved forward to advise the point man what I had observed. He also pointed out some strange configurations that were camouflaged behind and in the small bushes, trees and elephant grass. Upon further studying our surroundings the picture suddenly jumped out at us. We had walked directly into the middle of a company size base camp, complete with timber bunkers and built to have interlocking fire. The only thing that saved us from total annihilation was that it was unoccupied! This type of combat experience is what causes you to grow old faster than your natural body clock dictates. It made the hair on my neck stand up and I wanted to get the team out of there as fast as possible but in the safest manner I could think of. Since we weren't taking any fire from inside the base camp, I took a couple of minutes to visually check out the layout of the camp. It appeared that it had been abandoned for maybe six months or more based on the growth of the small plants and no area having been tramped down or recently cleared. There weren't any smells of campfires, human presence or food preparations, so I added that info to my estimation of when the enemy had last occupied the camp. I could see with my adjusted vision at least 6 bunkers in an arc pointing toward the front of our position. I believed there were additional bunkers to the left of our position, but they were so well camouflaged that you couldn't see them unless you walked directly to them. I had no intentions of exploring the camp because whoever had expertly built this site probably left a few surprises around for curious GIs. Fortunately the NVA were not known for planting mine fields around their base camps, at least not in South Vietnam. It definitely had all of the telltale signs that it had been built by some very experienced NVA/VC soldiers because of the near perfectly camouflaged positions and the tactical layout of the bunker system. The obvious intent of the complex was to hold off any large American force that had landed on the LZ and started to move off the LZ and into the jungle. A previous war reference would be how the Japanese established their camouflaged bunker systems inside the jungle or caves and allowed the GIs to walk right in front of them before they opened fire with deadly accuracy and interlocking fire.

After the quick visual recon, I signaled the team that we were moving out and had the point man take a 90 degree turn to the right so that we quickly exited the kill zone of the bunker complex and were back in thick bush and small trees under the double canopy of the large trees. It was like we passed through an invisible wall and were now back in the "natural jungle" surroundings and it definitely felt different and a hell of a lot safer! The whole team took a silent sigh of relief and we all knew we had dodged a deadly trap.

It would have been easy for me or any other team member to blame the point man for the missed signs of the base camp; however, a team doesn't function as 6 or 12 individuals. The team functions as one large body with 12 sets of eyes and ears, 12 smelling receptors and most importantly 12 highly trained and experienced brains that communicate with each other as one massive computer. If one member fails, we all fail!

That particular bunker complex was probably the finest example of a planned complex with natural jungle camouflage I'd seen in my first year as a Lurp. It caused me to post a little warning flag in my brain to pay more attention to things that seem out of place and not get so over confident that you could handle anything you bumped into. It also registered in my brain the direction/location not to return to because of the implicit dangers it represented to a Lurp team on the move. It would be especially true if the team was under attack and trying to move out to break contact with the enemy. You would have to believe that some of the enemy would be indigenous to the area and probably knew about the bunker complex. Thus, if they moved around the team and into the complex they would have the perfect impromptu ambush location. It also caused me to make decisions the following day that could have been disastrous for the entire team.

We moved out in a southeasterly direction for approximately 100 mikes when we came upon an area that was open to the sky but still had cover at the ground level. The point man signaled for me to come up to his location. When I got there I could see that the reason the jungle was open to the sky was that a very large tree, approximately 4 feet in diameter by 100 feet plus high had toppled over taking all of the smaller trees in the secondary growth with it. There was a large hole, 6 feet wide by 3 feet deep, where the root ball had been pulled up and out of the ground. It appeared that the tree had fallen over by natural causes, probably high winds, because there didn't appear to be any damage to the trunk, as if it had been hit by artillery fire or a bomb. There also weren't any secondary excavations in the area surrounding the downed tree that would have indicated some external influence that had caused the tree to be blown over.

Once I had visually surveyed the area and felt confident that this wasn't man made, we again moved out in a southeasterly direction. We started to climb a slight incline and after 100 + meters I halted the team. I could see to the east that there was light filtering down through the double canopy and I wanted to check it. We knew there was a high-speed trail in the area from our briefing and I felt this might be an area where the trail snaked through the jungle. I put the team in a circular defensive position. The point man and I cautiously moved in that direction. After approximately 25 meters, we saw that the jungle opened up and there was indeed a trail almost directly in front of us that ran primarily southwest to northeast; however, it was more then a trail. It was actually a truck road and had fresh tracks on it indicating that a dually type truck like a US Army Deuce and a half had recently used it. Our intel briefing had related the fact that there weren't and had not been any US troops in this AO for months. So the likely conclusion we made was that the enemy had a captured US deuce and a half in the area and was using it as a supply or troop transport. That caused me to have a somewhat increased pucker factor, but of course my gung-ho Lurp brain kicked in and I was thinking about being the first team to either blow up or capture an enemy vehicle. What the hell, if you have confidence in your team and you have the special equipment (LAW) to make it happen, why not dream big and plan for all contingencies. I could also see that the road/trail turned and headed primarily southwest up the continuing incline, that was now a small hill. The trail was well used and had all the indications that it was a high-speed trail and probably one of the primary trails in the area. The other thing that made this an excellent location for an ambush was that the trail formed a somewhat right angle and so from this location we would be on the outside of the right angle and have an excellent view of two directions while the area behind us dropped off and didn't have any trails that the enemy could use to flank our position. It also had the required overhead and front cover that would keep the team concealed and out of the scorching direct sunlight. It was a near perfect ambush site, I thought at the time. I decided to set up a linear ambush at the turn in the trail. The apex of the right angle would be the center of the kill zone. We returned to the team and we moved up into the ambush site. We posted a couple of Lurps on each end of the kill zone while the rest of the team set out their claymores in the kill zone and then in an arc to the rear to protect the flanks and as rear security. The area in front of the kill zone was relatively flat and at just a slight angle up toward the hill to our right. This allowed me to put 8 Lurps on the front of the linear ambush and the remainder on the flanks and the rear security. Since we expected to make contact with NVA soldiers in this AO, we brought two M-60 machine guns and approximately a 1,000 rounds for each gun. We also had one M-79 and one LAW. I placed the two M-60s near the right and left flank of the kill zone because it would give them a wide area as to their fields of fire. If any large force came down the trail from either direction both machine guns would be able to come on target and actually have interlocking fire zones. We were able to establish the ambush in a fairly fast time (25 minutes) because the terrain was cooperating with us and there was excellent concealment to our front and flanks. By the time everyone had cleared their individual area, like an animal making its nest, the day was rapidly disappearing and we settled into our ambush routine. Normally two of us were on guard and the rest just relaxing. It was around 1630 hours and the time was rapidly reaching the "bewitching hours" for increased traffic on a trail. We had been in position for approximately around 1.5 hours and I was on guard duty looking straight down the trail to our northeast. I just caught some movement to the southwest where the trail emerged from the thick underbrush, which was approximately 30 meters southwest of my position. I observed an enemy soldier rapidly approaching the team while walking down the trail. He was armed with a SKS and appeared to be a VC, based on his uniform and gear, but he was alert and carried his rifle at port arms. I allowed him to walk right up to where the trail turned northeast. He had no idea that he was walking into an ambush. I wanted to be sure that he wasn't the point man for a larger element. If he was, we would have let him pass and take the larger unit once they entered the kill zone. That is of course if there weren't more then we could deal with, maybe a squad of 8-10 men or less. That would be one of those millisecond decisions the team leader would normally make by initiating or not initiating the ambush. I was very proud of my team, because most of them saw him coming but no one fired until I fired. That represents extreme control of every team member's emotions and self preservation instincts. It also told me that they trusted without hesitation the life and death decision the TL had to make. A team leader doesn't gain that kind of respect by rank only, it is earned through hard work, timely and intelligent decisions and developing mutual respect for each team member's opinions and actions.

He was probably 10 meters away when I gave him a short burst in the chest from my M-16. He dropped like a rock and never moved. There wasn't any return fire from unseen enemy troops, so after several minutes I hand signaled the team to let them know myself and my point man were going out to search the body and recover the weapon along with his gear. We reached the body and I checked him out while the point man watched down the trail from where the

243

enemy had appeared. I recovered the rifle, his pack and web gear and I stripped the body naked. I intended to leave the body on the trail for psychological value to get inside the head of the enemy. I considered placing a grenade in the armpit of the enemy soldier so that when they attempted to recover the body it would explode and hopefully kill additional soldiers. I decided against it because at that point I thought we were getting extracted and we wouldn't be able to watch the body. I didn't want some experienced VC or NVA to check the body and recover an M-26 grenade minus the pin.

To a non-combatant, my attitude about simply shooting the enemy soldier like a jack rabbit in a field may seem somewhat cavalier or just plain soulless. The fact is that is the basic activity for war. The goal is to kill enough enemy soldiers that their forces are reduced to the point that they can no longer affect the outcome of the war. In fact the kill may be important to the war effort, but the hunt is what is important to the soldier, especially for a Lurp. It is his skills and techniques that got him to the point where he was in position to kill the enemy soldier. The kill occurred but it is not to be considered a notch in a Lurp's stock or to brag about it with fellow Lurp members. If a Lurp or any combatant enjoys killing then they are in the wrong business. War and its "God syndrome" can be very addictive and very destructive to the psyche of each individual combatant. It is important that each individual combatant moves on past the kill, to his team's efforts and their safe completion of the mission.

I advised the team to bring in their claymores and prepare to move out back toward the LZ, expecting that we would be extracted and returned to base or at least be extracted and dropped off at another location. That had been SOP (standard operating procedures) taught at Recondo School and what we had followed in our operating procedures since beginning recon/ambush missions. There were two extremely important reasons for this. First and foremost we were compromised as to our present location and that could be catastrophic for a team, especially in a VC & NVA very active area. Secondly, we had already moved out from the ambush location and I had left the body on the trail. Even if the enemy didn't hear the firing of our M-16s, it wouldn't be long before they found the body. Then there wouldn't be any doubt in their minds that there were US troops in the area. Hell, it was the same effective tactics that the enemy was using in this guerilla war we were fighting: Hit and Run; Hit and Run! If the CO didn't believe us all he had to do was review the enemy tactics over the last several years and except for the Tet Offensive, which was a military disaster for the NVA and VC. Those same tactics were used until the final offensive when South Vietnam finally fell in 1975.

As soon as we made contact and the enemy soldier was dead, I contacted HQ through a radio relay which at time was an Air Force O-1 Bird Dog, fixed wing aircraft with a call sign of Aloft. Essentially the Bird Dog was nothing more then a single engine Cessna tail dragger with no armament except for marking target rockets and a very thin skin. We had to use these aircraft as radio relay for the deployed teams, because there weren't any artillery bases in the area and we were at least 60 kilometers from any large US base. Our PRC 25 radios might reach 20 kilometers on a good day, so the lack of communication could be a death sentence to a Lurp team in contact.

From a dead start at the helipads it would take approximately 30 minutes for the helicopters, including the gunship, to spin up and be "on station" which was a long time for a team to be in contact, even a heavy team. We had moved approximately 100 meters back toward the LZ when the C&C ship arrived on station and I advised them of the ambush and the recovery of the equipment, which included a Vietnamese ID card and some writing on newspaper that was in his pack. I was talking directly with "6" who was our new company commander, as our second company commander had rotated back to the states. He had been in II Field Force HQ Unit and supposedly had both command and combat experience.

As soon as I gave 6/CO a Sitrep he asked me several questions as to what my intentions were. I thought that was rather strange because he knew what the SOP was after a team made contact. It was to extract and return to base on extract and re-insert in a different location. I advised him that I was moving the team toward the LZ for extraction. His reply was "negative" and that I was to Charlie Mike (continue mission). I requested that he at least have us extracted and re-inserted into another area. He replied that that was a negative and that we were to Charlie Mike. I could tell that he had made his mind up before he ever arrived on station and I was pissed about it, but RHIP (Rank Has Its Privileges), and I wasn't going to convince him other wise. I signed off with "Roger that!" To this day I don't know why he refused to extract us because he had placed us in a really precarious position and we would be vulnerable to an attack by the enemy since they knew we were in the area. It was a triple fucked situation; we were compromised as to our general location; we were too far out from any artillery bases for them to be able to support us; we had fixed wing aircraft for radio relay and if the bad weather came in and grounded Aloft, we wouldn't even have any communications capabilities.

To add to the problems, it was late in the afternoon and I had the infiltration route we had traveled through to get to the ambush site. I did not want to double back on the route we had had used because that was a cardinal sin and against every rule we were taught at Recondo School. Simply put, if the enemy had found your trail off the LZ and followed it and if they had also heard the shots fired on the ambush, they would know your approximate location. Kind of like having the mouse caught between two hunting cats that were following the trail from opposite ends. I also had no intentions of going back through the abandoned base camp because of all the negative possibilities within that scenario.

We had traveled back down the incline we had previously climbed up to establish and execute the ambush. Had we been cleared for extraction, I would have turned the team west and made a careful bee-line for the LZ. However, since the CO handed me a sack of shit decision to deal with, I had to decide what was best for the team and our safety. Hindsight says I should have moved further from the original ambush site; however, with what I considered three very dangerous locations – the trail/road to the southeast, the bunker complex to the north and the open LZ to the west – I had limited options. Since it was late in the afternoon, I didn't want to get caught moving at dark and have to find a quick location to hide the team for the night. The only direction I could have moved was up the incline to the southwest of the ambush site, but we would have been paralleling the trail/road and essentially the LZ to our west. I wasn't sure where the enemy had another base camp, but up the incline/hill would have been a good choice based just on military training with high ground being very important.

As we came off the incline and while still traveling north, we came back to the location where the large tree had fallen over. Upon looking at the location as a defensive position, it looked like the best place to stop for the night. I had a general idea about my surroundings and with a twelve man team and two M-60 machine guns I knew we could put up a hell of a fight if it came to that. I moved the team into the site using the large downed tree trunk as the front of our perimeter to the south. I placed the majority of my team (team 1-3) along the tree trunk because it offered excellent concealment and the log was like the front of a heavy bunker. The M-60 gunner was in the center of that placement and had an excellent field of fire to the south, southeast and partially southwest. The second half of the heavy team (team 1-6) was placed on the rear of the site with fairly good cover and excellent concealment. That half of the team formed the rear security, the right and left flanks, with the M-60 gunner to the right rear of the team. We were in what I believed was a good defensive position and if it went to total shit we could blow our claymores and E&E west, directly to the LZ which I estimated was 150 meters away.

Just by chance, Sgt Bolt, my ATL picked the hole created by the root ball as his position for the RON. He was approximately 8 feet to my south and about the same distance from the downed tree and the first member of our team. It was not an ideal setup because of the distances we were from each other, but again you have to adjust to the environment. Once the team was in position with their claymores out and their individual RON sites cleared, I made a circular visit to all of the positions to give each team member the decision I had made.

I decided to wait and listen to see if there was any activity up on the trail at the ambush site and if we would get probed during the night. I was fairly certain that the enemy didn't know exactly where we were, but knew we had not been extracted by helicopter. The other decision I made was not to move out right after we stood down from our first light alert. Again, I wanted to wait and see what tomorrow morning brought. If we didn't get probed during the night, I believed we could make a break in the morning, probably back toward the LZ away from the bunker complex, and then swing north and back into the jungle to find a new ambush site.

As I had anticipated, we started to have movement to the north, west and south. This was right after it turned dark and I think they were probably doing a soft probe to try to learn where we actually were. The most concerning was the movement to the west since a large group of enemy soldiers in that location could block our E&E to the LZ.

At approximately 0220 hours we heard movement up on the trail (150 degrees from our position), where we had left the dead enemy soldier. It sounded like they had brought an ox cart with an animal pulling it. I could smell some type of animal, maybe an ox or water buffalo, but since I had never been close to their domestic animals, I couldn't get a positive identification. I could hear the squeaking wheels on the axle and wood on wood sounds. They were apparently in the process of loading up the body. I somewhat regretted not leaving a surprise for them, but knew it would have been a 50/50 chance of them finding the grenade. A better solution would have been planting a toe pooper (anti-personnel mine) near the body and having one of them step on it. Of course we didn't bring any with us, primarily because we were loaded heavy with extra mags for our M-16s and M-60 ammo. The perfect solution would have been to drop artillery on them. At a 150 meters it would have been what they now call "danger close", we just called it too damn close but necessary for the situation. If the artillery being used were 8″ guns they were deadly accurate and could be walked in at less then 25 meters per shot. If they had been to the left or right of the target, it would have been easy to adjust the fire since it wouldn't have been in line with where the team was situated. The enemy were up the incline from our position, so I could have walked it down the hill with some accuracy without endangering the team too much; however, it was all wishful thinking, but just relates how one piece of equipment could have changed the outcome of what was to occur.

We also had some sounds of movement along an approximate 100 meter line from where we had killed the enemy soldier to our northeast. All of the sounds were approximately 50 plus meters from our location. At around 0330 hours we got a rock or dud grenade thrown near the east perimeter but nothing else happened. I was certain then that we were going to have company for breakfast in the morning and I didn't think they would be a very congenial group.

First light came around 0600 hours and it was a clear day, so if we needed gunships it wouldn't be a problem. As I had already decided we just sat quietly in our RON positions to see what the enemy did. I had no doubt in my mind that they were there, I just didn't know their numbers or what kind of weapons they had. Our heavy team was armed to the teeth with 11 x M-16s with probably 15 plus mags each; 2 x M-60 machine guns and at least 2,000 rounds of ammo for them; 1 x M-79 with probably 30 plus rounds, 1x LAW and I believe we had set out 8 claymore mines. The team was equipped almost as well as a full 30 man infantry platoon would have been and we were in good defensive positions.

After our initial first light alert status, I had placed most of the team on stand-down so they could rest since I don't think any of us slept last night with all of the enemy movement around our position. At just before 0800 hours we heard some new movement to the south of our position. It sounded like one or more enemy soldiers were moving through the bush in front of our south perimeter and directly in front of the downed tree. Sgt Bolt, who was in the stand down group, was asleep in his tree root hole. I was about to crawl over and wake him. I just caught the movement of an enemy soldier coming into the semi clearing created by the fallen tree. I could clearly see him, but he obviously didn't see any of the team. That confirmed what I had previously concluded that the enemy knew we were in the area, but they didn't know exactly where we were. There were now two enemy soldiers in my view and they were walking directly into the south perimeter with not a clue that they were dead men walking. It was at that time that I observed Sgt Bolt open his eyes. He had obviously heard the enemy approaching from a dead sleep. He was lying in his back and his M-16 was lying in his grasp on his chest, exactly how a sleeping Lurp should have been in control of his weapon. In one quick movement, Sgt Bolt put his M-16 in the auto-firing position, immediately sat up and fired a burst into the first enemy soldier who was probably less then 20 feet from him. I saw the second enemy soldier go down like he had also been hit, but I never saw him again after that.

Before the first enemy soldier had even hit the ground, it sounded like a hundred AK-47s all fired at once! Simultaneously, there were multiple explosions to our southern front, eastern side and to the rear of the team. I originally thought that the enemy had crawled in close to our perimeter and were throwing hand grenades into our perimeter. Then there was a louder explosion directly to the front of Sgt. Bolt's position. I felt a stinging sensation in my left shoulder and left upper chest. I quickly realized that I had been hit by shrapnel. I also realized that the explosions were from impacting and exploding RPGs to our front, the west and north side of our perimeter. A relief for me in some ways, because it told me the enemy had not crawled within grenade throwing range of our perimeter. The first RPG round that landed and exploded outside the south perimeter, hit three of us with shrapnel, including Sgt Bolt, another Lurp to the right of Sgt Bolt and me. I was now really pissed off at the enemy, my CO and myself for allowing this to happen. I was also pumped up with adrenalin, thought "fuck it" and made up my mind to personally kill as many of the enemy as I could.

I think the wound hurt, but between the adrenalin and the controlled anger I didn't have time to worry about it and only felt a small amount of pain during the entire firefight. Later, after self-analyzing the other times I was wounded during firefights I believe that I was able to block the pain out of my mind while in the fight! I also later realized that if I hadn't been facing to the west communicating to Aloft on the PRC-25 when the first RPG round blew up to our front I would have been seriously wounded or dead. Because I was facing to the west instead of the south, it caused me to get hit with multiple pieces of shrapnel on my upper left shoulder and upper left chest area about where the heart is. If I had been facing in the direction of where the first RPG round impacted, I would have taken the full blast in the chest. Based on the shrapnel that penetrated deep into my shoulder (so deep the doctors never tried to remove it during surgery), it probably would have penetrated my upper chest and that could have been very bad! Xin Loi GI.

The firing from the enemy never slowed down and it was pouring in primarily from the south and east of our position. The RPG rounds kept raining down on the area to the front and the rear of our position and they were coming in fast. One RPG round actually had an air-burst as it must have hit one of the few remaining small trees (2" diameter x 10 + feet high) inside our perimeter. This was very bad, because the RPG rounds are actually anti-tank rounds. When they blow, the light metal casing that covers the head of the rocket and its armor penetrating charge, break up into small dime size chunks of flying shrapnel that radiates out in a 360 degree pattern from the point of the explosion. Because it exploded approximately 10 feet above the ground, it blew out a lot of shrapnel over a large area and numerous Lurps were hit by the shrapnel.

Based on the amount and the time between incoming RPG rounds, I believed that there were at least two RPG launchers, somewhere up on the incline we had come down and probably about 100 plus meters

251

from our location. There was so much noise generated by the firing from the enemy and from the team that I couldn't hear them being fired which usually causes a loud whooshing sound and sometimes a smoke trail. I also noticed that there must have been a medium caliber machine gun (PKS 7.62 General Purpose Machine gun) on a tripod or bipod, because I could see it was sweeping above the perimeter by watching the tops of the small trees raining down inside the perimeter. They were being cut down about 4 feet above the ground, as if by an invisible chainsaw! The machine gun would swing from left to right and then back the other way on a very flat horizontal plane. It registered in my mind that the enemy didn't realize that the incline they were on continued on down to the level floor of the jungle where our defensive position was. This meant they were shooting higher than they should to bring effective fire on our position.

I also noticed that the second enemy soldier that Sgt Bolt had shot was no longer in view and I was worried that maybe he would try to crawl closer and throw hand grenades into our perimeter. I had continued to carry a willie peter grenade, even after Dicky Gross had been killed by the WP grenade in the accident inside the barracks. I had started carrying it on my left side, rear ammo pouch, believing that if I got shot from the front the three M-16 magazines in that pouch would possibly stop or deflect the round from hitting the willi peter. Wishful thinking at best, but what the hell it was better then worrying about it being hit and exploding while still attached to my pistol belt. I pulled the grenade off the pouch, pulled the pin and laid down on my back so that I could throw it right handed with a lot of power in an overhand hook throw. The WP grenade is heavy, probably twice that of the standard M-26 frag grenade, so you had to put some power behind your throw. I then quickly sat up and simultaneously threw the grenade as hard as I could in the direction of where I had seen the second enemy fall after being shot by Sgt Bolt. To my surprise I watched the WP grenade slowly rise up and then start to fall back down as if it was in slow mo. I actually thought it was going to land inside our perimeter where most of Team 1-3 was kneeling behind the fallen tree and shooting toward the south. That would have been a very deadly mistake and would have wiped out the team. To my great elation the WP grenade landed a couple of feet past the fallen tree on the outside of the perimeter and exploded, sending deadly fingers of burning willi peter in all directions, except to the rear because the trunk of the downed tree absorbed most of it. To this day I don't why I got such a weak throw with the grenade, because I was pumped up with adrenaline and should have been able to throw the damned thing at least 20 meters. Maybe I did the overhand hook throw incorrectly, because I had never played basketball in high school, so maybe it was just bad technique; whatever, Shit happens and you move on!

There was also the huge telltale, white mushroom cloud (50 feet in the air and about 30 plus feet in diameter) that rose from the location of the exploding grenade. This immediately caused two things to happen. The heavy machine gun fire from the incline to the south and also the RPG rounds begin to hit further to the north outside the rear of our perimeter. I later realized the enemy troops had obviously observed where the willi peter grenade had exploded and knew from experience that no one in their right mind would throw a willie peter grenade so close to their own perimeter. So, they adjusted fire, raising their aiming points, believing that we were actually further away from their position. It was just dumb luck that the grenade landed where it did and not in the perimeter. It had the positive side affect of causing the enemy to shoot higher and thus preventing more of the Lurps from getting hit by the defilade fire of the machine gun and probably from the numerous AK-47 sub-machine guns also firing into our perimeter. Some times Murphy is with you and sometimes Murphy is against you, but make no mistake; it is normally "YOU" that causes Shit to happen in the first place.

Even though it was extremely loud inside our perimeter from all of the weapons firing, I realized I was no longer hearing the steady heavy thumping of the M-60 firing, at least from the machine gun on the south perimeter. When I looked where my machine gunner, Sal, had been, I observed that he was face down behind the downed tree and had a lot of blood on his back with the machine gun lying next to him. He was, however, moving so I knew he wasn't dead. I left my position and crawled to where he was lying because I wanted to check on Sal and see if he had a fatal wound. I also wanted that M-60 operating, because it was all about fire superiority and I felt that the NVA/VC were outmatching our fire power at that particular time. I low crawled toward Sal's position, because there was a tremendous amount of shit flying around just over our heads and anyone standing would have been cut down in a flash. Once I reached his location I looked at his wounds under his camo shirt and saw that he had probably 15 or more flesh wounds on his back, probably caused by the RPG round that had exploded in an air burst above and in the middle of our perimeter. He also had some more wounds on his right arm, wrist and hand. I believe he was firing the M-60 when the RPG came in and exploded. His firing position caused him to take a lot of hits of shrapnel on his upper body and right arm. I got down next to his face and asked him how he was doing, he said he was in pain and wanted to know how bad he was hit. I could tell he was worried and I didn't want him going into shock! I told him, "Don't worry about your wounds, they're just superficial and I've seen worse wounds from fights between two GIs in a whore house then what you have!" I think he appreciated my comment, because he seemed to perk up, but was still unable to fire the M-60 because of the shrapnel in his right firing hand and wrist. Several of the other Lurps on both sides of Sal also had minor shrapnel wounds but they were busy firing their M-16s so I didn't try to even check them out. I decided to take the M-60 off Sal's back to my position to use it since I had carried the M-60 as a team member and loved the gun. Just then Spec. 4 Dick Moyer crawled up. He was the other M-60 gunner from Team 1-6 so I gave it to him and he started to check it out to see if it was still operational. Shortly after I heard it firing and saw that he was manning the gun and firing back toward the enemy on the south perimeter. Spec. 4 Moyer had obviously felt the same way I did about fire superiority and was able to get Sal's M-60 functional again to put some heavy fire on the enemy positions.

Since Dick had left his M-60 at his location with several of the team members from Team 1-6, I crawled to their location and picked up the M-60 and several 100 round belts of ammo. My intentions were to use it to increase our firepower and keep the enemy on our east perimeter at bay until the gunships arrived. I low crawled back to my original position cradling the gun in my upper arms and placed the M-60 on its bipod on the mound to my front. I started firing short bursts of rounds into the area on the east perimeter where I could tell the enemy was located. We had now been in the firefight for approximately 20 minutes on full auto response by the team. I'm sure that the team members were down to their last several magazines. I was pretty sure that we had probably at least several hundred rounds left for each M-60, especially since Sal carried a minimum of 800 rounds every time we went on a mission. He hadn't been firing very long when he got hit and he was a good gunner so I knew he hadn't just held the trigger down and blew through a lot of M-60 ammo without hitting anything in particular.

Approximately 25 minutes after the initial firefight began and as if on command the firing from the enemy fell off to just some harassment fire. I presumed that the enemy knew they wouldn't be able to over-run our position since we were still putting out a lot of effective fire, so they decided to cut their losses and Di Di Mow (leave quickly) the area before the helicopter gunships arrived. They must have left some troops on the east and south area, out side our perimeters to keep us pinned down while the majority of their personnel moved out. There was one enemy soldier that was particularly annoying because every time Sgt. Bolt sat up and fired the M-79 toward the probable locations of the retreating enemy, the enemy soldier would fire a round at Sgt Bolt. Apparently he was listening for the sound of bloop of the M-79 as the round left the tube of the grenade launcher. He was slowly zeroing in on Sgt Bolts location and it was pissing me off. I hand signaled to Bolt to wait while I got the M-60 in a position so that I could do a direct fire on the enemy's position. When I gave Bolt the signal, he quickly sat up fired the M-79 and ducked back down in the hole. True to form the enemy soldier fired another round at Bolt's location; however, two can play that game! I quickly fired approximately 20 rounds from the M-60 in the area I believed the enemy was firing from. I had Bolt fire another round from his M-79, but this time there wasn't any corresponding return fire from the enemy soldier. I don't know if I hit him, killed him or scared the hell out of him with the M-60 rounds, but he never fired another round from that position. Kind of like playing a deadly game of chess, with Sgt Bolt being the pawn, but with me making the winning move having the Queen, the beautiful M-60 machine gun, in position to deliver a deathblow to end the game.

At this time I heard the gunships coming into the area, so I set down the M-60 and picked up the PRC-25 radio hand piece and started directing fire into the locations I believed still held enemy soldiers. After the gun ships made several gun runs and not hearing any return fire, myself and two other non-wounded Lurps made a quick sweep of the area to the front of our southern perimeter. We found the first soldier that Sgt Bolt had shot and recovered his Ak-47, web gear and extra magazines. There was a trail through the low grass indicating that the second enemy soldier had probably been wounded and crawled back to the area where he could be helped by his fellow soldiers. We swept up the incline to a point where we were near the location of the original ambush. We observed an enemy soldier running west from out location and fired on him, but he disappeared into the heavy brush. I wasn't going to risk getting more Lurps wounded by chasing one enemy soldier. We headed back to our position and I signaled all of the Lurps to prepare to move out after recovering their claymore mines. I specifically advised them not to blow their claymores, because I was still not convinced that the enemy might have crawled in during the night and turned some claymores around.

By this time "6" was overhead in the C&C ship and advised me to move the team to the LZ for extraction. He also told me that a Platoon from D Troop, 3/17th Cavalry was inserting and would be sweeping the contact area. He requested that I leave three non-wounded members from my team to act as guides for the reaction platoon. Everyone from team 1-3 was wounded plus one Lurp from team 1-6. We had a total of 7 wounded Lurps, 6 with minor shrapnel wounds and 1, Sal my M-60 gunner with serious wounds (Note the actual number of Lurps on team 1-3 at the time of the ambush was only 10 Lurps; I had to check my diary to confirm the number). I was advised that all of the wounded would be flown by the two lift ships directly to emergency hospital at Long Binh and dropped there. The rest of the team would be flown back to Bien Hoa and the company where they would be dropped off to be debriefed. I advised Sgt Cowles to tell everyone in the debriefing not to use that particular area of the large LZ because I was now certain that it was being watched.

The response Plt along with the three unwounded Lurps swept the area where we had been in the firefight with the reinforced Plt of NVA and VC. They found two B-40 RPG Launchers on the rise to the south of our location. They also found expended casings from the medium machine gun they were firing at our position. To the east of our position, they found 30+ fighting positions in a north-south line, parallel to our position and 25 meters away. There were numerous blood trails leading away from those positions.

Further east, they found an entrance to a tunnel, which is probably how the NVA were able to get into their ambush positions without making any noise. Approximately 40+ enemy soldiers attacked us, including the known fighting positions; the two RPG crews; and the machine gun crew!

Simple math shows that we were fighting 4 times the number of enemy soldiers as we had on Team 1-3. I was very proud of the team, but I also knew that Lady Luck was with us on that day!

After the surgeons at 24th Evacuation Hospital performed individual surgeries, we were all sent to Cam Rahn Bay, 6th Convalescent Center to be given additional time to recover from our wounds and the subsequent surgeries. Several days after we were there several additional Lurps from 1st Platoon of Company F arrived at Cam Rahn Bay medical center, so I asked what had happened to them. Apparently the CO never listened to my recommendation not to use that particular part of the LZ, believing that it was being watched by the enemy. They told me that the day after our major firefight the CO ordered another heavy team into the same area. They got compromised on the first day and the CO refused to extract them. The following morning they got hit by an estimated NVA/VC Company (100 plus soldiers) just as they were leaving their RON location. Initially two Lurps were hit with rifle fire and seriously wounded. One had a head wound and died at the location. the team was pinned down with heavy fire and the Lurps told me that the enemy was so close that they could see the flash of their weapons as they fired on the team. They also said that they hadn't heard one noise that night and had no idea the enemy had set up a linear ambush on their RON sight.

The gunships were called in and made numerous gun runs with the 7.62 mini guns and 2.75 rockets. The enemy never broke contact and were in fact dedicating specific fire at the attacking gunships. Finally a FAC (Forward Air Control) was brought in and F-4 Phantoms Fighter/Bomber jets were used to make 20 mm cannon strafing runs on the enemy troops. It took numerous passes from the fast movers before the enemy finally broke contact and the team was able to move to the LZ. The Lurps told me that the 20 mm cannon rounds were hitting so close to their positions that they could hear the enemy soldiers being hit and screaming from their wounds.

The first lift ship came in and landed to pick up the now 3 seriously wounded Lurps, plus the body of the dead Lurp and two additional members of the team. As soon as it touched down a 51 caliber heavy machine gun from across the large LZ, opened fire on the sitting helicopter. It knocked out the engine and the team plus the helicopter crew started to evacuated the helicopter which was still receiving fire from the 51 Cal machine gun. In what was an obvious coordinated attack an enemy soldier stepped out onto the east side of the LZ, approximately 50 meters to the north of the damaged helicopter and fired an RPG round right into the rear fuselage of the Huey. It immediately burst into flames as the team and crew members were hauling ass away from the burning helicopter. It is unknown why, but the two unwounded members of the first Lurp team failed to exit the helicopter and perished in the rapidly burning helicopter. It was believed that they were probably both seriously wounded or killed when the RPG struck the thin aluminum skin of the Huey. Ironically the entire helicopter crew made it out safely as did the remaining wounded members of the team along with the body of the dead Lurp.

I was deeply disturbed by this information, because I was certain that the CO had received the information I had sent back from our contact. It was obvious that he chose to ignore it and a second team was almost annihilated by a significantly larger enemy force. They had three dead Lurps, most of the other team members had some form of physical or mental wounds, plus one completely destroyed Huey helicopter. So in two days based on bad decisions and apparent faulty leadership by our new CO, we had two heavy teams shot up and three dead Lurps. This was unprecedented in the short history of Company F, LRP and hadn't occurred before with the two previous COs. I never understood why the CO, who was Infantry and Ranger Qualified, ignored advice from his experienced NCOs. He caused the deaths of three Lurps and numerous other Lurps to be wounded. There would be future incidents with this CO and eventually the Platoon Leaders (Lieutenants) refused to comply/follow to the letter, his apparently uninformed and bad decisions. The costly decisions by the CO were not only reducing the mission tempo of Company F, because of the reduced number of teams that were capable of carrying out missions; but also, it was causing morale issues with the Lurps, who up to that point in the company, never had those issues. In fact Company F had the highest morale of any company I ever served in both in Vietnam and stateside!

My wish is that that CO lives with those unnecessary deaths burned into his memory and that he will take it with him when he dies. I can accept mistakes being made in real time in combat, but I cannot accept or respect an officer who apparently thought, because of his rank, that he couldn't or wouldn't make costly mistakes even when he had experienced Lurp officers and NCOs telling him that he was wrong! A simple analogy would have been: "If it ain't broke, don't fix it!"

It was also apparent to me that the enemy had adjusted their plans of attack against heavy lurp teams when they realized that a platoon of soldiers (30 plus) with some heavy weapons (RPGs and medium caliber machine gun) could not over-run a Heavy Lurp Team. They upgraded their plans and brought a company of soldiers (100 plus) with heavy weapons (large caliber machine gun and multiple RPGs) when they identified the location of a heavy team. They established a well placed linear ambush in complete silence that the heavy team walked into and could have been completely wiped out. Anyone who ever thought the enemy, both the VC and the NVA were stupid and cowardly, never stood face to face and toe to toe with them in an all-out slug fest! Sometimes it was just pure luck (and/or aerial firepower), who won or who lost. Either way there would be casualties in both perimeters!

Chapter 43

Face to Face Combat

There are various psychological affects for a trooper who has seen extensive combat in various forms, whether face to face contact with the enemy, assaulting a bunker line manned by the enemy, ambushing the enemy or being ambushed, hand to hand combat, etc. There are hundreds of other names and descriptions of the various forms of combat; however, they all come down to the same objective, kill or be killed!

As a Lurp on recon patrols (Long Range Recon Patrol, LRRP) or an ambush mission/disruption of enemy movement (Long Range Patrols, LRP) the contacts were normally very up close and personal operations. Most of our contacts were a max of 10 to 15 feet from the enemy. You could see them, smell them, hear them and in some instances see the damage you were inflicting on the enemy soldier by shooting them with your weapon, be it M-16, M-60 machine gun, M-79 grenade launcher and my favorite of all weapons, the M-18 claymore mine!

In his book *On Killing*, Lt. Colonel Dave Grossman, US Air Force psychiatrist during the Vietnam War, researched the psychological affects of one human killing another. He produced a chart as a result of his research entitled *Killing and Physical Distance* (page 98). It diagrams the most intense emotional reactions of a human's resistance to physically killing another human being. The highest intensity being the sexual range all the way down to the max range, which includes aircraft bombers and artillery! Number 5 on the list is close range, preceded by Hand to Hand Combat; Knife Range and Bayonet Range, respectively. I'll tell you that in a few instances we

261

could have reached out and nearly touched the enemy with the barrel of our weapon, if we wanted to. This occurred not because we trying to be brave or stupid, but primarily because of the terrain and the density of the bushes and trees. Most areas, especially in the single canopy jungle, were so dense that we had to be 10 feet or less from the trail to see what was walking into the kill zone. This could produce a 99.9 per cent chance of shooting and killing the enemy soldier or blowing him to pieces from the multiple interlocking fire of the claymores exploding in the kill zone. It also placed all of the Lurps on the team in a very precarious position, because that closeness to the trail had a two-sided effect. The enemy, while silently walking down a trail, may have been able to see you, hear you or smell you. So being up close and personal had advantages and disadvantages beyond the psychological affect. It also produced a very "DANGER CLOSE" situation because the claymores were designed to be used up to 75 feet (each claymore contained 1.5 pounds of C-4) from where the soldier was concealed; thus 10 feet could and did cause Lurp team members to be injured, sometimes temporarily (primarily loss of hearing) and sometimes permanent injuries (like the legs of the claymore or pieces of the claymore hitting the Lurp and causing external and internal injuries). The primary reason that the claymores were placed so close to our concealed positions was so that we could monitor the activity around the claymore. We didn't want the enemy to crawl in and turn the claymores around facing into our perimeter. That would have had a very dire consequence for the team. Also most ambushes established by a Lurp team usually contained at least 2 claymores directed toward the kill zone. I have been present when 6 claymores were detonated in the kill zone, an approximate 50′ length from one end to the other end of the kill zone. I can tell you that it completely deadens your hearing and fills the air with enough dust, debris and natural made shrapnel to block out the midday sun.

In one instance we detonated a claymore approximately 3 feet from our location, as we were hiding behind a termite mound and the claymore was on the opposite side of the mound. The results being that all 6 of us temporarily lost our hearing, burning plastic/shrapnel from the melted plastic case of the claymore came over top of the termite mound and I got a chunk of hot plastic in the interior corner of the right eye lid. The Lurp next to me, Dickie Gross' camouflaged shirt caught on fire from additional burning plastic landing on his back! Of course the concussion slapped our entire body with a pressure wave but didn't cause any internal injuries (maybe).

The anticipation of what was about to occur, the viciousness of the ambush attack using various weapons, and the death of the enemy, initiated by a Lurp team's ambush, caused the release of adrenalin. The human body production of the drug has been passed on from generation to generation since the beginning of ancestral man and it is still present for the direct survival of man in either the fight or flight mode. It is prodigiously released and surges through the body. It has different effects for each human, but all will feel the surge of power, the complete awareness of what is occurring around you, albeit sometimes in "slo mo" and the euphoria of being at the top of your game. Some people like to call it The God Syndrome, but in reality it is the highest of highs and the super human realization that it doesn't get any better as life on earth for a mere human soldier. Some soldiers become addicted to this rush of adrenalin and they seek out ways of repeating it, either in the form of volunteering for extreme combat operations or the overwhelming desire to extend their assignment in the combat zone so they can stay in combat to seek out its effects. If a soldier reaches that level of addiction, he becomes a danger to himself and also a danger to his fellow soldiers. It doesn't matter what their age was or what their combat experiences were. They simply became addicted to the rush of the adrenalin and pursued it at all costs to themselves and in some instances, at a cost to the team members that they were serving with. This is where it becomes critical for the team leader, the platoon sgt and the first sgt to be aware and have the ability to communicate with each of their enlisted personnel so that they may detect a change in the man's personality, his daily habits and the length of time he is spending in the field as compared to other team members. If the addicted one happens to be a team leader or senior NCO then that oversight should be assumed by the officers of the company. There isn't a simple solution and the longer a war continues, the more likely some of the soldiers fighting that war will fall victim to the adrenalin fix and deviate from their normal persona. Simply sending the soldier back to a state side assignment doesn't fix the problem and may in the long run create more psychological problems for that addicted soldier. The US Army in Vietnam didn't have a fix for the problem or in most instances did not even recognize that there was a problem.

Most soldiers eventually returned to a US assignment and they brought the problem with them. I'm not sure that being labeled as a soldier suffering from PTSD was correct, but the addiction may have been a side track of what was considered the primary characteristics of PTSD, created by fighting in intense combat operations. Wherever it fell into the PTSD classification it was a problem and once again each soldier handled it differently. It could manifest itself in the extreme, like committing violent crimes to incapacity from illegal drug use. I feel that the standard drug of choice for masking the problem was alcohol since it was legal, could be purchased anywhere, any time. A drunk soldier that was off duty was just considered a normal thing that men did when they weren't working. PTSD is one of the rocks around the neck of Vietnam Vets that are still being carried by us. Most of us will take it to the grave with us. Of course, other wars were just as violent and those combat soldiers suffered from it also, but the major difference being that most of the returning soldiers from the other wars were welcomed home as heroes! The Vietnam Vet was treated like a war criminal and so there was a double hit to the psyche of each Vietnam Combat Veteran upon returning to the World. I personally believe that is why Vietnam Vets are much more affected by PTSD. If nothing else came as a benefit of the Vietnam War, it forced the VA to start to examine and treat PTSD in a clinical sense. Our sacrifices also paved the way for future returning combat vets to be respected by the citizens, to open the doors for acceptance (mostly) by the military hierarchy and to allow the troops to overtly attend treatment facilities, such as the Vet Centers.

The absolute solution for veterans is to never have to go into combat and thus be subjected to its horrendous acts. It will probably be a long time before that scenario occurs on earth, if ever.

Chapter 44

Explosives 101

At the MACV Recondo School we were taught some basic explosive identification and what explosive worked best to handle a certain problem facing the LRP team. It was probably an hour or two at most. Because of this training and the testosterone in our young male bodies, we basically assumed that we were now experts with explosives. The primary explosive we were taught to use was Det Cord. It looked like clear plastic quarter inch tubing with a white powder on the inside. It came in rolls of up to 100 feet + and it was primarily used to connect multiple explosives charges and/or claymore mines together so that they would explode almost simultaneously. It was one of the explosives known as a "cutting charge" because it burned at 25,000 feet per second. As an example, you could put one wrap of it around a 55 gallon steel barrel and detonate it. It would cut the steel barrel in half like a giant chop saw. Two wraps of det cord worked also but anymore than that, it would start to bend the edges of the barrel inward because of the excessive force it produced. We used it exclusively in the company area for cutting the shit barrels we needed for the latrines. It was not uncommon for someone to be cutting barrels in the area behind the latrine. It didn't make a loud explosion noise, more like a very loud "Snap", but it could be heard some distance away.

We had two main uses in the field for det cord; first we used it to "daisy chain" a series of claymores together, especially if one Lurp had control of multiple claymores. It allowed the Lurp to detonate all of the claymores with only one detonator. It also added redundancy to the process since if one of the blasting caps in the well of the claymore didn't explode then the det cord had sufficient force to activate/explode the C-4 in the claymore mine. We used it in that configuration for a short while, but it had several shortcomings, primarily that it was white in color, so it had to be camouflaged with natural material so that the enemy wouldn't see it. Secondly being in a roll, you might carry 10 to 15 feet of it, it had to be unrolled and cut to length if possible and the cut ends sealed. That meant that you spent excessive time along the trail in the kill zone. If you just used the detonation wire in the claymore bag with the electric blasting cap already attached for that purpose, it would save time and reduce the individual Lurp's exposure in the kill zone.

We did, however, normally carry some det cord, because of its cutting abilities. If the team was in trouble in contact and they needed to be extracted ASAP, they could find a semi-clear area for a LZ where the helicopter could attempt to land. Or at least hover while the team climbed on board, even in the middle of a hot LZ/fire fight. Invariably there was always one tree that stood in the middle or along the edge of the LZ that prevented the Huey from coming in to pick up the team. Thus at least two brave souls would crawl out to that tree, wrap it numerous times around the trunk with det cord and maybe add a pound of C-4 as a kicker charge. They would either put a time pencil detonator on it that would explode in 10-15-30 seconds depending on which one they were carrying or they would just attach a claymore wire with the blasting cap on the end and roll out the 75 feet as they crawled back to the team. They would detonate the det cord and possibly the C-4, which would normally cut the trunk of the tree in half, causing it to topple over. I'm not sure what the largest trunk you could cut, but the det cord made quick work of anything at or below a 10 inch diameter. Of course not being expert tree fellers, sometimes the tree fell in the wrong direction and landed on the troopers. I observed that happen while I was still with the 173rd. They dropped a tree to make an LZ and it fell on a trooper breaking his arm. That was a million dollar wound because he got med-evacuated out when the helicopter landed to drop off food and ammo.

The second most used explosive was C-4. It was extremely stable, but it exploded/burned at such a high speed (26,400 ft per sec) that it could also be used as a cutting charge when properly deployed. It was kind of our all-purpose explosive and someone on the team normally carried it. Its secondary characteristic was that it burned at a fairly high temperature and could easily be lit with a match or cigarette lighter. Of course the Lurps, like all good GIs, learned to use it to heat up C-Rats or water for the freeze dried Lurp rations. I never allowed anyone to heat a meal in the field on my team. I thought it compromised our position with the light from the flame and the smell of cooking food. I suspected that some teams did heat some food out in the bush, especially during the cold dry season or the very wet monsoon season. I stayed strictly within the protocol taught by 5th Special Forces at MACV Recondo School, because the instructors had field tested them in combat and they were still alive, so one would have to believe it was Gospel!

The third type of explosive we carried was TNT demolition blocks. They were in approximately one pound blocks with an OD green hard paper cover, approximately 2 inches square and 6 inches long with a well at the top to insert a detonator. What made TNT better to use on say a wood and mud bunker was that it was a bursting/smashing charge as compared to C-4's cutting abilities. We used it sparingly because we normally didn't plan on blowing up bunkers, since it tended to let the enemy know you were in the area. It would work well for blowing up an enemy stockpile of ammunition or explosives, but so would C-4.

On one particular mission I decided to carry a 5 pound block of C-4; a one pound block of TNT, a short length of det cord and a couple of detonator time pencils. I was inspired by the fact that we had a platoon of Navy Seals staying in our company area. They were working with us on some special patrol areas that were rumored to have large bunker complexes. In fact on one mission carried out by another Lurp Team they located a large abandoned bunker complex with smaller bunkers on the perimeter and one large command bunker located in the center. The complex had trenches cut to each bunker and they were all connected. The Team contacted our TOC and some of the Seals along with sufficient explosives were dropped in by helicopter to blow up the bunker complex. One of the Navy Seals (Pappy) was an expert with explosives. It took him and other Seals several hours to place all of the explosives while the Lurp team provided security. When the explosives were in place the Seal Team members and the Lurp team moved back so that Pappy could detonate the explosives. According to the Lurps who witnessed the feat, when the detonation occurred, with only a muffled explosion, the walls of all the bunkers blew inward and the roof of each bunker fell on top of the walls, completely destroying the complex. This was a successfully completed mission by an experienced, explosive expert.

So not to be out done by the Seals, I had decided that if we found a bunker complex I was going to blow it up just like the Seals did. We did in fact find a small bunker complex along a river bank which included a dug-in personnel bunker about 10 feet long, by 4 feet wide by approximately 4 feet above ground and approximately 2 feet below ground. There was also another two-man bunker/bomb shelter that was probably 6 feet square on the outside dimensions, but was only big enough for two small people on the inside. We set up an ambush on the bunker complex for a day with no action occurring. When we scheduled to be extracted, I decided to blow up the large bunker like the Seals had. I had been carrying this damn 5 pounds of C-4 for the entire mission and I wanted to use it after all that extra effort it took carrying it. While the rest of the team provided security, I crawled in the larger bunker and decided to place the entire 5 pounds in the corner of the bunker against one roof beam consisting of an approximate 6-inch diameter cut off tree. After forcing the C-4 into the corner as best as I could and with limited time and explosive experience I used some det chord attached to a 30 second time pencil to detonate the C-4. After pulling the pin on the time pencil we all sought cover in the jungle behind trees to prevent being hit by the flying debris from the 5 pounds of exploding C-4 and the blown apart bunker roof. There was a small, muffled explosion with a small amount of debris and dust flying in the air, but no blown up roof of the bunker. We went back to inspect the bunker and the sole damage was an approximate 9-inch diameter hole in the mud roof. Nothing else was damaged except for my pride. Not giving in, I set my sights on the two-man bomb shelter, which had no apertures to shoot out of and only a small wooden door for the two small persons to crawl inside. They closed the wooden door by placing it on the inside of the doorframe. Anyone with even a small amount of explosives training would have recognized that this was an almost air tight bomb shelter and that the walls were probably as least a foot thick based on the comparison of the outside and inside dimensions. Of course I initially missed that point and now being very short on time before the extraction occurred, I came up with an impromptu bunker buster. I took one claymore mine, one pound of TNT and placed the claymore blasting cap in the well of the TNT and then set the claymore facing up on top of the TNT. I closed the air-tight door and backed off the max of 75 feet, the length of the claymore detonating wire. Since the last bunker buster was a dismal failure, the team was more relaxed about this second attempt so we all sought shelter behind the long personnel bunker, which was less then 50 feet from the bomb shelter. We were all thinking that this was also going to be a dismal failure. I attached the clacker, the device that sent a small electrical charge down the wire to the electric blasting cap attached to the block of TNT and fired it. There was a very muffled explosion and then the entire two man bunker raised up off the ground about 10 feet and blew outward in a 360 degree pattern with broken logs and large chunks of hard as concrete mud walls falling out of the sky all around us and the immediate area of where the bunker had been. It was an outstanding success and completely destroyed the bunker although also almost hitting and injuring some of the team members including myself. I felt I was vindicated on my ability to use explosives; however, thereafter I stayed with just ambushing the enemy, calling in gunships, artillery, or air strikes on them, which I had been trained to do and had developed an expertise on how to do it! I left the "blowing up shit" to the true experts! Xin Loi GI!

Chapter 45

C-4 and a Lurp's Cookout

For every designated military use for a certain explosive, Lurps/GIs found other ways to use it to assist them. Probably the best use of C-4 in a non-combat role was to heat water for our freeze dried Lurp rations or to heat a C-Rat in its metal can. A piece of C-4 about the diameter of a quarter and maybe quarter inch thick would bring a canteen cup of water to a boil in less than a minute. It was a common scene around the back of barracks at night to see several small fires of C-4 burning at any given time, because someone was hungry or wanted a hot cup of coffee so they heated up the water to prepare the meal. What we didn't realize is that when you lit C-4 on fire it becomes unstable and is liable to explode if it is hit with a shock wave. One of our fellow Lurps taught us that lesson one night when he was drunk and broke off a piece of C-4 about twice the size he needed. When his water was boiling and seeing that he still had a lot of burning C-4, he decided to stomp it out. Well, the burning unstable C-4 plus the shock from the stomping action (on concrete) caused it to explode, blowing off the heel of his jungle boot. After he picked himself up and checked his now sober body, specifically his stomping foot he realized he wasn't injured. The rest of us in attendance slowly crawled out of our reactive, low profile, eat dirt mode, and realized that this could be a problem. The underground, internal company message center quickly passed along the info to every Lurp in the company, so that someone else didn't use an even larger piece of burning C-4 and blow off his foot while maybe also wounding a fellow Lurp, who was joining in the late meal. After that incident, we were somewhat more careful with using C-4 to cook; however, we had an unlimited supply of C-4 in the ammo bunkers, no one cared that you were eating a late meal, so why mess up a good thing.

Chapter 46

Search for a PoW Camp

On numerous occasions Company F was used by one of the alphabet agencies to verify intel that they had obtained from "reliable sources." Of course we were never told what those sources were. The Company F Commander was given the orders from higher command. Unless it was absolutely outside of our training and experience, we, the Company, accepted the orders and acted on them. We got updated intelligence briefings on the information they continued to collect and where we would be conducting the missions, but not much more than that. It was normally down to the team leaders to work out the details and then brief their individual teams. That info dictated what type of weapons we would carry, who carried what weapons and how much ammo for those weapons along with the time and probable route we would use to ingress and egress the target area.

On this particular mission we also received some special equipment to use during the mission. Two unique types of weapons included silenced M-3, 45 caliber, Second World War Era Grease Guns and Second World War era British Sten guns that were also silenced in 9 mm caliber. We did also receive some silencers for the M-16s but they extended the barrel by about 14 inches and had to have special ammo to fire through them. They were a pain in the butt and we didn't use them because of that.

The second specialized weapons we received were explosive bolt cutters that we were suppose to use to cut the chains the prisoner had on their ankles. They were circular and had a hardened steel chisel-head like device that was used to cut the chains by placing them inside the circle of steel so that the explosives would drive the cutting head against the chain and cut it. They were heavy and probably weighed 4-5 pounds each. Each team carried a couple of the bolt cutters, but we never used them.

The original ops plan was set as a heavy team with 12 Lurps that would conduct the recon/rescue mission. That was changed the day before the missions were activated. The most likely reason being because we couldn't field enough Heavy Teams to cover the area with saturation type patrols to find the camp. The intel agency had information on the general location of the alleged camp, but didn't have exact coordinates of the camp. It was basically in an area near the Cambodian border and between two east/west imaginary lines. That was common for the intel given to our teams on our regular recon missions. What most people don't realize is that even with 500,000 troops in country, Vietnam had large areas, especially in the dense jungle, that were not patrolled by any friendly troops, thus the enemy roamed free and with little concern about bumping into American or Allied troops. It is one of the reasons that Lurp Patrols worked so well in those areas. It was the reason Lurp Companies were formed, to recon an area to locate the enemy, then either strike them in ambushes or call in artillery and air strikes to destroy the enemy and their equipment. If we found a large concentration of enemy troops or a base camp then we sent that intel to HQ/II Field Force and they decided if they wanted to send a company or battalion of troops, armored cav units or air mobile units to attack the base camp and the enemy manning it. Either way the Lurp teams had accomplished their responsibilities for finding the enemy. Also depending on what type of attack was planned the Lurp Teams would continue to patrol the area and when possible pick off small numbers of enemy troops using the trails. It would further disrupt their command and control and supply lines which in the end would assist in denying the enemy a specific area of operation.

My team had originally been assigned to be a heavy team with Sgt Carter's team, but when that was changed at the last minute we had already loaded our gear into our packs, so I didn't want to change

273

the entire load out. We basically kept everything that Sgt Carter had assigned to our team, which meant we were loaded very heavy. Sgt Carter being an old trained Ranger had anticipated a heavy contact with the enemy if we found the PoW Camp and if it held American and/or Allied PoWs. Thus he loaded out the team as a ranger squad that was going to go heads up with the enemy. I have no doubt that is what we would have done, if we had remained with Sgt Carter's team as a heavy team. This was probably the heaviest load we ever carried, approximately 85 + pounds per man with all of the extra ammo, claymores, explosive bolt cutters and C-4/det cord. As it turned out we did more recon patrolling then an outright attack on the enemy.

We were to be inserted late in the afternoon as a Lurp team 1-3, not too close to the area we were suppose to be searching for the PoW Camp. Again this was the TL's decision because too far out added extra time and risk of exposure, but too close and the mission was compromised before we ever got on the ground.

The first day we moved a short distance from the LZ and set up our RON sight and hunkered down. We didn't hear or see anything around us that night. We knew we had a clean insertion so it was time to get down to business. We had a fairly straight line patrol march on the second day, but we ran into some single canopy areas and they were a bitch to move through. The problem was that all of that tropical sunlight was making it to the floor of the jungle and every plant in the jungle grew with abundance. We were trading off at point because in some places we literally had to climb our way through the jungle because it was so thick. I actually tried to fall over at one of our rest stops, but it was impossible because of the thick vines and vegetation. This caused two problems, first and foremost we were making noise and leaving a trail, which was exactly what you didn't want to do on a recon patrol. Secondly it made moving a lot slower and so we were behind our time to get to our projected patrol area. Also it told us that the camp wasn't in this particular area because an aircraft/helicopter crew could look down into single canopy and see what was there.

As usual the clock started as soon as we hit the LZ, because just like a nuclear sub crew we only carried limited food and water supplies to conduct a 4 night, 5 day patrol. Yes, we could be resupplied but that would compromise our secrecy and our location, so we might as well just be extracted and re-inserted after receiving supplies or just call it a completed mission and return to the base camp. After that 5 day patrol period and being on high alert for 24/7 the team was burned out and needed to rest for several days to make up for all the burned energy and loss of sleep.

As we moved out on the second morning, we realized we had a tail, two enemy troops that were following us. Probably LZ Watchers who had seen us insert and were now following us. We did a series of turns and maneuvers including an impromptu ambush on our own trail, but apparently we had lost the enemy or they figured out that we knew they were there and decided to di di mow to fight another day. We had also entered an area of double and triple canopy so it made it easier to move and cover our trail from the two enemy troops following us.

Either way we were compromised, which meant we had lost our advantage of secrecy and also opened the possibility of the enemy setting up an ambush on our route of march. This just put additional awareness/stress that we were now the hunted instead of being the hunter.

We spent a fairly sleepless RON, believing that we were probably going to get attacked in the middle of the night, but nothing occurred and we didn't have any type of abnormal movement outside our perimeter. We moved out early because we were now within the patrol area and we slowly meandered our way through the AO looking for signs of a base camp/PoW Camp. The trails we found were not very fresh and we only heard one distant signal shot during the whole time we were in the area. Around mid-afternoon of our third day we noticed an unusual clearing in the middle of triple canopy. First of all, the brush and small trees had been cut out and the trail to it was not well used but had been obviously made for a reason. As we carefully circled the area, still in the thick brush we observed a one man Tiger Cage suspended from a medium size tree (40-50 feet tall) in the middle of the clearing. It also indicated sleeping areas on the ground for approximate 4-6 personnel based on the crushed grass and clearing out of sticks, leaves and other forest residue that had fallen out of the higher trees above the cleared out area. After observing the area for several hours, myself and one other Lurp slowly crawled out to the cage to try to learn if it had been recently used. The cage was probably about 4 feet in diameter and approximately 4.5 feet tall. Kind of like a large bird cage made out of bamboo. It had a door secured by vines and was suspended probably a foot off the ground with vines to a branch of the medium size tree. I determined that it had been used in the past, based on small signs like broken and dying grass under the cage. It probably had been a week or more since it had been used. It didn't show any signs of active use say in the last day or two. What this appeared to be was a type of temporary holding cell, which the guards and the PoW would use for one night and then move along to the next location, probably within one day walking distance. Intel in past had advised us the VC/NVA when moving a PoW, would travel in small groups with maybe one or two PoWs. This was to prevent being observed by our aircraft or patrols and if they were attacked they were attacked and killed they might only loose one or two PoWs.

This was similar in operation to what the pony express/stage coach lines used in the 1800s to move long distances, with a stop-over, resting/overnight location and then back on the trail to the next rest area. We backed off from the cleared area and set up an observation/ ambush site to see if anyone would show that night. Nothing occurred, though we were on high alert thinking that possibly a late patrol might show up with a PoW.

In the morning we saddled up and moved a short distance to see if we could find any other similar camps or try to find the main trail the enemy was using. Around 10:00 hours we got a fly over from Aloft and received a message to move to an LZ for extraction. Apparently between other teams being compromised or finding little if anything in the area, the intel agency believed that the PoW camp was in a different area . Or maybe that the enemy knew we were there, so they moved all of the PoWs across the border into Cambodia. We were disappointed that we didn't make contact and have a chance to rescue a PoW, but we were also happy to be extracted from this high stress Lurp patrol. We never learned the reason why the operation was shut down, just a thank you very much from the intel agency and don't call us we'll call you if we need anything else.

Chapter 47

Last Chance for the Grim Reaper to Collect My Body and Soul

I got a lucky break from combat on an assignment to work the R&R Center in Hawaii. It was shown to me by Sgt Bill Schimdt, the company clerk, who was a close friend of mine. He was getting ready to DEROS back to the world, but had read a teletype about the Army recruiting Staff Sergeants and higher NCO ranks to work at the R&R Centers that were controlled by the Navy. You had to have been in country for at least one year and have a Purple Heart. I qualified, so I applied through II Field Force HQ and by some miracle, I actually got selected. I had to extend my time in Vietnam by 30 days to make the next rotation of personnel to the R&R Center. It was a 90 day TDY (Temporary Duty Assignment) which means I got extra pay while on the assignment. For me as a Staff Sgt, it was approximately $500 a month since I had to rent an apartment for the 90 days, because there weren't any US military barracks in Australia.

When the three weeks passed and I was on a roster to board an aircraft out of Tan Son Nuht Airport, I got a ride down and headed for the aircraft. As I came up to the Air Force Sgt. checking the personnel manifest to get on the aircraft, I showed him my ID and he checked the list. He looked at me and said that I had been scratched from the manifest by the R&R coodinator for the Army. I was literally five steps from the aircraft stairs, but had to turn around and head back to Bien Hoa. To say I was pissed would be an understatement, since I had extended an additional 30 days to make the rotation date. Granted, I was not going in the field, but I was training the Company D personnel on the proper methods of setting up claymore mines

278

and how to integrate them into a comprehensive kill zone. Some were very receptive and some had the attitude that they already knew everything necessary to be a Lurp in Vietnam. Xin Loi, GI!

I did some searching and found out who the Liaison Person was for the Army and that his office was located over in the Long Bien Base. I managed to catch a ride over there the next day and found him, Second Lt. Johnson (an alias). As soon as I introduced myself he started apologizing stating that the Navy had sent a TT stating that they didn't need any more Army Personnel in Hawaii. He said he had an opening in Australia and I could have it, if I wanted to wait two more weeks, so I said, "Hell yes!"

I eventually made it to the R&R center in Sydney, Australia, and did my 90 days in Paradise in Sydney, as a member of the R&R staff. We basically checked in the GIs coming from Vietnam and got them up to speed on Australian customs and made sure they each had a hotel to stay in. After that we exchanged their money and sent them on their way. In 7 days they were back to catch a return flight to the lovely tropical paradise of Vietnam. We also had to work as the liaison person for the R&R center one night a week. You basically had to be the liaison to Australian Shore Patrol and police departments when GIs got in trouble. The usual cause was getting drunk on Australian beer and getting into fights with other GIs. Go figure, like they didn't have enough fighting while in Vietnam. The results were that they were put on the first aircraft back to Vietnam.

At the end of that outstanding assignment, I rotated back to Vietnam and was now assigned to Company D, 151st Infantry, LRP, who had assumed Company F's role as the Long Range Patrol Company for II Field Force. Their company was located about a mile east of our old company area and I was housed in one of their temporary barracks to wait for about a week before DEROS and returning to the USA.

The very first night I was back In-Country, I got totally shitfaced drunk with First Sgt. Butts who was also waiting to DEROS. Company D had an NCO Club in their company area and that is where we spent the evening. I think I drank 8 Rum & Cokes that evening and I also had brought back a bottle of Drambuie that I stashed outside the club. First Sgt Butts and I closed down the club and then went out back to have a shot of the Drambuie. First Sgt Butts took a long drag on the bottle and then handed it to me. I also started to take a long drag, but as soon as the warm, sweet liquor hit my stomach I knew it was coming back up. I must have puked for at least a minute or more, which the first shirt thought was rather hilarious. Then he said, "Good luck" and headed out to his bunk. I did the same and fortunately it was down hill since I was falling down drunk, but had a general idea where my barracks was. Dejavu the first night with the 173rd in Dak To.

That was the last thing I remember until I woke up some time in the sunny morning, lying in a muddy jeep track about 50 meters east of my barracks in an open field. I had no idea how I got there and it had obviously rained during the night because my fatigues were wet and I had sunk several inches down into the soft mud of the jeep tracks. Fortunately, it wasn't a well-used track so no one ran over me during the night, although I felt like someone had. I managed to get up and stumble to my barracks and fall into my bunk. No one had missed me because I wasn't on the new company's roster, since I was essentially a hold over from Company F, waiting for my DEROS date. I never moved the rest of that day or night, until the next morning when I needed some water. After a short drink of warm water, I went back to bed and slept all day until that evening when I managed to go take a shower. I was so nauseated that I had no desire to eat anything. Finally on the third day I managed to make it to the chow hall for the evening meal, where I ate sparingly. Two more days past before I was fully recovered from what was essentially alcohol poisoning. I believe that if I hadn't thrown up some of that alcohol after drinking all evening with First Sgt. Butts, I probably would have been found dead out in that jeep trail. Probably nobody would have really given a shit about me being DOA, since most of the Company F Lurps had already transferred to other Lurp companies. Xin Loi, GI!

Two days later I was on a Freedom Bird Flight out of Tan San Nuht Airport and arrived at McChord Air Base about 14 hours later after a refueling stop in Hawaii. I have to say that as the pilot advised that we were out of Vietnam air space, I literally felt a weight come off my shoulders for all those responsibilities as a team leader of a Lurp team. I was very proud of the fact that I hadn't had any KIAs on my teams, even though most team members had collected at least one Purple Heart, along with my two plus 3 wounds from "friendly fire". I knew some of that was because of my skills as the TL and the teams' skills, but also because Lady Luck had been with me most of the way and had kept Murphy and the Grim Reaper at bay most of the time. I thought I was good to go with the rest of my life and that Vietnam was just one phase of my young Life. Neither I, nor most of the combat exposed GIs returning from Vietnam, had any idea that we were all subconsciously bringing back to the "WORLD" most of what we had experienced in combat, especially those up close and personal near-death experiences in firefights with the enemy.

Chapter 48

The Grim Reaper Collects
another Soul

Actually, the Grim Reaper had collected another soul while I was in Australia. When I got back to Vietnam, I brought back a fifth of good whiskey to give to Lt. Johnson, as a thanks for sending me to Australia.

I traveled over to Long Binh several days after I had returned and recovered from my alcohol-poisoning incident. When I got to the Office of the R&R Coordinator, I saw that a new Lt. was in charge. I asked for Lt. Johnson and got this blank stare. The new Lt. informed me that Lt. Johnson was dead, KIA'd over a month ago. He said that Lt. Johnson was off duty and sleeping in his bunk on the second floor of the Officers' Barracks, when a 107 mm (4.21 inches in diameter) rocket was fired at the base and came through the roof of Lt. Johnson's barracks. It actually hit him in the chest and passed through his body, his bunk, the floor and blew up on the first floor causing a lot of injuries and major damage, but Lt. Johnson was the only one killed. The chances of that happening, even in a war zone, had to be 50 million to one. The 107 mm rockets were Russian made, unguided, just propped up into a firing position and fired in the general direction of an Army/ Air Force base. They were usually fired 5 or more miles from a base and were more of a terror weapon than an accurate military barrage weapon. Sometimes, however, they hit a target.

I was completely blown away (no pun intended) when I received that information from the new lieutenant. Lt Johnson had had one of the safest assignments in Vietnam and one of the best jobs for a lower ranking officer. I could only think that it had really been his time to,

"Get His Ticket Punched" in Vietnam. There simply wasn't any other reasonable explanation for his death.

The Grim Reaper – plus one. The US Army – minus one.

Xin Loi, GI!

"There is no instance of a nation benefitting from prolonged warfare."

– Sun Tzu, The Art of War